OCT   1988

BLEACHERS

BLEACHERS

A SUMMER IN WRIGLEY FIELD

LONNIE WHEELER

CONTEMPORARY
BOOKS

CHICAGO · NEW YORK

Library of Congress Cataloging-in-Publication Data

Wheeler, Lonnie.
   Bleachers : a summer in Wrigley Field / Lonnie Wheeler.
      p.   cm.
   ISBN 0-8092-4641-4 : $16.95
   1. Wrigley Field (Chicago, Ill.)—History.   2. Chicago Cubs
(Baseball team)—History.   I. Title.
GV863.I32C458   1988
796.357'06'87731—dc19   88-1834
                                                                   CIP

Copyright © 1988 by Lonnie Wheeler
All rights reserved
Published by Contemporary Books, Inc.
180 North Michigan Avenue, Chicago, Illinois 60601
Manufactured in the United States of America
Library of Congress Catalog Card Number: 88-1834
International Standard Book Number: 0-8092-4641-4

Published simultaneously in Canada by Beaverbooks, Ltd.
195 Allstate Parkway, Valleywood Business Park
Markham, Ontario L3R 4T8 Canada

For my father, who gave me a great gift when he made
a baseball fan out of me. (He also put the baby spoon
in my left hand so I would be a switch-hitter,
but we won't get into that here.)

And for Martie, who did everything else while I was
off in faraway bleachers, and never complained.

Contents

Acknowledgments

I'd like to thank Mike Murphy, for sharing his experience; Ned Colletti of the Cubs, for access; David Black, who talked me into this; and all my friends in the bleachers: Mark Wilmot, Norb Kudele, Jerry Pritikin, Marv Blum, Al Yellon, Steve Schanker, Leonard Becker, Joe Barach, Howard Hankin, Elsie Foydl, Mike Roche, Marcy Schauwecker, Jim Cote, Dancing Annie, and the rest.

Introduction————————————

CERTAIN IMAGES SEEM to find an audience in my head—little glimpses of things that somehow, seductively, persuade me to follow them to somewhere real.

When I was a kid, I saw a movie once that had a boy and a dog and a house in the back country, and I have an image of the boy and the dog walking down some Tobacco Road sort of road that I remember as North Carolina but could have been Georgia or Virginia or somewhere else. I don't know what the movie was, and I'm not sure I'd recognize it if I saw it again. But that vague image of the dog and the boy and the house and the woods and the road was the way I imagined North Carolina, and I was compelled to go there and see what it felt like. On spring break from college one year, when other kids went to Florida, I drove alone to North Carolina.

My infatuation is with real places. I think of a real place as one that feels different than other places, and there aren't very many of them left in America. An image I had—I can't even say what the image was, exactly; it was just an indistinct but unmistakable *something*—persuaded me that the bleacher section of Wrigley Field was such a place. I decided to spend the baseball season there and see what it felt like.

People ask me how I got the idea for this book, and I don't really know. I think it got me. It was just there. I had never bought that business about climbing a mountain because it was there, but I think I know now what the guy meant. He meant that he didn't know why he did it. I think what he meant was: "Don't ask me. Ask the mountain."

In a way, I find it hard to believe that nobody has ever written this book before. On the other hand, perhaps it had to be done by somebody to whom the bleachers were not a familiar fact of life, but a fetching image. I had been to the bleachers only once before; I don't believe I could have done this book if I had been raised in them. I don't believe I would have wanted to. I would have realized that the bleachers were unique and precious, but I don't believe I would have been able to step back and see how they blended so smartly into the American landscape.

I grew up in St. Louis when Harry Caray announced the Cardinal games, and Wrigley Field was that strange daytime place where Curt Flood was always climbing the vines. I moved to Cincinnati and went to ballgames at Riverfront Stadium, which is located in the middle of a parking garage and was the first stadium to have an entirely synthetic infield. Wrigley Field, with its brick and grass and ivy and sunshine and bleacher bums and tragicomical Cubs, seemed like another world.

The bleachers seemed like a world within that one, an arcane but quintessential subculture. They seemed like baseball's stomping ground—companionable, passionate, fundamental, unaffected, and gloriously human. I imagined them as the place where the game met the people; as the place where a ballgame felt like a ballgame, and a season felt like a season.

I imagined that the bleachers at Wrigley Field were what baseball was all about, and that if a book could capture the bleachers, it could capture baseball.

April

I'D ALWAYS THOUGHT of Wrigley Field's bleachers as the place where real baseball fans go when they close their eyes and click their heels three times. On television, I'd seen all those home runs disappearing into the thick crowd in the cheap seats in left field, and I imagined those same happily suffering souls, shorn of their shirts and pretenses, sticking it out together through all the bittersweet seasons.

I had been to the bleachers only once in my life, on a crowded Saturday with my wife. I didn't know what they were like on weekdays or hot days or windy days or most days, and yet I knew, as baseball fans instinctively seem to know, that a bleacher seat at Wrigley Field was the best place in the world to watch a ballgame. I thought of the bleachers as a window on baseball, and the view as pure as if the glass had been broken out on a foul ball by the kid next door. I thought of them as the balcony over baseball's summertime serenade. I was going to spend the season there, and I thought it would be baseball heaven.

On Opening Day 1987, it was apparent that I had underestimated the place. To the 3,260 people packed into them—

3

plus standing room—the bleachers were much more than benches beyond the outfield. They were a neighborhood, a bar, a depot, a beach, an office, a church, a home. They were a ward of Chicago, and I stood against the fence behind the four-dollar seats in left field on Opening Day and felt like a stranger. It was strange being a stranger in a ballpark, sort of like being at a party where everybody figures you must know somebody they know. People hugged each other, friends lost over the grim Chicago winter and found again with the first pitch. They shook hands with the beer vendors. Two women I had never seen before, stockbrokers named Mimi and Kate, asked if I wanted something from the concession stand.

It was Yankee Doodle Tuesday in Chicago, Opening Day and Election Day all wrapped up in an apple-pie April seventh. No other place observes both baseball and politics with the same fervency as Chicago—it is equally judgmental of its aldermen and its outfielders—and to a stranger, the afternoon seemed as privately provincial as it was classically American. Outside the ballpark, a large black man walked in front of an important-looking procession, and I reasoned that he must be the incumbent mayor, Harold Washington, with his entourage. I asked the guy standing next to me about it. He looked at me like I had underwear on my head and said, "Vrdolyak." I explained that I had taken the large black man for Washington, and the guy said, "That was probably the bodyguard. Are you from another planet?" It seemed that I was. Place called Ohio.

The bleachers were a world that a visitor could admire for its sights and society, but he would have to live with the natives for a while before he could understand them. More and more, ballparks were ballparks, and being in one was like being in another shopping mall with five shoe stores, a chocolate-chip cookie shop, and patient husbands sitting around the fountain. But the bleachers were *somewhere*. They were a place settled and developed by a city and a sport, indigenous turf, a tract of Americana whose essential nature could not be contained by the brick walls of Wrigley Field, or the streets named Clark, Addison, Waveland, and Sheffield. In a way, the bleachers were bigger than the ballpark. They were an icon, a culture, a Windy City fingerprint. They were an open floor on which a big town danced its parochial polka. And the music started on April seventh.

For the charming if somewhat curious branch of mankind known as Cub fans, spring is a sanguine time of the year. Every spring holds the blithe hope that perhaps this is the season in which Satan will grow weary and ease up on the headlock in which he has diabolically held Chicago's mightily struggling National League baseball team since its last world championship in 1908.

The phenomenal aspect of the Chicago Cubs—the thing that makes them different from any other professional sports franchise in the Americas (other than the fact that they have gone longer than any other without a championship, the closest being the crosstown White Sox, who won the World Series in 1917, and then the Boston Red Sox, who beat the Cubs in 1918)—is that, despite their colossal legacy of losing, the scope and fidelity of their constituency is unmatched and unmitigated. There is no census taken on such a thing, but for whatever reasons—cable television, Wrigley Field, day games, cuteness, whatever—it is eminently probable that the Cubs have more and better fans than any other team in the Western Hemisphere, if not beyond. More people watch them on TV than any other team. It's the Cubs that merchants and farmers talk about around the coffee tables in Tennessee and Nebraska. Early in 1984, before the Cubs caught the country's imagination with their joyous rush to the division title, a newspaper in the major-league wilderness of Casper, Wyoming—a place where Chicago's WGN superstation was not available to cable subscribers—conducted a readership survey to determine the most popular baseball team in the area, and the Cubs outpolled the second-place Yankees by nearly four to one.

There is nothing like it in all of sports. The Red Sox have the same sort of long-suffering history and traditional appeal, but they have won pennants, and the devotion attending them, while heartfelt and powerful, is essentially confined to New England. The Yankees and Cowboys and Notre Dame have all been winners. Going into 1987, however, only once in the previous fourteen seasons had the Cubs won more games than they had lost. Excepting 1984, incredibly, they had never been closer than five games to the league or division champion since 1945, when they won the pennant. They had contended for first place on rare occasions—their great collapse of 1969 is all too vividly remembered—but nowhere near often enough to interest a less constant congregation. There was no conventional explanation for their massive, madcap popularity. Neither was there any end to it in sight.

In the spring training they had just concluded—after a season in which they finished in fifth place in the National League East, thirty-seven games behind the Mets—the Cubs had drawn more than 106,000 fans to HoHoKam Park in Mesa, Arizona, and broken the all-time preseason attendance record that they had set in 1985. This was despite the fact that a trip to Arizona was not nearly as expedient by car or as economical by airplane from Chicago as most of the Florida camps were to the Eastern major-league cities. It was the traditional wont of Cub fans, however, to schedule their vacations in March or October, depending on their particular form of optimism. There were those who chose to indulge in the winsome wishful thinking and 73.6-degree average high temperatures of Maricopa County's East Valley, and there were those who reserved a week in October on the fat chance that the Cubbies might reverse the wrongs of recent decades and carry the banner of the great American underdog into the World Series. The latter usually ended up at Disney World or somewhere, but there had been nothing to divert the gush of good hope into the sunny, sensible city of Mesa.

It was the Cubs' good fortune, also—either that, or their doing—that Illinois had contributed more than any other state to Maricopa County's population boom in the late seventies and early eighties. The Cubs were practically the home team. After Cub telecasts went out over cable in 1982, announcers Harry Caray and Steve Stone became so popular in greater Phoenix that they opened two restaurants there. By the middle part of the decade, the Cubs' arrival had become a grand event accompanied by a great convergence of blue upon the East Valley—official seventy dollar Cub satin warm-up jackets in the cool Mesa mornings; Cub shorts and shirts and hats and visors and earrings and pins and buttons in the comfortable Mesa afternoons. Cynics and St. Louisans might find metaphor in this great expression of blue coming from Cub fans, but it is just a color, not a mood. There isn't a baseball fan anywhere who doesn't feel warm late-summer possibilities in the buoyant breeze of spring. With the Superstition Mountains at their backs in the early spring of 1987, the Cubs looked as they had in so many early springs before: like they could be contenders. It would depend on the pitchers and the kids.

It would depend, really, on things about which little could be presumed. A baseball season never really begins; it just sort of emerges out of the accumulated yesterdays, each new team having its genesis in the several before it, and the previous three years had reported ambiguously on the competitive state of the Chicago Cubs. The seminal event in their recent history had been the intoxicating divisional championship of 1984, but two years later, the Cubs appeared before the mirror with their clothes wrinkled and their breath reeking, staring at the glass and wondering what happened.

Although the circumstances were certainly extenuating—in 1985, all five of Chicago's starting pitchers had been injured—the fact was that the first-place finish had been followed by a fourth and a fifth. The players had remained essentially the same through it all, the principal exception being that Shawon Dunston had taken over at shortstop for Larry Bowa. Midway through the 1986 season, however, Dallas Green, the powerful president and general manager, had fired manager Jim Frey and replaced him with a quiet, lanky, former weak-hitting shortstop and mildly successful Yankee manager named Gene Michael, known otherwise as Stick. With that symbolic if arguable change, at least Green had indicated that he recognized a troubling pattern. This was not

an easy acknowledgment for the big executive, a man of prodigious ambition and ego who had basked in an air of infalli-
bility after 1984. Having hand-made the Cubs by trading for
Ryne Sandberg, Keith Moreland, Gary Matthews, Larry
Bowa, Ron Cey, Dennis Eckersley, Steve Trout, Scott Sanderson, Dick Ruthven, Bob Dernier, and Rick Sutcliffe,
Green had reason to regard himself as the team's great deliv-
erer. But as the years went on, the humbling, inevitably mor-
tifying process of Cubness was overtaking him and the men
he brought to Chicago. The team didn't run, didn't pitch,
didn't hit in the clutch. Green's pre-owned ballclub had been
a dream machine in 1984's fast ride, but nobody thought to
check whether the odometer had been rolled back.

By the time they arrived in Mesa in 1987, the second-hand
Cubs were leaking oil, but at least their chrome still had a
shine. Several of the stars—Sandberg, Jody Davis, Moreland,
Leon Durham, Sutcliffe, reliever Lee Smith—were ostensibly
still in their primes. Dunston's was presumed to be arriving
anytime, and any of numerous young or unfamiliar players—
outfielders Rafael Palmeiro, Chico Walker, Brian Dayett,
and Dave Martinez; and pitchers Jamie Moyer, Greg Maddux, and Drew Hall—had the opportunity and apparently
the capacity to make a difference. And then there was Andre
Dawson.

After a decorated ten-year career as an outfielder with the
Montreal Expos, during which Dawson hit twenty or more
home runs seven times, won six Gold Gloves, was Rookie of
the Year, Player of the Year, the best player in Montreal
history, and, according to a *New York Times* survey of major
leaguers in 1983, the best player in the game, there wasn't
another team in the big leagues that showed the least bit of
interest in Dawson as a free agent in the early spring of 1987.
The Expos themselves had offered two million dollars for two
years, but Dawson, whose tender left knee had been at odds
with Montreal's artificial playing surface, was intent upon
playing in an outfield that earthworms could inhabit. He was
also a better hitter in the daytime, had a .346 career average in

the natural light of Wrigley Field, and made it clear that he wanted to be in Chicago. Sutcliffe said he'd chip in one hundred thousand dollars of his own salary if the Cubs would sign Dawson. But when Dawson and his agent, Dick Moss, showed up at HoHoKam Park on March third and told Green he could name the price for a new rightfielder, the Cubs folded their arms. Finally, Moss handed Green a blank contract and said that Dawson would sign it that way, with the salary to be determined by the Cubs.

Green still demurred, insisting that no single player could improve a team from 70–90 to 90–70. "In my heart, I don't feel we need Dawson," he said. He called the whole thing a circus, and said that Moss "wants to put on a dog and pony show at my expense." Accustomed to being the man in charge, Green was on the defensive. If he signed Dawson, he would compromise his stand against free agency; worse, he would do what he had said he didn't want to do. If he didn't sign Dawson, there would be a public uproar and a hole in right field. And another factor was at work. The Cubs' attendance had declined slightly in 1986, and if they continued in their mediocrity—most of the forecasts placed them fourth in the National League East in 1987, ahead of only Montreal and Pittsburgh—they would forfeit all of the momentum that remained from 1984. The Cub rage would be over. And if that happened, the Tribune Company, owner of the Cubs, would of course have to reevaluate its executive personnel.

By the end of the week, Dawson was a Cub. Green was surprised that a player of such repute could be had for five hundred thousand dollars. For his part, Dawson was surprised that he would be offered the lowest salary of any of the Chicago regulars, with the exception of Dunston, who had less than two years of major-league experience. But the contract did hold out the possibility of more money—one hundred fifty thousand dollars if Dawson made it through the All-Star game without going on the disabled list, and another fifty thousand if he made the All-Star team.

After the late start, Dawson had a good spring. He hit a

home run against the Brewers in Chandler and then two more against Seattle in Tempe. It was enough to provide Cub fans with the optimism they required to begin the season.

The Cubs were playing the Cardinals, which was dumb. There were 38,240 people at Wrigley Field, and there would have been that many if the Cubs had been playing the Bombay Bicycle Club on Opening Day. The Cardinals would sell out Wrigley Field on Christmas, but anyway, in the wisdom of the National League, it was Sutcliffe against John Tudor to start the 1987 season. Vince Coleman grounded out for the Cardinals, Ozzie Smith did the same, and a guy in the left-field bleachers announced that he was headed downstairs for playoff tickets.

Sutcliffe worked out of the first, and then Bob Dernier, whose leadoff ability had declined to an unacceptable standard the previous two years, started the Cubs out with a single to left. This brought up the possibility of stealing a base against catcher Tony Pena, a former All-Star whom the Cardinals had acquired in a trade with Pittsburgh. "It's not a good idea to run on Pena," a Cub fan in the bleachers told his buddy. "I'm still pissed they got him." Ryne Sandberg, the teen-idol second baseman who had grown a mustache over the winter and shaved it after eighty-seven percent of people responding to a poll by the *Chicago Sun-Times* said they didn't like it (though he denied that was the reason), doubled. Then Dawson, batting for the first time as a Cub, hit a ground ball that was muffed by Tom Herr, the second baseman. Keith Moreland, an erstwhile outfielder who had been moved to third base for the season despite the skepticism of many who had watched the wide-legged Ron Cey for four years—a longtime Cub fan, Sara Davis, had expressed the prevailing sentiment one day during spring training when she said, "Moreland's a helluva nice guy and he'll do anything they ask him to do, but he's too fat for the job"—drove in a run with a fly ball, and after an inning the Cubs led 2–0. Vrdolyak was still in the game at that point, too.

He was also *at* the game, and if the mayoral vote had been

taken inside Wrigley Field, Vrdolyak would have probably won in a walk, much in the manner that St. Louis eventually did. The Cook County Democratic Party chief referred to himself as the leader of the party's "white wing," and the Wrigley Field crowd was and traditionally is as white as any yuppie or European precinct in Chicago. It was no coincidence that while Vrdolyak—who was running on the Solidarity Party ticket despite his Democratic position—and Republican candidate Donald Haider worked both the ballpark and the nearby taverns on election day, Washington was nowhere to be seen around Wrigley Field. It *was* an interesting coincidence, though, that the election and the first game fell on the same day. It meant, if nothing else, that Chicago was guaranteed at least one winner on April seventh.

By the third inning, though, it was becoming apparent that the Cubs would not be among that number. Sutcliffe, who had been handed the Opening Day assignment despite a miserable 1986 and a lackluster spring training, soon developed an acute disinclination to throw the ball over the plate. He walked five Cardinals in the third inning alone, and didn't even finish it. The Cardinals scored a run for every walk, and Kate and Mimi left for Murphy's Bleacher Bar across the street.

As the deficit lingered, the Cub fans, showing no effects from the long winter layoff, pulled out their old tricks. The first target, of course, was Sutcliffe. As the wealthy pitcher left, a red-faced middle-aged man standing behind the seats in right-center field and wearing one of the seventy dollar satin Cub jackets (it was 46 degrees) screamed, "You're a bum, Sutcliffe! Take the money and run, you bum!" The same guy picked on Dawson moments later, when the new rightfielder came to bat. The previous time, batting with the bases loaded, Dawson had hit a massive drive to left that the wind blew foul, then popped up. "Dawson, you're a bum!" the man hollered. "Did you get a hit with the bases loaded? No! You're a bum! Welcome to Chicago!"

The fans in right field yelled at the St. Louis rightfielder, Tito Landrum, and Landrum pointed to the scoreboard.

Then they yelled at left field in the traditional Wrigley Field salutation. Right field: "Left field sucks!" Left field: "Right field sucks!" And so on. Inspired, the people on the Waveland Avenue (left field) rooftops took up the chant, their object of course being right field. Unappreciative of the support, the fans in the left-field bleachers turned and hollered at the roof people. "Scabs!" they called out.

Then Jerry Pritikin's plane flew over. Pritikin, a fifty-year-old superfan who called himself the Bleacher Preacher, had hired an airplane to carry the banner HARRY CARAY FOR PRESIDENT. It was a nice touch; Caray, the beloved announcer, was home in California recovering from a stroke. It was also expensive for a man without a job. "Sure, it costs," said Pritikin, "but I've got a reputation to uphold."

Pritikin had just moved back to Chicago from San Francisco, where he had worked as a self-employed photographer and publicist, and he intended to be at every Cubs home game in 1987. He made every game but one in 1984, after he won a lawsuit and used the money to spend that summer at Wrigley Field. This time, though, there was no job or settlement to fall back on. "I'm a professional fan," said Pritikin.

The manifestations of this were several. Pritikin wore a hat with a propeller on top and a T-shirt with BLEACHER PREACHER on the back. On the front of his shirt was the question, HOW DO YOU SPELL BELIEF?; and the answer: C-U-B-S. His self-appointed duty as the Bleacher Preacher was to save lost baseball souls who cheered for other teams, which he did by invoking the names of Bill Veeck, Sr., the father; Bill Veeck, Jr., the son; and Charlie Grimm, the Cubs' holy spirit. Occasionally, he brought to the games a voodoo doll depicting a particularly evil opponent and invited fans to stick pins in it. He made signs, gave out awards, and presented Cub decals to anybody who threw back a home-run hit by somebody on the other team.

What Pritikin did not do, though, was drink beer. In the bleachers, this distinguished him as much as the propeller on his head. In my naivete, I had not understood the vested partnership that beer held in the bleachers. It was a firm of four: sun, people, beer, and ballgame. The pecking order was interchangeable, depending on the crowd, the weather, and the score.

On Opening Day, the crowd was large, the weather was chilly, and the score was 9–3. When the game ended, an older couple walked slowly down Sheffield Avenue. The man was wearing a Cub jacket over a Cub T-shirt from 1984, and on top of his head was a popcorn bucket turned upside down with the bottom torn out. Through the hole in the bottom were stacked beer cups too numerous to count.

The bleachers had always been an interesting place, but it wasn't until the late sixties that anybody knew it. "I remember the day the Bleacher Bums thing really started," said Mike Murphy, a sales representative and bleacher historian. "It was 1966, the year Leo Durocher took over as manager and said the Cubs were not an eighth place team like they'd been the year before—and sure enough, they finished tenth. There was a September game, and the Cubs and Mets were battling it out for ninth. I got there early and I was the only kid in the bleachers. I was catching all these home-run balls and I didn't have anything to do with them. I stuck a couple in my jeans, and then I started playing catch from the bleachers with Billy Williams. I took a nose count that day, and there were thirteen people in the bleachers. Twelve of them were in left field. When there are only twelve other people, there's nothing to do but talk to each other. This was the beginning of a little friendship among the fans out there.

"Then, lo and behold, the next year the Cubs actually took over first place in July when they swept the Reds in a double-header, and there were about forty-three thousand people in the ballpark. The bleacher popularity really started in '67. The twelve or twenty of us who knew each other kind of sat together. We were a raucous group. Then, when the Cubs became a hot story in '69, all of a sudden everybody wanted to join the bandwagon. There were four newspapers in town then, and they were all trying to get an angle on the Cubs. One time a reporter came out and asked, 'Who are you guys?'

We said, 'Ah, take a hike. We're just a bunch of bums out here.' The next day the headline said something about 'bleacher bums' this or that, and all of a sudden all these TV crews are out there looking for the Bleacher Bums. Before we knew it, NBC was out there, the *Wall Street Journal.* We started wearing yellow helmets because when we went to St. Louis the Cardinal fans threw things at us; pretty soon, they're selling yellow helmets on the street corner. The Bleacher Bums became synonymous with Cub fans in general. We didn't set out to make ourselves a group. The press made us a group. The press created us."

The original Bums gradually dispersed, some moving out of town, others into the grandstand. When the bleachers became the rage, left field was the first place to break up. Even those Bums who remained in the bleachers transferred to other parts of it. By 1987, a new generation of regulars was gathering on weekends and staking out the left-most section of the bleachers, next to the private family area where alcohol was not permitted. In the main, though, left field had become the place for young drunks, school kids, and out-of-towners.

It was also the best place to catch home runs during batting practice, and on Thursday—Wednesday had been an off day—Jack Clark of the Cardinals was hitting batting-practice home runs that were being caught by kids who didn't look old enough to be out of school. The kids were keeping the balls. "Hey," yelled Jerry Pritikin, the self-appointed defender of bleacher tradition, "throw 'em back. Have some Cubbie pride. Didn't you guys go to spring training?"

Though it is the most celebrated, left field is actually the smallest of the three basic sections of Wrigley Field's bleachers. The right-field section accommodates more than twice as many people as the left, and generally better baseball fans. The two sections are physically and symbolically divided by a patch of center-field seats that was closed off to fans on April 19, 1952, when Cardinal manager Eddie Stanky complained to the league office that his hitters—Stan Musial, in particular—lost sight of pitches as they blended in with the light shirts in the bleachers. Immediately next to the empty area, in right-center, is where for decades a group of men with names like Sleazy and Moon and Za Za and Pip and Three Hundred Sam and Charlie Seventy-Nine and Jeweler Joe and Mister B and Mama Doll and Baby Doll made bets of all sorts, big and small, every day. Things changed in the bleachers, and all but a few of the boys stopped coming. Still, the back rows of the right-field bleachers remained informally reserved for the old and the wise.

The top section of the bleachers—the only straightaway center-field seating in the ballpark—is a trapezoid that starts out wide at the bottom part, which hangs over the concession stand, and tapers upward to narrow rows sheltered by the huge manual scoreboard. The few regulars that choose center field sit in the front row, which, although separated by altitude and the aisle that is the main left-to-right thoroughfare of the bleachers, is sort of spiritually joined with the back row of right-center. Bill Veeck, the great baseball Barnum and man of the fans, sat on the rail in center field before he died in 1986. Veeck's bleacher wisdom was this: "I have discovered, in twenty years of moving around a ballpark, that the knowledge of the game is usually in inverse proportion to the price of the seats."

A few of Veeck's buddies were still sitting on the rail in 1987, but apparently an old man wearing a Cub painter's cap and eating nachos by himself on Thursday was not one of them. Maybe he was, though. I didn't really get that far.

It was early. There weren't any other people around. "Been a Cub fan all your life?" I asked him.

He ate another nacho, leaving melted cheese on his lower lip. "Long as I been here."

"How long is that?"

It was getting longer all the time. "Thirty-five years," he said finally.

"Were you a fan of another team before then?"

"Nope."

"How do you think they're going to do this year?"

I wondered if he heard me. Maybe he was hungry. There were certainly a lot of nachos per serving. " 'Bout the same."

I left him alone, but resolved that I would have him talking by the end of the season.

A little later in center field, there appeared a young man (or an old teenager, I wasn't sure which) with long hair, an earring, a cigar, a beer, keys on his belt loop, and pink tennis shoes. Next to him—right next to him—was a young man (this time I was sure) of comparable age, pale and slim, whose hair was light and short, probably just cut. He was wearing Bermuda shorts and reading the financial section of the *New York Times*.

The Chicago players were removing their caps for the national anthem as two guys found seats down below. One of them looked around respectfully and said, "Can you imagine towers of lights surrounding this place?"

"I can't imagine it," said the other.

"I can," said the first.

Near them, a father explained to his son how to use his scorecard to identify the pitchers for other games posted on the scoreboard behind center field. The pitchers at hand, meanwhile, were Steve Trout of the Cubs and Danny Cox of the Cardinals, and both of them did well in the early going, Trout's success owing in part to a splendid diving catch in the second inning by centerfielder Dave Martinez.

Against Cox, a righthander, Michael had started Martinez and Chico Walker next to each other in center and left. Neither were rookies, but both were getting their first full chance in the major leagues and would begin the season in platoon with Dernier and Brian Dayett, respectively. The Cubs seemed to be awakening to the reality that, despite Wrigley Field's liberal home-run possibilities, they would not become a complete or consistent team until they introduced more speed and defense into their scheme. Martinez received a standing ovation for a splendid catch. One obviously veteran Cub observer, however, refused to rise. "Let's give him a couple of years," he said.

Despite the sound intentions, Walker, leading off, and Martinez managed just one hit in nine tries between them on April ninth. St. Louis's swift men, on the other hand, had little trouble reaching and running the bases, and stole six of them, four coming when Coleman twice swiped second and third. The Cardinals looked as though they would be an alert team in 1987, and their fans in the left-field bleachers enjoyed it immensely. One girl taunted the Cub fans by yelling, "Forty-nine years! Forty-nine years!" No one called her on the fact that forty-nine years had nothing to do with anything. It had been forty-two years since the Cubs had last won a pennant, seventy-nine since they won a World Series.

Their give-and-take notwithstanding, though, the Cub and Cardinal fans in left field got on rather amiably. It happened that the Grateful Dead were in town, and a large group from St. Louis—Dead fans who had met in the Busch Stadium bleachers—had come to see both them and the Cardinals. Some of the left-field Wrigley regulars were also Deadheads. In their trademark tie-dyed T-shirts, they were known as Gary Matthews fans, but their hearts beat to the Dead. It was a peculiar bond. "There's a unity of Deadheads," one of the St. Louisans said. "We may have different teams, but we all love the Dead. There's really a strong relationship between Deadheads and baseball."

The Cubs lost again, 4–2, their last run coming on a homer by Dawson in the eighth. Whitey Herzog, the Cardinal manager, said that Dawson would be good for twenty homers and ninety RBIs if he could stay healthy.

It was 42 degrees on April fifteenth, and the northeast wind was blowing hard off Lake Michigan, across Lake Shore Drive, over the condos and the elevated train tracks and Murphy's Bleachers and the huge old manually operated scoreboard behind center field that Bill Veeck put up in 1937. It passed over the outfield fence, stirring the bittersweet and ivy, still brown from winter, that Veeck planted in '37, and at last fell in with the various veteran pitches of Steve Trout and Rick Reuschel.

Pittsburgh's Reuschel, the roundish but resourceful former Cub, was making good use of his meteorological advantage, and Trout was weathering nearly as well. The Pirates scored a

run in the second inning on a home run by another former
Cub, Mike Diaz, but were deprived of four in the fifth when a
long drive by Barry Bonds with the bases loaded was arrested
by the wind and collared by Martinez. In the bottom of the
inning, the calamitous Trout came up limping after beating
out an infield hit. "Hey, Trout," came the lonely call from
right field. "This is the fifth inning. Do you want to go out
now?"

"Geez," the man said to nobody specifically, "I've never
seen that guy go more than seven innings."

Sure enough, Trout left after seven. Reuschel, meanwhile,
pitched on in shirtsleeves, working scorelessly through the
eighth. That was when I came upon Mark Wilmot in the back
row of the right-field bleachers.

I knew immediately that Mark was a baseball fan of the
highest order. For one thing, he was keeping score in ink and
carrying White-Out. For another, he had several newspapers
with him. And, most important, he didn't yell or cheer a lot—
although the game was progressing very much to his liking. A
history teacher at a city high school, he had ventured to the
game on this day to watch Reuschel, his favorite pitcher, and
also, it being cold and Wednesday, he knew the crowd would
be negligible. Despite the fact that the Cubs had won three of
four in Philadelphia—the final victory coming after Jamie
Moyer took a no-hitter into the ninth inning—there were
scarcely more than five thousand people at the park. "There
are too few days like this," Mark said. "The crowds ruined
it."

Mark had been coming regularly to the bleachers since
1966. He sat in left field at first, but moved to the other side in
1969 when his privacy was interrupted. Actually, his favorite
place to watch a ballgame was a backwater minor-league
park in some place like Beloit or Kenosha. He read *Baseball
America,* the publication that covers the minor leagues and
college; he was serious about the game and went to great
lengths to be informed. That was why he had taken such an
immediate and intense dislike to Dallas Green. He thought
Green, indirectly but squarely, had presumed him to be a
fool.

"Dallas Green," he said, "came in here and said that the fans are complacent, that they're used to losing. It was like, 'You guys are stupid for supporting this club.' And then he proceeded to run down everything about the ballclub. He just came in here and said, in effect, we've got garbage here. I took that personally. That was me he was talking about. You can't dump on people that way. You've got to have fans like that. You've got to build on that base. I'm not really a Cub fan anymore. I'm a fan of this ballpark. I don't hate the Cubs, and more often than not I pull for them, but I hate Dallas Green so much. I want to run him out of town."

In the ninth inning, Mark's favorite pitcher lost his victory when Reuschel's reliever, Don Robinson, surrendered the four thousandth home run hit by the Cubs in Wrigley Field history. Jody Davis delivered it against the wind to tie the game. In the tenth, though, the Pirates won when they scored twice against Dickie Noles and little-known rookie Lester Lancaster, the last run coming home on a balk by Lancaster with two outs and the bases loaded.

"Lester," a fan yelled, "pack your bags!"

The next day it was cold again, and the Cubs could do nothing against Bob Kipper, a twenty-two-year-old pitcher from the Chicago suburb of Aurora. In the sixth inning, the Pirates—picked for either last or fifth in the division, depending on the state of the Montreal Expos—scored four times against Ed Lynch when Dunston dropped a pop foul and Andy Van Slyke followed with a bases-loaded triple. At that point, a teenaged fan sitting under a blanket in the center-field bleachers ripped off his Cub hat and pulled a Bears stocking cap over his ears. "Man, I'm sick of the Cubs losing," he said. It was the fourth home game of the year.

In the left-field bleachers, a carpenter in a leather jacket screamed at Dernier in center, informing him tactlessly that 1984 had been his career year. Dernier was not amused, but the carpenter's friends were. Finally Dernier turned and pointed past the Cubs' clubhouse, indicating he would meet his antagonist in the parking lot after the game. With that, the carpenter became a hero to his buddies. Inspired by his friend's bravado, one of them got up and walked over to a blonde woman in a red coat sitting in the first row behind the fence. A few moments later, he waved his hand disgustedly and reported back: "She's married."

Kipper pitched the first complete game of his year and won 6–0. The Cubs had played four home games and lost them all, scoring six runs in the process.

It was a troubling sign—not so much a pattern emerging as an apparent reality. Like most teams, the Cubs were customized to suit their ballpark. With its lush background and close fences, Wrigley Field was known as a friendly park to hitters. Although the home-run distances were comparatively deep down the lines—355 feet in left field, 353 in right—the outfield wall swerved in toward the playing area to accommodate the bleachers, and the alleys in left- and right-center registered at 368 feet, an intimate proximity on days when the swift southern air made light of every foot. But the problem with building their team around their ballpark was that, unlike most teams, the Cubs had two ballparks. There was Wrigley Field with the wind blowing in, and Wrigley Field with the wind blowing out.

The Cubs' new jingle, recorded by the Beach Boys to the tune of "Barbara Ann," declared, "Wind blowin' out, wind blowin' in, whichever way it's blowin', the Cubs are gonna win." But it wasn't so. For generations, the Cubs had been sending out teams of brawny men whose pop-ups would become home runs when the summer wind was gusting toward the streets. This myopic philosophy not only precipitated some wretched road records but often made them unfit for even their own park. In the five years previous to 1987, the wind had blown in at Wrigley Field thirty-five percent more often than it had blown out. On such forbidding afternoons, the day was often won by speed and pitching. It was a cold, windy May day in 1917, in fact, when Hippo Vaughn of the Cubs and Fred Toney of the Reds pitched the only double no-hit game in baseball history, the Reds finally prevailing in the tenth inning.

As long as the wind shifts, there will be gossamer days at

Wrigley Field when the score soars into the teens and occasionally the twenties. But the precedent is there on behalf of pitching. The last time the Cubs won the pennant, in 1945, their home-run total was only one higher than the lowest in the National League. They led the league in earned run average that year, and won as many games on the road as they did at home. By the end of the decade, their pitching had decomposed, but it wasn't Wrigley Field's fault. In fact, according to the formula used in the authoritative *Baseball Encyclopedia*, when the Cubs fell to last place in 1948, Wrigley Field was the worst hitter's park in the National League.

Instead of attending to the pitching, however, the Cubs tried to compensate by stocking up with sluggers. First they traded for big Hank Sauer in 1949, then, in 1953, for seven-time home-run champion Ralph Kiner. Ernie Banks's first year was 1954. These fine men sent baseballs soaring into the breeze, but the Cubs never finished in the first division in the fifties. Billy Williams and Ron Santo joined Banks in the sixties, but the Cubs didn't get out of the lower half of the league until Ferguson Jenkins, in his first full Chicago season, won twenty games in 1967. With Leo Durocher managing in his truculent manner and Jenkins winning twenty every year, Chicago maintained moderate success without interruption through 1972. But Durocher was fired that season, Jenkins traded after the next, and the Cubs didn't break even again until Reuschel won twenty games in 1977. They didn't have a winning record until Sutcliffe won the Cy Young Award in 1984.

While a team has obviously never lost a game by hitting home runs, the Cubs' postwar preoccupation with power had just as obviously precluded the very elements with which teams such as the Cardinals and the Dodgers and even the Reds sustained success in the last three decades. The Cardinals' modern tradition of speed dates back to the acquisition of Lou Brock—ironically, from the Cubs—in 1964. Brock, of course, became the all-time stolen base leader. Meanwhile, the last Cub to lead the league in steals was Stan Hack in 1939, with seventeen. The team record for stolen bases, sixty-seven, was set by Frank Chance during the Roosevelt presidency—Teddy's.

Chicagoans have an innate sense about the weather. In the early spring, the city's weather is a Canadian import on most days, but every now and then a warm current will visit from the Gulf. In Chicago, they understand the wind like they understand stuffed pizza. North Siders have been known—perhaps apocryphally, perhaps not—to keep balloons blown up for wind-checking purposes on baseball mornings, or else to wake up, throw open a window and hold out a Cub pennant. They are also uncommonly aware of the sun and its potential for the afternoon.

So it was that on Good Friday I arrived at Wrigley Field embarrassed to be wearing a jacket and a sweater vest. Still a hopeless outsider, I was apparently the only person in Northern Illinois to be duped by the past two days and the A.M. chill. To everybody else, it was day one at Wrigley Beach. Ladies and gentlemen, start your suntans.

At 11:30—Wrigley Field opens two hours before game time, which was 1:20 on April seventeenth—the grandstands were barren and the bleachers were full. As though he were playing Frisbee in the sand, Mike Fitzgerald, a catcher for the Montreal Expos, was tossing a baseball back and forth with happy young people in the bleachers. He would try to catch the return throw behind his back, generally without success. Ultimately, of course, one guy kept the ball and the game ended.

In upper-center field, a man sat down next to me, removed his shirt, applied suntan lotion, then scooted down the row next to two girls. He lifted weights. A lot of guys who took their shirts off in the bleachers lifted weights.

There were also a lot of people with funny hair. When I was growing up, baseball fans didn't have funny hair. But in 1987 it was as if baseball, through the medium of cable television, had cut a video and joined up with pop culture. Some of the girls in the center-field bleachers had spiked hair and tattoos and wore leather jackets and silver belts and a lot of black on their persons and sunglasses like Madonna.

In left field, six kids turned toward the WGN camera set up between the left-field bleachers and the section that's closed off. They had GO CUBS spelled out on their chests. Television. No other baseball team is so steeped in television. The Cubs' home schedule has been televised locally since 1947; since 1982 practically every game has gone out nationally over WGN's superstation. The Cubs are on television; therefore they are. By 1987, sitting in the bleachers at Wrigley Field had become a ceremonial participation in a rite endorsed and glorified by television. Would those six kids have written GO CUBS on their chests if the bleachers weren't on television? Would they have been at the game? The day before, with the temperature in the forties, two teenagers had taken off their shirts as they sang "Take Me Out to the Ballgame" during the seventh-inning stretch, then turned toward the camera and raised their arms triumphantly for the folks at home. The bleachers had become a studio—no lights, but camera and action.

To many, consequently, the most important baseball-related employee of the Tribune Company wasn't Dallas Green or Ryne Sandberg or Rick Sutcliffe; it was Harry Caray. To them, Harry Caray was a great old guy who made baseball fun and sang badly in the seventh inning and liked to party as much as they did—Cub Fan, Bud Man, they called him; the Mayor of Rush Street—and was the star of Cub television. To them, he was baseball. It was ironic. I smugly regarded this as superficial fandom, as contemporary and ephemeral and insubstantial, and not at all what baseball is really about. And yet, when I was a kid, Harry Caray was baseball to me, too.

It was radio then, not TV, and it was St. Louis, not Chicago. My friends and I would periodically and routinely lapse into Harry's voice, using Harry's words. "One" . . . you had to say *one* like a top spinning . . . "strike" . . . a little emphasis there . . . "and a ball, the runners lead away, the stretch, the pitch, HERE it is . . . swung on, and there's a drive" . . . he had been describing home runs in this imitable way for more than forty years . . . "way back . . . it might be outta here . . . it might be . . . it could be" . . . the ball couldn't take this long to leave the park, could it? . . . "it iiiiiiiiiiizzzz . . . a HOME run."

Wait a second. "HO-ly cow!" That was what baseball sounded like. It sounded like Harry Caray in the backyard in the summer. And the key word there is *sounded*. Baseball used to have a sound; but the sound was being replaced by a look. Everything was changing, except for Harry Caray. I began to take a warmer view of the young people around me who stood up and raised their beers every time the camera turned.

Meanwhile, at She-Nannigans Irish Pub & Sports Bar on Division Street, people were signing their names to the world's biggest get-well card to send to Harry in Palm Springs. He had been been playing gin at a country club there in February when the cards fell from his hand. It was a mild stroke, and he was expected back at the microphone on May nineteenth. In the meantime, WGN had arranged a lineup of guest announcers to fill in. It was a master move that put nobody on the spot and kept alive the sense of a good time that Harry manifested. On Opening Day, the guest announcer was Brent Musburger of CBS, who had said, "Before I die, I want to do the Cubs." Others included columnists Mike Royko and George Will, Cardinal announcer Jack Buck, NBC announcer Bob Costas, Hall of Famer Stan Musial, actor George Wendt, and, on Good Friday, comedian Bill Murray.

"Leading off for the Expos will be Casey Candaele," announced Murray as Montreal's first batter stepped in against Sutcliffe. "Well, he's no good."

The Expos *weren't* very good, actually. Dawson had left them. Their other superstar, Tim Raines, was a free agent whom, incredibly, no team had signed. Their best remaining player, Hubie Brooks, was injured. Their best young player, Andres Galarraga, was hurt early in the game Friday. That left Tim Wallach pretty much by himself.

"Here's a stupid single to center by Wallach," said Murray. "Boy, I hate this guy. He always hits the Cubs."

Montreal's best relief pitcher for the previous several seasons, Jeff Reardon, had been traded to Minnesota. Two of their best starters, Charlie Lea and Joe Hesketh, were lost to injury. Their best remaining starter, Floyd Youmans, was overweight. And Youmans was getting pounded by the Cubs, particularly Jody Davis, on April seventeenth. Davis hit a two-run homer in the second inning, then doubled in the fourth and scored on a single by Sutcliffe. When that happened, Youmans, not one to call the pumpkin plump, began making remarks about the prodigious heft of home-plate umpire Eric Gregg. Gregg ejected Youmans. "You hate to see that happen," said Murray. "Especially when we're hitting him so well."

While Sutcliffe finished off a shutout, in the center-field bleachers a young fellow in a flowered shirt held his lighter underneath the pants of one of his friends from the English muffin factory where they worked. The fellow was of Eric Gregg proportions, and all at once he stood up and began sniffing purposefully. "I smell chocolate," he said. His muffin friends scrambled madly to get out of his way.

Tom Foley was the last batter. "Is that terrible Foley up there again?" said Murray. "Hey, Foley! Strike out, Foley! I hate everything you stand for!" Gregg called Foley out on strikes and Sutcliffe had a four-hitter.

The shutout was encouraging for Sutcliffe and the Cubs, and it made me think back to a late March afternoon in Mesa, when the exhibition game was over and a few good fans remained at HoHoKam Park to talk baseball and watch batting practice. I had met a bleacher fan named Marcy Schauwecker who had been visiting with a former bleacher fan named Barry Spector—he had gotten married and become an attorney and bought tickets in the grandstand—and we had talked about the unique and aesthetic aspects of the Cubs and Wrigley Field. "The first time I saw Wrigley Field," Marcy said, "it was breathtaking. It was the color. I think the Cubs were playing the Reds, and with the blue and red uniforms and the green grass . . . I've never seen anything like it since." The conversation had gone on about lights, the impact of cable, the Cubs' appeal to women—the whole package of Cubness—and somewhere in the course of it, this woman who had been so taken by the tones of Wrigley Field pointed out optimistically that Sutcliffe was working on a new pitch.

This was what was really important in the spring: finding a reason to believe that the Cubs would do well in the year ahead. Sutcliffe had been having problems all spring, but he had three RBIs and a stolen base on Good Friday, and the new pitch, whatever it was, was evidently working.

The networks love Wrigley Field. With its bricks and ivy and sunshine and bleacher bums, it is the most photogenic of major-league ballparks. The Cubs were on network television Saturday, April 18, despite the fact that they were playing a team for which a man named Wallace Johnson batted third. I don't believe I'd ever seen anyone so bereft of credentials as Wallace Johnson batting third in a major-league lineup.

If nothing else, though, the Expos were a likable team. In their bright red warmup shirts, they looked good playing pepper in the lush green outfield. Pitcher Randy St. Claire surreptitiously signed a baseball that a kid lowered on a string from the left-field bleachers. And Fitzgerald was at it again, this time trying to throw a ball through the hole reserved for Montreal's eighth inning in the scoreboard. Fortunately, Fitzgerald had made friends in the bleachers. Otherwise, throwing at the scoreboard would not have been amicably received. Once, Tim Foli of the Pirates threw a ball against the scoreboard before a game, and Jerry Pritikin complained to the Pittsburgh management. The next day, Pritikin put Foli's name on his voodoo doll and entertained much pin sticking. Bleacher fans regard the scoreboard as a family heirloom. They thought it inexcusable, for instance, that the Cubs had allowed it to go unpainted for so long. On the other hand, Pritikin had considered 1986 to be a worthwhile year, because even though the Cubs finished in fifth place, they had removed the Budweiser advertisement from the base of the scoreboard. Wrigley Field fans take the same attitude toward ads on the scoreboard that the Sierra Club would take toward taco stands along the trails of the Grand Tetons. But Mike Fitzgerald had participated playfully in the spirit of Wrigley Field, and when, after countless attempts, he finally put a ball through the top of the eighth inning and it disappeared, he turned and sprinted off the field in triumph.

It was a beautiful Saturday. A young man took his seat singing, "Heaven . . . I'm in heaven. . . ." A guy explained Wrigley Field's universal appeal to his girlfriend. "Even if the Cubs are bad," he said, "the weather's usually good."

The generally agreeable afternoon weather is one of several reasons why the Cubs unquestionably have recruited more female fans than any other baseball team. The bleachers are a most sociable tanning salon. This factor is of increasing consequence, also, to the legion of bodybuilding modern men who have shown a willingness to invest time in their unshirted appearance. The Cubs merchandise sunshine. Bill Veeck, who never owned the Cubs but should have, said once that if a baseball team tried to sell tickets just to the real baseball fans, it would be out of business by Mother's Day.

This is not to say that there isn't a significant number of women who are real Cub and baseball fans; there is. Many of them are homemakers who used to listen faithfully to morning host Wally Phillips on WGN and leave the radio on for Vince Lloyd and the Cubs. Some are television housewives who prefer the Cubs to soap operas; a ballgame is ideal daytime television, because it doesn't have to be watched from a stationary position. All over America, fathers hand down the love of baseball to their sons; in Chicago, mothers also hand it down to their daughters. It's a family game. For decades, the Wrigleys pounded home the theme that their ballpark was a family place. They promoted it like a big picnic. It was like their Doublemint gum: double your pleasure, double your fun.

A college girl sitting next to me on April eighteenth said that she preferred Sandberg without his mustache and that her favorite players were Dernier and Martinez. Dernier had played well in '84; why Martinez? He was cute, she said.

As the Cubs took a 1–0 lead in the first, a young woman named Deborah who said she was twenty-six and the head of freight billing at the office of a large corporation gave advice to the college girl and her friend about relationships. She also kept telling me, "Put in your book that I have a big chest." I explained that the book was nonfiction. Deborah's last name was Polish, prompting the guy next to her to say "Do you know why so many Polish names end in 'ski'? Because they can't spell 'toboggan.' " His name was Greg Martin, and he was from Denver. He worked for Continental Airlines and could fly wherever he wanted, so he had flown to Chicago to go to Wrigley Field. He would visit ten ballparks during the season. Wrigley Field was first.

Montreal got four runs in the second inning against Greg Maddux, and Chicago did very little against Bob Sebra, although Chico Walker managed to steal two bases. That gave the Cubs thirty straight stolen bases without being caught—seventeen of them in 1987. That was very good, but, on the other hand, if you took a chance on something thirty times in a row and it worked every time, wouldn't you think that maybe you should be taking more chances? Meanwhile, two of Deborah's friends, Italian sisters who were also in freight billing (it was the day out for freight billing) tugged mischievously at men's shorts as they walked past. One of the sisters said she wanted to remove her shirt and pretend she was wearing Playtex swimwear.

The Cubs lost, 4–2, their fifth defeat in six home games. But it was early in the year and the sun gave everybody warm shoulders. A band of black horn players and a drummer was set up on the sidewalk outside Gate N. The band played "Wipe Out" and "Louie Louie" and "Tequila," and the young white baseball fans gathered around. Some of the drunks danced like Pee-Wee Herman. A little kid picked up coins and put them into a horn case.

The sidewalks were hot on Easter morning. On residential streets just south of Wrigley Field—Aldine and Roscoe and Newport—little Hispanic girls in blue dresses skipped into neighborhood churches.

Not ten years ago, half the names on the poll sheet of the 44th Ward were Hispanic. The Hispanics had followed the Asians, who followed the Eastern Europeans, who followed the Swedes and Swiss and Germans who settled the community of Lake View in 1836. They grew celery, and Lake View consisted of truck farms. Chicago had become chartered as a city in 1837—it was celebrating its one hundred fiftieth anniversary in 1987—but Lake View didn't become part of it until 1889. After that, it boomed residentially, growing by more than fifty percent to nearly one hundred thousand people by 1920. When there was a housing shortage after World War II, the ones in Lake View were divided into two-flats and three-flats. The neighborhood became more dense and less gracious. The bothersome noise from the north-south el (the elevated rapid-transit trains) and the deterioration of the houses that weren't built of brick and stone gradually turned Lake View into a low-rent district. The neighborhood population peaked at a hundred twenty-five thousand in the fifties, as Japanese and Filipinos clustered around Clark Street, leaving a legacy of inelegant but worthwhile restaurants. Despite their number, the Asians were not an assertive presence in the community. But the Hispanics were. The streets were dominated by Hispanic gangs like the Eagles and the Latin Kings.

The neighborhood was almost entirely Hispanic when Jim Murphy, a former policeman in the gang crime unit, moved in on Sheffield Avenue in 1972. "I was the only English-speaking person in the neighborhood," said Murphy, who bought Ray's Bleachers at Waveland and Sheffield and renamed it Murphy's Bleachers. "You had to carry a gun to take your trash into the alley. People didn't realize how bad it was. It was fine during the daytime, but at night the street gangs came out."

One day in the seventies, Bill Westman was walking down Wilton Avenue near Grace, two blocks from the bleacher gate, when a car came barreling down the one-way street the wrong way. "There was a bar there, and a group of kids in front of the bar," said Westman, a Century 21 realtor on Clark Street just north of the ballpark. "These kids in the car were sitting up in the window sills, with their guns on the roof of the car, and they started shooting at the guys in front of the bar. I was about half a block away, and all of a sudden I heard a whistling sound, a shot going right over my head. I think they were shooting at me, too. There were a couple of guys shot, lying in the street. I ducked into a doorway." He said that people were afraid to walk east of Clark Street.

By 1987, Lake View was nearly eighty percent white, most of it yuppie. The Lake View Citizen's Council—one of the groups opposing lights at Wrigley Field—had resisted urban renewal for the neighborhood, which returned to style through what was colloquially called "gentrification." That meant that the handsome brick and limestone walls were washed down, second-floor porches fortified, linoleum removed, kitchens remodeled, and extra bedrooms turned into dens or solariums. The Lake View population was down under one hundred thousand again, but real estate was up. Houses that could be bought for twenty to thirty thousand dollars in the early seventies sold in 1987 for three hundred thousand. Rent multiplied six to eight times in that period. But young professionals paid the rates because the neighborhood is close to lovely Lincoln Park, the lake, and downtown; it is self-sufficient and interesting; and the homes were built with German craftsmanship. The only weak feature in most of the houses is the sandy surface of their basements, where Lake Michigan used to be.

The prosaic, white-chested edifice of Wrigley Field occupies a square block very near the heart of Lake View gentrification, most of which has occurred south and east of the ballpark on streets with maple and mulberry trees. Because of the high rises near the lake, the numerous courtyard apartment complexes, and the broad lower-rent buildings on the corners, Lake View is much more dense than its quiet residential character suggests. In fact, it is one of the densest neighborhoods in the country, an eclectic community with countless pockets of ethnic groups.

In that way, it's different from almost any other neighborhood in Chicago. Where Mayor Daley grew up in Bridgeport on the South Side, the Irish didn't dare cross over into the black neighborhood, or even the Slavic neighborhood, that bordered theirs. Lake View, though, is Chicago's Ellis Island.

Streets like Broadway and Halsted are a mixed bag of yuppies, punks, pimps, bag ladies, basketball players, fashion plates, artists, hustlers, businessmen. The adjacent residential streets provide addresses for Jews, blacks, Germans, Poles, Japanese, Puerto Ricans. Lake View has the largest concentration of senior citizens in Illinois, and the largest gay population. Restaurants across the street from one another specialize in Thai food and barbecued ribs, Mexican and Ethiopian, sushi, and Vienna beef hotdogs. Southport is ethnic, Broadway is garish, Belmont is busy, Halsted is gay. If one had to choose a single square mile that contains the most complete cross-section of the United States, the most fully and fundamentally American place in the world, he could start measuring at home plate, Wrigley Field, Chicago, Illinois.

On Easter morning, however, none of the little Hispanic girls in blue dresses were lined up outside Gate N. Instead, there was a guy wearing a hat bearing the likeness of two female breasts in a bikini top. Another fellow had a hat with a middle finger sticking out of it. Another wore a T-shirt with the letters DAMM, which stood for Drunks Against MADD (Mothers Against Drunk Drivers) Mothers. There was also a group of students from the University of Illinois, one of which, mindful of the struggles of the Cubs' young centerfielder, asked his friend, "So, do you think Martinez is gonna win the batting championship?"

Martinez, in fact, had batted himself out of the lineup by Easter. Walker was in center field and Dayett in left, even though Montreal was pitching a right-hander, the long-beleaguered Lary Sorensen. When Dayett came out to take his position in the first inning, the left-field fans applauded him, aware of the chance he was getting. Dayett was thirty years old and had batted only 249 times in the big leagues despite a two-year stretch in the Yankee organization during which he hit sixty-nine home runs. He was not a fast or cunning player, and his swing was not the stuff of cinema; consequently, opportunity had not worn out its knuckles on his door. To Cub fans, this made Dayett the underdog's underdog, the outfielder whom fate had treated utterly Cubbishly. A woman

named Karen Fox had driven all the way to Des Moines,
Iowa, just to watch Dayett play in 1986. When he came to the
plate one time during spring training, a man stood up and
yelled, "Dayett, if you don't go north, we don't go north!"
Dayett knew the fans were on his side, and on Easter afternoon he turned and acknowledged them with a grateful smile.
Then the Expos scored three in the first against Moyer, who
was making his first start since the near no-hitter in Philadelphia.

When Montreal took the field, their man in left was somebody named Alonzo Powell. It was looking as though Raines
would sign again with the Expos on the first of May, when
free agents were allowed to renew talks with their former
teams, but in the meantime Montreal pretended that Wallace
Johnson could bat third and Alonzo Powell could play left
field. "Give me a P!" shouted the weekend regulars in the left-
field bleachers. "Give me an O . . . Give me a W . . . Give me
an E . . . Give me an L . . . Give me another L . . . What's it
spell?

"Powell!"

"Fee-fi-fo-fum! Powell is a fucking bum!"

One of the left-field regulars said "stinking bum" instead.
His name was Steve Herzberg, and he came to every weekend
game with his wife and wore tie-dyed T-shirts and stood in
left field blowing bubbles and yelling at outfielders and umpires. "Hey, Powell!" he boomed in a great bleacher voice.
"You're a bum, Powell! When Raines comes back, you're in
Double A! Double A, Powell!"

He was taking pictures of the second-base umpire. "Look
at Eric Gregg," he said. "He casts a shadow over the entire
right side of the infield."

Jerry Pritikin sat in left field, too, when he sat. Usually he
walked around the bleachers carrying signs and converting
non-Cub fans and trying to get on television. His shtick was
for publicity, in part, but it wasn't a put-on. Being a good fan
was a very serious thing to the Bleacher Preacher. He wanted
somehow to make a living at it, and if he did, it would be an
honest living. He had been infatuated with baseball from the

time he was a small boy and sat in the living room on Sunday nights, drinking root beer and listening silently while his father and a friend waited around the radio for Walter Winchell to come on and talked about Chance and Three-Finger Brown and the great Cub team of 1906, and Fred Merkle of the Giants not touching second base in 1908. Pritikin grew up on Roscoe and Broadway, a few blocks south of the ballpark, and as a kid he would hang around after the games and turn over seats in the grandstand, for which he would be rewarded each time with a pass to the next game. He was Jewish, and his idol was Hank Greenberg. When the Cubs played the Tigers in the 1945 World Series, Pritikin, eight years old, begged his father to take him to see the Series and Greenberg. "You're too young to go to the World Series," his father said. "I'll take you the next time the Cubs are in it." Henry Pritikin was unable to keep his promise, because he died in 1981. "The last thirty days of his life he didn't say anything," said Pritikin, "except for one time, when he woke up and said, 'We gotta get rid of Kingman.' That was the only thing he said the last thirty days of his life."

Easter Sunday, Pritikin's brother and his family sat with Jerry—they call him Jerome—in the left-field bleachers. Allen Pritikin, a successful businessman, doesn't have his brother's zeal for the Cubs, but he cared for the game nonetheless. His father had raised him on baseball heroes, and he had raised his own son the same way. "When we were kids, people came to the ballpark to see individuals," he said. "I was a Cardinal fan because of Stan Musial. Once I took my son to a game during school, so I wrote a note to the teacher. The note said, 'My son won't be in school today. He's going to see Willie Mays.' " His son and his son's fiancée had come with Allen Pritikin to watch the Cubs and the Expos. "Your dad thought he'd see you playing ball here," Allen said to his son, "and my dad thought he'd see me playing here."

Sorensen pitched six innings, held the ineffectual Cubs to one run, and was relieved by another undistinguished journeyman, Andy McGaffigan. In the seventh, McGaffigan threw a pitch close to Dunston, and then threw another one close. Dunston dropped his bat and sprinted toward the pitcher, swinging wildly when he got there. The pitcher ducked, and Dunston, never slowing down, tumbled over him. Both teams rushed onto the field, and in the bleachers, security guards stood ready at the outfield walls so that nobody jumped over.

McGaffigan pitched three perfect innings for his first save, and the Cubs, 1–6 at Wrigley Field, gladly left for St. Louis.

In St. Louis, Jody Davis won a game with a ninth-inning homer and the next night Dawson, batting .157, beat the Cardinals with a grand slam. The Cubs lost once, won three straight in Montreal to go 9–8 for the year, and when they returned home on April twenty-eighth, they were only a game behind the Cardinals. What's more, St. Louis's best pitcher, John Tudor, had broken his leg on Easter Sunday when he tried to cushion young Mets catcher Barry Lyons as Lyons came barreling into the St. Louis dugout in pursuit of a foul ball. The Cardinals' catcher, Pena, had also been hurt. The Cubs were tied with the Mets, and the Mets had problems, too. Dwight Gooden, the league's best pitcher, was away from the team at a drug treatment center, and New York's top reliever, Roger McDowell, was on the disabled list. The Cubs were in better shape than anybody. Dawson was the National League Player of the Week.

As they flew back from Montreal, some of Cubs looked out their windows and saw another jet whoosh past. "Not now," cried Dayett. "We've won three in a row."

The Giants were in town Tuesday, with former Cub Mike Krukow pitching. When they arrived in Chicago, Krukow had taken charge of the tradition in which a San Francisco rookie applies red paint to the testicles of a horse named Winchester, on which General Philip Sheridan rides in his statue at Belmont and Sheridan avenues. Sheridan, a Civil War hero, had led the effort to preserve order in Chicago after the great fire of 1871, and every National League bus passes the statue on the way to Wrigley Field. In the statue, the horse is rearing, and the players know this monument as "The

Horse's Balls of Chicago," and league tradition has held that looking at the testicles can bring bad luck to a hitter who is going well. The Giants added their own little touch, and in 1987, infielder Matt Williams had been appointed by Krukow to perform the honors.

In the back row of the right-center field bleachers Tuesday, a very husky man, already tan, was reading the *Daily Racing Form* with his shirt off. Next to him, two old-timers in roadster hats, remnants of the Damon Runyon days, sat silently, one in a winter overcoat and the other with a scarf around his neck. Another old man read a newspaper pulled from a grocery bag stuffed with them. These men had seen Krukow pitch in Wrigley Field many times before, but seldom better than he was pitching Tuesday.

His opponent was Sutcliffe, who gave up a run in the first and then held his own for a while. Moreland helped him with an impressive backhanded stop at third base, which pleased the woman next to me, a twenty-four-year-old banker named Jackie in a skirt and high heels. "When Cey and Bowa were on the left side of the infield, every ball they waved at," she said. "Every ball."

Later, Jackie was talking to the man she came with—they were on a long lunch hour—and she was obviously upset about something, waving her arms about vigorously. She turned and explained. "Oooh, it just makes me so mad," she said. "Michael, and Jim Frey before him—it seems like their goal in life is to make Lee Smith a millionaire. They only bring him in when it's a save situation. It's ridiculous. I mean, he's pretty good, but he's not Reardon." That was impressive. She didn't say that Smith wasn't Sutter, or wasn't Gossage; everybody knew that Sutter and Gossage had been superstar relief pitchers. Reardon had become the best reliever in the National League before he was traded in the off-season, but only the good fans knew it—and so comfortable was she with this fact that she didn't have to use his first name.

I asked Jackie how she felt when the Cubs blew their two-game lead in the playoffs in '84. "I was impossible to live with for days after '84," she said. "The worst was the fourth game (when Steve Garvey, the player Cub fans hated most, beat them with a two-run homer in the ninth). I was going to Notre Dame then, and we played Miami that day in the rain. It was a miserable day. Here I am sitting in the rain watching my team get murdered by vermin, and then I have to go inside and watch that."

The sixth inning Tuesday was almost as bad, the Giants scoring five runs against Sutcliffe. Undaunted, however, two guys in right-center tried to get friendly with three nurses. They teased them about being yuppies. Finally, one of the nurses tired of it. "We're not yuppies," she said fiercely, "and I resent the hell out of that. We're nurses. We work nights. We wipe ass. We're not impressed."

Durham homered, and the Cubs scored twice in the seventh. Across the aisle from the nurses, a group of firemen drank beer and made small bets. One of them kept betting a dollar that every batter would reach. "Reach" was the term used by the old bettors to mean that a batter would make it to second base, but the fireman didn't know that. He kept betting a dollar that a batter would reach *first* base, with no odds. "Buck he reaches," he would say. "Buck he reaches." He was losing, of course. There isn't a player in the major leagues who reaches base half the time.

The Giants won, 6–2. "Rick Sutcliffe made fifty thousand dollars today and he lost," a man said loudly from the back of the bleachers. "I want everybody to know that!"

In eight home games, the Cubs had managed but one victory. In the clubhouse, Durham groped for a solution. "We may need to bring the billy goat back and see what he can do," he said.

When the Cubs made the World Series in 1945, William Sianis, owner of the Billy Goat Tavern, had a box seat ticket for his goat, but P. K. Wrigley wouldn't let the animal in the ballpark. So Sianis put a hex on the Cubs. There are worse explanations for why the Cubs lost that Series and hadn't · been in one since. The curse was perpetuated by Sianis's nephew, Sam, until Dallas Green welcomed both him and *his* goat, number XX, to Wrigley Field for Opening Day in

1982—for which Sam and the goat were so grateful that they turned the hex on the Cubs' opponents. They came back in 1983 and 1984, the last time being the first playoff game against the Padres, which the Cubs won.

Despite his disrespect for the supernatural powers of goats, Wrigley was rather taken with the notion of a hex. He once actually hired a professional Evil Eye, a squirrely, disreputable little man who was paid five thousand dollars—with an extra twenty-five thousand dollars if the Cubs won the pennant—to sit behind home plate and cast spells over opposing pitchers, none of whom cooperated. But unlike the Evil Eye, the goat was a figure of some repute within the hex industry. And he hadn't been to Wrigley Field in 1987.

The sun was out early Wednesday, and in the back row of the bleachers a woman held aluminum foil under her face. Two long-time bleacher men sat down in right-center. "I've got to get to all the games I can before the kids get out of school," one of them said. A high school girl named Heather threw out the first pitch, underhanded. In the grandstand, her friends cheered. "Pathetic throw," said a guy in the bleachers.

The wind was blowing out for the first time all year, and the Giants took a quick lead against Greg Maddux, the Cubs' baby-faced pitcher who was the youngest player in the National League. Chili Davis doubled off the left-field wall in the first inning and Candy Maldonado followed with a wind-blown pop fly that Martinez, back in the lineup, dove for and missed. "I'll bet that Martinez won't be starting on June first," said one of the bleacher veterans, a retired jeweler named Joe Barach.

"No, that Martinez is going to make this team," said the other, Leonard Becker. "He's going to hit, he can run, he's going to make this team."

Dawson homered in the bottom of the first, and the fans in right field stood and chanted his first name as he came out to take his position. In the top of the third, Jeffrey Leonard hit a pop fly and Sandberg, who had coped with Wrigley's tricky winds for five years, backed up with the intention of catching it easily. The ball landed in the dirt by first base and a run scored.

Leads are capricious on windy days at Wrigley Field, however, and Martinez led off the Cubs' third with a single that Maldonado booted, and booted again, in right field. Walker and Dawson followed with a single and a double, but minutes later, Matt Williams, the rookie who had touched up General Sheridan's horse, tied the game with a home run onto Waveland Avenue. It was an eventful game that was about to become excruciating for both pitchers. The next batter, Chris Speier, hit a line drive that struck Maddux in such a place as to raise his voice. Then San Francisco's pitcher, Roger Mason, sent a one-hopper into right field, but Dawson, not conceding the single, fielded it and threw a ninety-mile-an-hour fastball that beat Mason to first base by a step and a half. It was something I'd never seen before, although Becker probably had.

A retired businessman with thick gray hair and a goatee that made him look like a foreign intelligence agent, Becker had been sitting in the bleachers for more than fifty years, most of the time in right-center with dozens of other men who were willing to lay cash on their knowledge of the game. They were the ones about whom the play *Bleacher Bums* had been written. Most of them had died or stopped coming when the Cubs eliminated the bleacher pass gate—a separate entrance where some of the regulars could get in without a ticket if they knew the right person—and when the bleachers got crowded with yuppies and yahoos. But Becker lived only a half mile from the ballpark, and he could walk or ride his bicycle. He loved the game too much to stay away. He didn't bother with weekends or 3:05 starts, but for the 1:20 weekday games he would buy a ticket outside and then find a seat at the end of a row in front of the concession stand so he could hop up and watch replays on one of the televisions. He especially liked smart plays. He had been impressed in the first inning when Maldonado tagged up from first base and advanced to second on a deep fly to left. After seeing the Dawson replay, he was still excited. "He's alert!" he declared crisply. "He's a major leaguer! That was worth the price of admission!"

I mentioned to Becker and Joe that I suspected Ernie Lombardi, the lumbering old catcher from the thirties and forties, had been thrown out at first base a few times like that.

"How do you know Ernie Lombardi?" Becker asked.

"I bet you can't tell me his nickname," said Joe.

"Schnozz," I said.

"Schnozz, sure. But he had another one, too. Bocci."

By the bottom of the fourth, the wind had started to reverse itself, and in center field Chili Davis dropped a fly ball hit by Dunston. Then Martinez hit a line drive to center and Davis, either confused or deceived by the fickle breeze, watched it whiz over his head for a triple. The Cubs scored three times, and the inning went on long enough for Dawson to get an infield single. It was 6–3, and in front of Leonard Becker and Joe Barach, a guy in a loud print shirt smoked marijuana and complained when a blonde cocktail waitress in the next row placed her feet next to him. "I need my space," he said.

Dickie Noles came in to pitch. One of the bleacher regulars, a young businessman, told Becker he was flying to Montana the next week. There was a six-hour layover in Denver, and the Triple A team there had an afternoon game; he could put his bags in a locker at the airport and get to the ballgame and back before his flight left. Meanwhile, the guy in the loud shirt left, presumably to get some space, and another the same age sat down, wearing a suit. The latter was a waiter in a French restaurant, and his boss, Jean-Pierre, had told him to go to the ballgame because the restaurant wouldn't be busy that day. The bleachers were busy, though. Becker gazed at the crowd around him and turned to Barach. "We're finished here," he said. "I can see it happening. School's not even out, and look at it."

Joe agreed, but said he would be back anyway, with his eight-year-old grandson. He had brought each of his grandchildren to the bleachers from the time they were six to the time they were twelve. "Once they come out here five years or so, that's it," he said. "They're hooked."

In the sixth, Dawson tripled to complete his cycle. It was a rare thing—the second thing he'd done in the game that I'd never seen before. Dawson had hit for the cycle once before in his career, but there are many fine players who never do. Just the previous week, Pittsburgh's Junior Ortiz had tripled to give him the cycle for his *career*, 208 times at bat. After he did it, Ortiz kept the baseball.

In the eighth, a fan behind home plate climbed the screen. "Craziest game I ever saw," said Becker.

Dawson singled for his fifth hit in the bottom of the eighth, and the Cubs won their second home game of the month, 8–4.

When it changed directions in the middle of the afternoon Wednesday, the wind had brought in more cold Canadian air. The warm weather that had seemed so promising as it heated up the Chicago pavement on Easter morning had skipped off to Oklahoma or somewhere. On the last day of April, the Cubs rubbed their hands as they waited to get into the batting cage.

"How'd you like summer in Chicago?" Billy Williams asked Dayett.

"Where was it?"

"It just passed."

The wind was blowing crisply toward home plate from center field, and Gary Matthews was hitting fly balls short of the fence. "Gonna play the elements, go with the ball?" Williams asked him.

Dayett stepped in, hit a fly high to left, and shouted, "Wall!" The ball didn't even reach the warning track.

"Wall!" scoffed Sandberg, laughing. "Wall!"

Moreland, who was in a bad slump anyway, borrowed Matthews's bat. It was heavier than his own. "I'll hit one out with this bitch," he said. He couldn't. His fly balls fell harmlessly in the grass. "What do you think?" he asked rhetorically, wondering if a home run would be possible in the forbidding wind. "Do you think it'll go? I don't think it'll go."

Finally Matthews hit a ball over the fence in left and Jerry Mumphrey hit one over the fence in right. Mumphrey turned to Moreland. "It'll go, Zonk," he said.

To the side of the cage, Matthews leaned on his bat and talked about the peculiarities of Wrigley Field and the stigma of being thirty-six with bad knees. It was a difficult time for him. In 1984, he had been one of the Cubs' most popular players; when he took his position in left field, the bleacher bums saluted him, and he saluted them back. But even his fans knew his days were over in the outfield. In spring training, a man in a Cub hat had watched Sarge hobble down to first base and yelled, "Cut him. He needs a wheelchair to get down there." He named a retirement home that he thought would be suitable for Matthews. The Cubs had resolved to go with faster, younger players in left field, and Matthews hadn't started a game all season. Dallas Green had said he wanted to trade him, and Matthews, though he loved Chicago, was eager to go to the American League, where he could be a designated hitter. But he hadn't hit often enough to show that he still could. "You know, Chili Davis had trouble with those balls in the wind and sun yesterday," the Sarge said. "If it had been me out there, they'd be saying I can't get to the ball with my knees."

On the other side of the cage, Durham yelled something to the Giants' Chili Davis about the wind, and Davis spread his hands as if to bunt, a two-fold message. He was teasing Durham that he was going to lay one down in his direction, and he was also saying, "Hey, with the wind like this, you don't think I'm going to *swing*, do you?"

The wind was an inscrutable third party in the tactical struggles waged between hitters and pitchers. When it was blowing out, hitters looked for a high pitch they could lift, and pitchers, knowing that, tried to throw low. But then a hitter, knowing *that*, might come to expect a low pitch and adjust his swing accordingly; a low-ball hitter might do quite well against the wind. On the other hand, some pitchers did well throwing against the wind because it improved their breaking stuff. When the wind was blowing the other way, against the hitter, a pitcher might serve up more high strikes than he normally would, daring the high-ball hitters to challenge the elements. "I just try to hit line drives," said Dawson, after hitting a string of them against Glenn Brummer, the batting-practice pitcher. "You can't really adjust to the conditions, because the pitcher is aware of it, too. If you get defensive, he might come at you more than he normally would. It's a cat-and-mouse game within a game."

When Gate N opened across the ballpark, the old man with the painter's hat bought some nachos and took his place in the upper center-field bleachers. I still wanted to get him to open up. I told him I hadn't seen him the day before.

"I was here," he said.

I told him there were some things in that game that I'd never seen. He looked at me and ate nachos.

"Take it easy," I said.

In the left-field bleachers, it was a slow day for Moe Mullins. Mullins had bought a bleacher ticket for nearly every game so far, but he was yet to stay for one. He was there to catch batting-practice home runs. He, along with several others, had been doing this for more than twenty-five years, and in that time he had caught about fourteen hundred National League baseballs. His friend, Rich Buhrke, had accumulated about sixteen hundred. "But he counts spring training," said Mullins, a purist. "I went to spring training this year, and I got twenty-seven balls. I don't count that. It's too easy. It's like robbery."

Mullins grew up in Wrigleyville—the neighborhood name used for the portion of Lake View within four blocks or so of the ballpark—and at lunch break from LeMoyne School on Waveland he used to run over to the ballpark and get on the field to catch batting practice balls for the Cubs and the other teams. Even after that was disallowed, he never paid to get in until 1983, when the Cubs eliminated the bleacher pass gate. That changed things for a lot of the regulars—the common lament was, "Why should I pay four bucks to get into the ballgame?"—but Mullins just started buying tickets and standing by the back fence of the bleachers, gloved and ready.

He worked a late-afternoon shift in the warehouse of an air freight company, so he would drive to the ballpark early and park across the street in one of the spots vacated by the police when their morning security meeting broke up. Until the gate opened, he would catch balls out on Waveland and Kenmore, the little street perpendicular to Waveland where Dave Kingman once hit a home run onto the porch of the third house (some say it was the fourth). When he went into the ballpark, Buhrke and some of the other guys stayed outside on the street, and Mullins helped them out. As balls were headed over the back fence of the bleachers, he would signal his friends which way to run. Almost anything in the bleachers, though, was his. If he stood in left field, he could cover from the family section in dead left to the WGN camera in left-center. Both his knees had been operated on, but he still had his range. A ball would arc toward a spot six rows in front of him, and while everybody there would reach, Mullins would sprint over, stand on a chair and stick up his glove just as the ball came down. He knew how to play the hitters, too.

Mullins probably got more balls from Ron Santo than from any other player, but Santo wasn't the best batting-practice hitter. "The best I ever saw," he said, "was Mike Anderson when he was with the Phillies. That guy was awesome." Anderson hit all of twenty-eight home runs in his big-league career. The best team in terms of pregame power was the Braves around 1972, with Hank Aaron and Darrell Evans and Earl Williams and that crowd. The most balls Mullins ever caught in a day was twelve, twice. He gave a lot of balls to a Little League team, and some to the local team for which he was player-manager. When batting practice was over, he went to lunch; he wasn't much of a Cub fan. "If the Cubs lose, that's better for me because there are fewer people out here," he said.

There were always guys pushing and running over people for balls hit into the bleachers, though, and as they did so on the last day of April, Jerry Pritikin held up his newest sign: THOU SHALT NOT KILL FOR A BASEBALL. Pritikin had just been offered a job by an advertising agency. He described the possibilities as very lucrative, but he didn't know what to do. He wanted a job where he could tie promotions into baseball, and he wasn't sure he could do that with the agency job. One of his clients would be Dental Implants.

The north wind was still whipping when the game began,

and Jamie Moyer made the most of it, keeping the Giants hitless until the fifth. The Cubs squandered a two-run lead in the sixth but went ahead again in the bottom of the inning when Martinez, who had held onto his position and was looking more and more like he would be long-term in center field, tied the game with a single, and Walker hit a sacrifice fly to put the Cubs ahead, 4–3. That was still the score in the seventh inning when Dunston made two sensational plays in succession. First, he flashed across the diamond to pick up a slow roller by Speier, sprawling as he threw to Durham and ending up ten yards from first base. Then Mike Aldrete, a left-handed batter, hit a crisp grounder between shortstop and third, for which Dunston dove headlong, then popped up acrobatically and threw low and hard to Durham, who scooped the ball smartly out of the dirt.

In right-center, Becker was ecstatic about what he'd witnessed. "That's the best play you'll see all year!" he shouted happily. "What a play. Oh, that was marvelous. I'm glad I saw that."

At the end of the inning, left field chanted, "Right field sucks!" and right field responded in kind. Somebody spotted a guy in blue not chanting and started up a new version. "The guy in the blue sucks!" he shouted, and soon the cry was taken up across the bleachers. "The guy in the blue sucks!"

Becker, meanwhile, was still marveling over the play pulled off by Dunston and Durham. "That was really something," he said. "What a scoop-up! What a scoop-up!"

In the manner to which the banker Jackie had alluded, the Cubs brought in Lee Smith to hold the lead in the eighth. The Giants tied the game. In the ninth, with Smith still pitching, Speier doubled and Harry Spilman, a pinch hitter, singled him in to put San Francisco ahead, 5–4. Spilman then stole second base—his first stolen base in ten seasons of major-league baseball—and was immediately removed for a pinch runner.

In the bottom of the ninth, against San Francisco's Greg Minton, Walker walked, and with two outs Dawson had his chance. He slashed a ball toward third and the crowd rose, but it was foul. Again he slashed a ball toward third and again the crowd rose; again, it was foul. The count went to 3 and 2, and I thought of the cat-and-mouse game Dawson had talked about three hours earlier. Minton was a veteran right-handed pitcher; he knew that if Dawson got the ball in the air it could at least tie the game and maybe win it. Dawson knew his job was to get the ball in the air, but he knew that Minton knew it, and Minton was a sinkerball pitcher, anyway. With the count 3 and 2 there was also the possibility of Minton walking Dawson semi-intentionally, but that would put the tying run in scoring position for Durham, a hot and left-handed hitter. Nonetheless, Minton could use the open base to his advantage by keeping the ball away from Dawson's power and not worrying about a walk. But Dawson wasn't likely to let a close pitch go by.

He swung hard at Minton's sinker and rapped another ground ball toward third, this time into the glove of Matt Williams.

Outside, a young guy in a green fatigue jacket passed out against the wall of the right-field bleachers. People took pictures of him as he lay there.

May ————————————————————————

THE IVY TURNS in May. By the first day of the month, the top leaves were already green and the outfield walls were beginning to take on the civilized country look that P. K. Wrigley was so eager to see in 1937.

The ivy had been Bill Veeck's idea, actually. The Wrigleys were always pushing the fresh-air-and-sunshine theme at the home of the Cubs, and P.K. decided it would be appropriate to redecorate with an outdoorsy, sort of National Park motif. Veeck, who was Wrigley's right-hand and leg man, had admired the ivy that covered the walls of Perry Stadium in Indianapolis and easily persuaded Wrigley to borrow the concept. It was Veeck's intention to order the ivy at the end of the season and plant it in the fall, giving it time to take root by the spring of 1938, but Wrigley was not sympathetic to the requirements of time, and a day before the Cubs were to return for their last homestand of the year, the boss called Veeck and told him he was bringing friends in to see his beautiful ivy-covered walls. For his part, Veeck was not a man who was sympathetic to excuses. He found out that ivy could not be planted in a day, but that bittersweet could, so he purchased both and stayed up all night with grounds-keeper Bob Dorr, weaving the two over the outfield bricks and holding them in place with copper wire.

The ivy, many would say, is what puts the ubiquitous adjective in Beautiful Wrigley Field. Actually, the bricks are underrated in that regard, but the ivy does look comelier every year in the lineup of polyester ballparks. Its loveliness is not only in its verdant complexion, but in the attitude it expresses, an appreciation of aesthetic virtue too often bygone in a sport of the heart. In terms of both identification and whimsical worth, there is only one other feature in one other ballpark that is anything like it—the Green Monster left-field wall at Fenway Park in Boston. The difference between the two is the difference between Wrigley Field and Fenway. The vines are seductive; in the fetching but cruelly manipulative manner of Wrigley Field, they lure outfielders into their soft leaves and let them crash against the bricks. The Monster is Fenway's great symbol of duplicity, a stark, looming standard that perpetuates hope in its proximity and heartbreak in its height.

In the 1945 World Series, the Cubs' Andy Pafko had to search through the ivy leaves to find the disappearing line-drive hit by Detroit's Roy Cullenbine. Bill Buckner once hit a hide-and-seek homer into the vines. Curt Flood used to climb them to catch long drives—or so Harry Caray said on the radio. The ivy, truly, has been bittersweet.

Anyhow, it was a significantly better idea than the Chinese elm trees that Wrigley put on the steps to the scoreboard in center field. That, too, was a notion that came from Veeck, who offhandedly said that trees would look nice behind the ivy; but Veeck imagined rows of them reaching over the back of the bleachers from Waveland and Sheffield avenues. Wrigley wanted them right there in the ballpark. So Veeck had footings made at substantial cost, planted the full-grown trees, and then watched the wind blow the leaves off. Wrigley said to try again, but the wind wouldn't stop even for him. Veeck estimated that he planted ten sets of trees before the chewing-gum magnate was convinced the plan wasn't going to work. But the footings remain, and when the bleachers are crowded—which has become most of the time—healthy young people hop atop them for private accommodations.

The scoreboard, meanwhile, has weathered much better, although it, too, very nearly joined the ranks of Wrigley Field fiascos. In his book, *Veeck—as in Wreck*, Veeck explained that he was racking his brain for a new scoreboard concept in 1937 when an eccentric inventor walked in off the street with plans for one. The coincidence was compelling, the design was sound, and the order was placed. But a day before the delivery date, Veeck phoned the inventor's workshop and was met with no answer. Hastening over, he found the scoreboard half-built and the factory deserted. With no time to squander, Veeck swiftly hired a team of electricians from a switchboard company, brought in the Wrigley ground crew, and together they finished the massive thing in a night—twenty-seven by seventy-five feet—hauling it piece by piece to the ballpark and assembling it where it still stands handsomely overlooking the bleachers: so high, haughty, and distant that it has never been struck by a batted ball.

While other scoreboards sing, dance, illustrate, calculate, explode—that was Veeck's doing, too—and cost millions of dollars, Wrigley's makes do with a periodic paint job and a few hale fellows to put the five-pound steel numbers into the appropriate innings of the appropriate games. (The first time my wife visited Wrigley Field, she asked, incredulous, "You mean there are *little men* back there?" Actually, the men are on the order of burly. The ranking member of them, Art Sagel, sits in a leather chair that badly needs reupholstering, from which he can look through the window of an uncompleted inning and watch the game below, or even gaze upon the house four blocks away where he was born.)

An obligatory electronic message board was attached to the bottom of the big board in 1982, but the basic information comes in still colors—white and yellow on green. The balls, strikes, outs, batter's number, and hit/error indicator are made up of white balls that resemble lights from a distance and are operated speedily and mechanically from behind home plate. The hits for both teams are totaled in a yellow line on the order of: VIS 10 HITS 9 CUBS.

The rest of the board is occupied by line scores from other games, which go up inning by inning and remain there. Nothing is more frustrating to real baseball fans than modern gizmo-graphic scoreboards that flash cryptic partials from other games at random intervals. Wrigley's scoreboard is what it purports to be—a board for scores.

The scores come in on a tickertape, and the men carry twenty-inch numerals up a fire-escape staircase to post them in a stack of games that reaches three stories high. Actually, the American League's expansion to fourteen teams caught the system a little short—there is room for only twelve teams to be listed in each league—but that only serves to humanize the old board a bit more, necessitating that a little baseball judgment be exercised as to which game people care about the least. This is an infrequent problem, anyway, inasmuch as games in other parks usually don't begin until Wrigley's is long over. If one ever sees a picture of the Wrigley Field scoreboard with games going on throughout both leagues, he knows the picture was taken on a Sunday.

The scoreboard is Wrigley Field's link not only to the rest of baseball but to the world outside. One could keep track of a Cub game simply by standing on Sheffield or Waveland avenues and monitoring the balls, strikes, outs, innings, and runs. The antiquated clock atop the board serves the neighborhood better than a high-tech message center outside a suburban bank. And passengers going home from work on the el can tell whether the Cubs won or lost that day by checking the flag flapping above the scoreboard: blue for victory, white for defeat.

The won-lost flags are actually more indulgent than informative, because any Cub fan worth Rich Nye's resin bag knows what the boys have done before he starts home. To the serious Cub fan, the flags that matter above the scoreboard are the ones that represent the standings of the National League. The significance of them is not the standings—a serious Cub fan looks at the standings before he looks at the bottom of his cereal bowl—but the direction in which they whip as he approaches the ballpark. If the pennants are straining toward Murphy's, there will be a fine burst of home runs and a splendid chance of the home team winning. If they're pointing at the pitcher's mound, well, on such a day it is wise for the Cub fan to assume his bleacher seat with expectations in check.

On the first day of May in 1987, the world was well, the wind blowing out. The bleachers filled up as the ushers in the grandstand stood with their hands in their pockets. Against the Waveland Avenue fence in left field, Moe Mullins stood with his glove on his hip and noted that Durham was swinging authoritatively in batting practice but that Moreland's slump lingered on. In the right-field bleachers, a woman held up a sign: BEWARE OF THE KILLER D'S—DERNIER, DUNSTON, DURHAM, DAWSON, DAVIS, DAYETT. Unfortunately, DiMaggio did not come with the set.

The Cubs were playing the Padres. A young beer vendor named Howard poured eleven Buds for a group from an office—it was Friday—and explained to one of the women that San Diego's manager was Larry Bowa. "He used to play for the Cubs," he said. "He was a really bad shortstop. Now he's a manager and his team's in last place."

I sat in the upper section of center field, under the scoreboard, thinking that things would be pretty straight there. Then I looked across the aisle and saw a guy in a leather jacket, chains, black sunglasses—the whole urban-punk bit—and platinum hair shaved in back and on the sides and combed straight up, a couple of inches high, on the top and in front. Once, when the squeaky-clean Ryne Sandberg appeared at a bookstore on Diversey Avenue for an autograph session, a group of kids resembling this fellow had wandered in to see what the fuss was about. "Eeoou," one of them said in that urban-punk sound of contempt, "he must be, like, with the Cubs or something." I tried to imagine this guy kicking around trades with his buddies. That didn't work, but he was, nonetheless, a contributing party to the social balance and phenomenon of the bleachers. He may or may not have been a baseball fan, but the same could be said of the other three thousand in the cheap seats. Like them, he was there.

Scott Sanderson, back from the disabled list, was making his second start for the Cubs, and on his first pitch, the Padres' Joey Cora drove a ball to center field that Martinez caught on the run. Dunston got Sanderson out of trouble in the second with another of the terrific two-out plays he was beginning to make with convincing regularity. In the third, Moreland made a difficult stop and throw. But the next batter hit an unchallenging grounder to his left, and as he casually picked it up, his look was visibly overconfident. He had played well at third base, and suddenly—was it the influence of the good play he had just made?—it seemed as though he thought it was all so easy. Moreland was a tough, conscientious guy, a former defensive back at the University of Texas and a work-ethic ballplayer. One wouldn't have expected such a lapse coming from him—and maybe there really wasn't any—but from the bleachers, there was something about Moreland's casual gait as he approached this simple play that made it appear he was going to throw the ball away, which he did.

Sanderson escaped the inning without further incident, however, and then the thin, brittle pitcher startled everyone in Wrigley Field by stepping into a pitch from Eric Show and bouncing it high off the pavement of Waveland Avenue. The run went up immediately on the big manual scoreboard in center field. Two innings later, it was accounted for on the electronic board in the third-base grandstand. The bleacher regulars were so accustomed to seeing misinformation on the electronic board that they paid no attention to it. "That thing must be run by Dallas Green's nephew," one of them said.

Moreland, unaffected by his earlier error or by Moe Mullins's appraisal of his batting stroke, homered in the fourth, and the Cubs led 3–2 after six. Sanderson was being well served by an excruciatingly slow curve, but by the seventh it was all that he had. Dickie Noles relieved him with two men on and allowed them both to score, assisting with a balk and a wild pitch. It was 5–3 when Manny Trillo, the veteran infielder who was employed for his savvy and not his power, homered in the bottom of the seventh. Dawson tied the score with his seventh home run in the eighth against reliever Lance McCullers, and the Cubs won the game later in the inning when Dunston drove in his first run of the year. Maddux, the kid pitcher who had been struck below the belt two days before, was pinch running, and barreled fearlessly into San Diego's rookie catcher, Benito Santiago.

On the WGN radio talk show that evening, the callers gushed over Maddux's fortitude, and they asked Dallas Green about the bullpen. "If they're not doing the job, you've got to keep sending them out there. That's the only way they're gonna get any better," said Green, surprisingly frank for a member of baseball's sugar-lipped fraternity of hired executives. Another fan asked, inevitably, about Gary Matthews. It was an awkward situation. The Sarge was a man and player about whom the fans felt warmly—he had given away caps with sergeant stripes to people in the bleachers in 1984—but he couldn't run. "If you want to get him off the ballclub," Green said coldly, "you have to take about anybody."

"Do you think you'd have to take a young prospect?" the caller asked.

"Yeah," said Green. "Or a body."

For Ryne Sandberg Poster Day, the Ryne Sandberg posters came rolled up and wrapped in plastic. All over the bleachers, people were hitting their friends with them; it was as irresistible as twirling their whistles is for lifeguards.

It was a chilly May Saturday—Kentucky Derby day—and as the players jogged in the outfield, a guy in the left-field seats shouted at Trillo. "Good job yesterday, Manny." Trillo waved back. There was a smell of a Magic Marker in the vicinity. A big fellow in a blue shirt with white flowers was making a sign: DAWSON IS DYNAMITE. He paused in his work to yell at the San Diego pitchers, several of whom were known for their right-wing politics. "Hey, Show [pronounced like 'how now'], you Communist! You too, Dravecky! Show, you Hitler!" Then to McCullers: "Hey, Lance, way to pick up that save yesterday, buddy." The other Padre pitchers got a chuckle on that one.

In right field, two middle-aged women wore yellow baseball caps with the words, GARVEY SUCKS. For the first time, people talked about the pennant race. "You don't think the Cardinals will hold up, do you?" . . . "I still gotta believe the Mets'll be there." . . . A girl on the aisle didn't stand for the national anthem. It was her prerogative, but it seemed odd nonetheless. How can one go to Wrigley Field and dislike America? What about mutual exclusivity?

The first two Padres, Cora and Garry Templeton, hit safely against Steve Trout. A loud fan in right field was fed up already. "The Cubs are chokers, man," he shouted. The same guy tried to start up "Left field sucks." Nobody was ready. He waved his hand in disgust. "Right field sucks, too."

In the fourth, with the Padres leading, 1–0, Dawson homered deep to left. It was his eighth homer already, and when he came out to right field to start the fifth inning, the fans there stood up spontaneously and bowed to him. A few of them did it, and then a lot of them did it, extending their arms and doubling over at the waist in a sort of innocent idolatry. They had done the same thing for Matthews in the past, but Matthews was hobbling and Dawson was hitting home runs. In the week *after* he had been Player of the Week, Dawson had hit for the cycle, gone five for five, thrown a runner out at first base, and hit two game-tying home runs. It was the best week of baseball I'd ever seen, and apparently the best the people in the right-field bleachers on May second had ever seen. It was enough, anyway, for them to all hail, bow down, and worship their new deity, Awesome Dawson, who tipped his cap and seemed rather embarrassed by it all.

Durham followed Dawson's homer with another, and in the fifth, Trout singled and then appeared to hurt himself diving back into first base. Trout was always hurting himself or appearing to. "Get up, Trout!" yelled a gray-haired lady from Elmhurst. "You can be hurt next week!"

The lady was with her thirty-two-year-old daughter. Both of them wore Indiana University National Champions sweatshirts. "I started bringing her and her friends in '69," said the mother. "One of the parents would have to bring the kids down here at five in the morning so they could get in line for tickets, then come back and pick them up after the game. I decided that was crazy—I like baseball. So I started going with them."

By the seventh inning the Cubs were trailing again. Then, with two men on base, Sandberg hit a pitch from Ed Whitson high off the fence behind the left-field bleachers. All over the stadium, Cub fans waved their Ryne Sandberg Poster Day posters, producing an eerie, black-light effect, and marking another in the endless litany of metaphysical moments that seem to leave little doubt as to which game God keeps up with. Why was it that Roberto Clemente had exactly three thousand hits when he died in that plane crash? Why is Hank Aaron the first man listed alphabetically in *The Baseball Encyclopedia*? Why did Don Denkinger miss that call in the 1985 World Series and the Royals win it the next day, when nobody knew yet that Kansas City's manager, Dick Howser, would die from cancer less than two years later? Of the forty-eight players eligible to win the Chicago-San Diego game of May 2, 1987, why would it be the man whose picture was on the posters given out at the gates? Why are the Cubs the Cubs?

They would hit four homers in all on Derby Day. As Jody Davis came to bat in the eighth inning, a dark-haired woman in the right-field bleachers implored him to be seated on her face and to do various other personal things in her company. Obviously aroused, he homered all the way across Waveland to Kenmore Avenue.

The Cubs had won eight of eleven games. In St. Louis that night, Todd Worrell blew a three-run lead in the eighth against the Dodgers.

A young woman from the University of Illinois showed up

Sunday shivering in shorts. "It was 70 degrees and the sun was shining when we left Champaign," she said. At Wrigley Field, it was gray and 44.

Elsie Foydl, Al Barrett, and Marv Blum sat bundled up in front of the concession stand. The ramps from Gate N are wind tunnels that blast into the bleachers in right- and left-center, and it is often about fifteen degrees colder there than it is in the small, comparatively unpopular area shielded from the lake's cold breath by the beer and all-beef hot dog station. When the weather warmed, Elsie, Al, Marv, and a few wise others would move over by the ramp in right-center to catch the breeze, but this was gray May. Marv sat with a trash bag over his legs.

Al had picked up Elsie after eight o'clock Mass. She was sort of his ballgame buddy and guardian. Al never worried about himself, so Elsie did it for him. He was eighty-five, probably the oldest regular in the bleachers, and he had been going to Cub games before they even moved north to Wrigley Field, which was 1916. They used to play on Chicago's West Side, and Al, who lived nearby, would pick up bottles at the ballpark to get in for nothing the next day. Now, he paid his four dollars and assumed his place inconspicuously, wearing a Cub hat and tinted glasses, marking his scorecard, and rarely looking around except to greet friends and smile quietly.

Al and Elsie and Marv didn't bet on the games, but they had sat in the same place for decades and watched the action around them. One of the old-time gamblers, Honest Abe, was there Sunday, sitting stiffly off by himself in a winter coat, scarf, and a Bears stocking cap. There was nobody to bet with him. He left in the second inning. By then, the Cubs were already leading behind Sutcliffe. The Padres weren't hitting him, and a guy in line at the concession stand innocuously commented that he was throwing well. "It's only the third inning," said another.

Dawson batted in the bottom of the third, and Jerry Pritikin ran over to left field to try to catch the ball in case it was a home run. It was a single. When he came back through on his rounds, the Bleacher Preacher complained that the fans in left field weren't what they used to be. He liked group participation. He liked to make a sign or come up with a slogan and have everybody pick up on it. They used to do that in left field, but now they would just turn around and look at him and maybe say something about the propeller on his hat. Pritikin wore the propeller so that, when he saw somebody in a Cardinal or a Pirate hat, he could say, "Gee, that's a funny-looking hat you got on." But the fans in left field were getting younger and drunker and they didn't know who he was. They didn't care. "You can't tell them anything," he said. Then he walked off toward right field.

It wasn't the same there, either. Elsie and Al and a few others were precious relics from a time when people were institutions in the bleachers—people like Caleb Chestnut, who, day after day, would slowly light his pipe and then, to the edification of a regular and respectful audience, embark on a meandering lecture embracing finance, politics, and the pitiful Cub pitching staff. He wouldn't admit to being a Cub fan. Before he died in 1977, one of his last pieces of wisdom was that the ruination of baseball would be lawyers. Then there was Papa Carl, a painter who would regularly arrive at Wrigley Field before sunrise to be first in line for bleacher tickets, sticking his bag and black sweater in the grating of the gate to save his spot. Much to the wrath of those not in his circle of bleacher friends, he would also save spots in line for those who were, then save seats inside. He would hustle up the ramp and feverishly tie cardboard to cover as many places in right field as he thought his entourage would require that day. Once, on Opening Day, he roped them off. Nobody argued with Papa Carl about the rules of the bleachers, though, because he made them. Couples being publicly affectionate were his favorite targets. "Hey," he would yell out, "my wife's picture is in my wallet."

But Caleb and Papa Carl and most of the old gamblers were gone; in right-center, as Sutcliffe mastered San Diego, Marv was talking to two guys in their thirties named Mike and Doug who kept standing up and turning around so that they could look at the girls above them in the center-field section. They were the ones who had been hitting on the nurses the other day.

"I see Raines don't need spring training," said Marv. He was in his early sixties, short and blunt and friendly, with a flat neighborhood manner of speaking and a round cigar that he seldom lit. He had noted with interest that Tim Raines, in his first game back with the Expos after missing a month as an unsigned free agent, had gotten four hits against the Mets Saturday, including a game-winning grand slam in the tenth inning.

"Did you see who he hit it off?" asked Mike. "He hit it offa Orosco."

"Yeah," said Marv, cackling, "you shoulda seen him. He said, 'Shit!' I was watching it in Fencik's bar."

Mike lived at Lake Shore Drive and Irving Park Road, several blocks northeast of Wrigley Field, and when he watched the game on television at home he would often hear the roar of the crowd over the audio of the set, then hear it again, live, five seconds later as it swept across Waveland and Grace and Sheridan. On Sunday, several chubby girls from Indiana were sitting in front of him and Doug, and the two of them somehow got the idea that the girls were going to buy them a beer. At least, they drank one that the girls paid for, which led to a long and rambling argument that led nowhere. Elsie was getting annoyed. Finally, grudgingly, Doug paid the girls back. Then he and Mike turned around and started catching peanuts that a girl was throwing down from the section above. "Throw the whole bag down," said Mike.

"Why don't you sit down and watch the game?" said Elsie. Elsie was a tiny, red-haired spitfire with a soft heart and a fierce sense of propriety about the bleachers. She was sort of Mother Bleacher, and wasn't in the least timid about reprimanding those who did not subscribe to proper bleacher decorum.

One of the chubby girls stood up to do "Left field sucks."

"Sit down," said Elsie.

Dawson doubled in the fifth and homered in the seventh.

The fans in right field bowed down to him. It looked as though he would be Player of the Week again, except that in Philadelphia, Eric Davis of the Reds was hitting three home runs, one of them a grand slam.

It was plain to see, meanwhile, that the Padres were awful. Cora, running off of first base, rounded second on a deep fly ball that was caught by Walker in left, then forgot to touch second again as he backtracked to first. Minutes later, he and Templeton let a ground ball roll right between them.

"Do you want a beer or something?" Mike asked Elsie as he got up to go to the concession stand.

"I don't drink beer," she said.

"Coffee?"

"Okay, coffee."

He was trying to make peace with Mother Bleacher. "When I scold them, they buy me coffee. I have that effect on people," Elsie said. She shook her head. "Why do they come to the baseball game?"

"It's like a damn singles bar," said Marv. The Cubs led, 4–2, and Lee Smith, in relief of Sutcliffe, got the last two outs in the ninth. Durham had two RBIs. Sandberg made a diving stop. Dawson, Sutcliffe, Smith, a three-game sweep. . . . It was going just like it was supposed to. "We've got an awesome team here," said Durham in the clubhouse afterwards.

The Cardinals and Dodgers were rained out in St. Louis. The Cubs were half a game out.

Monday, May 4, was Slice Tote Bag Day, and the fans in the bleachers were wearing them over their heads. The Dodgers were in town, and so was the sports department of the *Cleveland Plain Dealer.*

The Cleveland guys were out on the road to watch baseball, which was yet to make a legitimate appearance in their hometown. They were going to the White Sox game after watching the Cubs—one of the rare occasions when both teams would be home—and then to Milwaukee on Tuesday, all the while carrying along the banner: BASEBALL ORGY 87. They also carried a tape recorder, and two of them—strictly for their own purposes—were announcing the game from the left-field bleachers.

In front of them, a large, jolly fellow had come with a young woman named Laurie who had recently moved from Nebraska. Someone mentioned Ernie Banks, and Laurie asked who he was. "Who's Ernie Banks?" the jolly fellow repeated loudly enough to make certain she was embarrassed. He grabbed her hand. "Which finger do you want to lose?" He was in for an even more shocking disclosure when it came out that she had never been to a baseball game that the home team had won. Of course, chances were the Cleveland guys hadn't, either.

The Dodgers' rainout in St. Louis the day before had not worked in the Cubs' favor, because it meant that Fernando Valenzuela would pitch against them instead of the Cardinals. The good news was that Trillo, Sandberg, and Durham hit home runs against him. In what had become uncharacteristic, Dawson did not.

Despite the manly competitiveness he had recently shown, however, Greg Maddux was not yet up to the task of beating the great round Mexican. The Dodgers scored three times in the third inning, although the large fellow in the left-field bleachers did his jolly best to cut the rally off. He thought Maddux had Franklin Stubbs picked off second base. "All right," he shouted, standing up purposefully, "this is America! Let's take a vote! All those who think he was out, raise your hands. Okay, there's six, nine, thirteen . . . that's enough! He's out of there!"

On Orgy Radio, meanwhile, the play-by-play and color men were having a little disagreement over the merits of Moreland at third base. His error had led to an unearned run for the Dodgers, and though he had played the position satisfactorily so far, it was apparent that he didn't have the reflexes or the range to do it well.

"I disagree with Michael about that," the color man said. "You've got to move Trillo to third and get Moreland the hell out of there."

"You've got to remember Moreland's had some awfully good years with the bat."

"Yeah, but this is the major leagues."

Valenzuela was not his frequently dazzling self, but he got Trillo, Walker, and Dernier with the bases loaded in the sixth inning to keep the score tied, and nobody with the Cubs' interest in mind was disappointed to see him removed for a pinch-hitter in the eighth. With Frank DiPino pitching for the Cubs, the pinch hitter, Mickey Hatcher, hit a troublesome fly ball toward the line in right field. Foul space is scant in Wrigley's right field and the territory is treacherous; the visitors' bullpen is a dangerous impediment, and the brick wall, although covered in pads, arrives on the heels of the foul line. Dawson caught the ball as he ran into the pads. The guy next to me shook his head. "Is Dawson earning his keep," he said, "or what?"

By the time the ninth began, shadows covered the left side of the field—it had been a 3:05 start—and the fans in the third-base grandstand had evacuated for the warmer seats along first. In the left-field bleachers, Orgy Radio had come to a rough spot. The color man reported that his partner was having a little problem with the Old Style. There was also the matter of getting to the White Sox–Yankees game on time if this one went to extra innings, but that was easily resolved. "Screw the White Sox," one of them suggested, the others agreeing readily.

When the bottom of the ninth arrived, though, it was imperative and inevitable that the Cubs should win. They had received scoreless relief from Ron Davis, Ed Lynch, DiPino, and Dickie Noles, and a team cannot squander such rare fortune as that. With two outs, Sandberg doubled against Ken Howell. Dawson was the batter with first base open. The Cleveland broadcast team said the Dodgers should walk him intentionally. Their manager, Tom Lasorda, disagreed. "No way they pitch to Dawson here," said a guy in a Cardinal hat, who might have fondly remembered a similar situation in the last game of the 1985 playoffs, when Lasorda allowed Tom

Niedenfuer to pitch to Jack Clark with first base empty and Clark homered to win the game. In this case, a single would win the game.

Dawson singled up the middle. The Cleveland guys made haste for Comiskey Park, and the large, jolly fellow gave Laurie a hug. "Now I can take you anywhere," he said.

Cub fans whooped and hollered as they dashed down the ramp to Sheffield Avenue, where they lingered and danced on the sidewalk and hollered some more. They poured into Murphy's and the Cubby Bear and the Sports Corner, and gradually, grudgingly, they dispersed.

One fellow walked east on Addison, alone, his Slice tote bag over his head, and he sang as he went along. "I'm Popeye the sailor man, boop boop! I'm Popeye the sailor man. . . ." Then he stopped singing and started shouting: "Andre! Woo-woo! Andre! Woo-woo!" When he came to Halsted he turned left, and I watched him fade off happily into the North Side of Chicago.

On the morning of Tuesday, May 5, nobody in Chicago had to hold the newspaper upside down to read the standings. The Cubs were in first place. Not only that, but Ernie Banks was the guest announcer.

At fifty-six, Banks was still a strikingly, sweetly handsome man. Even when he played, he seemed too pretty and graceful to be the devastating home-run hitter that he was. He hit 512 of them, all with the Cubs, between 1953 and 1971, and did it with an effortless, utterly coordinated swing that sugarcoated the sinew he had developed picking cotton in Texas. The most memorable thing about Banks, though—the thing that made him Mister Cub—was the undaunted optimism he maintained through nearly two decades of incessant losing. Some said that Banks's disposition was phony. What if it was? There are songs about putting on a happy face, about smiling when your heart is aching. Banks and his infield sidekick, Gene Baker, were the Cubs' first blacks, and they played in one of America's most segregated big cities; had Banks been surly, he might have been gone early. Instead, he showered Chicago with homers and happiness. If the indomitable, sunny spirit that envelops the Cubs can be attributed to any single man or player, the man and player is Banks. Every year, he would predict a pennant on the North Side. Every day, he would come to the ballpark and say it was a good day to play two. He rhapsodized about Wrigley Field and even Phillip Wrigley. He loved the Cubs, and because he did—and they did—the fans felt the same way about him. His number, 14, flies on a flag atop the left-field foul pole.

As the Cubs took batting practice on the morning of first place, Banks came onto the field looking good in dress shoes, lavender slacks, and a plaid sweater. Bill Madlock, the former Cub and batting champion who was playing for the Dodgers, walked past Banks, touched him on the arm, and said, "It's a great day for two!" Banks loved it. After his retirement, he had been employed by the Cubs in a community relations capacity for as long as the Wrigleys owned the team, and the Tribune people kept him on for more than a year after that until they decided it wasn't working out. He took a job in Los Angeles, but he missed Chicago and he was missed.

The Dodgers' Bill Russell was throwing batting practice, and Banks stepped into the cage. He let a pitch go by that he didn't like, then swung with ridiculous ease and laced a double down the left-field line. People smiled. Steve Stone, his broadcast partner for the day, tried to pull Banks aside to get ready for the afternoon, but somebody wanted a picture of Mr. Cub. Then the fans along the first-base fence started screaming his name—girls ten and twelve years old whose parents might not have even met by the time Banks retired from baseball. They probably didn't know what position Banks played, but he was the greatest modern Cub, and his flag flew in left field.

Over to the side, other Cubs talked about being in first place. They had been there two years before, the season after the division title, until the starting pitchers became collectively infirm. The pitchers on this team were younger and healthier, if not better. The defense was better. Dawson was incredible. "Whether we are contenders or not, the first of

June will tell you that," said Moreland. "But I tell you, we're getting that feeling every day that, hey, we're gonna win this baseball game."

In the bleachers, Jerry Pritikin held up a sign: THIS IS D YEAR. Eighteen thousand people were in the park on a Tuesday afternoon early in May, with Jamie Moyer pitching against Bob Welch. Moyer, a Pennsylvanian who had pitched in college for three years before advancing swiftly through the Cub farm system, was a prematurely resourceful left-hander with an intelligent change-of-pace pitch and an encouraging ability to escape from nervous situations. He retired Mike Marshall with the bases loaded in the third, but not before the Dodgers produced the only run of the game's first seven innings.

Welch was disposing of the Cubs routinely all the while, but the dearth of activity on the field did not affect the beer-abetted enthusiasm of a banker in the bleachers, who had come from Fort Wayne and who intended also to see the White Sox and Yankees that night. "I'm going to make all five divisions in one day," he said merrily. "The NL East, the NL West, the AL East, the AL West, and Division Street." The latter was the location of Chicago's liveliest night spots.

A louder, younger drunk, however, was more disconcerted by the Cubs' impending defeat. He leaned uneasily against the rail on the far side of the right-field bleachers and vented his frustration upon the Dodger nearest him, rightfielder Marshall. For lack of a better imagination, he decided upon a handy and personalized insult. "Marshall!" he screamed. "You're a homosexual!" It didn't help his mood when the Dodgers scored twice more in the eighth on a home run by Madlock.

Dunston tripled and Mumphrey singled for a run in the Cubs' eighth, but Welch eluded further trouble when he got Dawson to pop up. There was no bowing when Dawson returned to his position for the ninth, but there was plaintive petitioning from Marshall's good friend, who was aware that the Cubs had won four straight and had apparently invested in a fifth. "Andre!" he pleaded. "You can do it! You tell 'em, okay? You tell 'em, Andre. I don't want to go home and tell my old lady I lost."

On a hit and two blown double plays, the Cubs put the tying runs on base in the ninth. It was then demonstrated that a Cub rally, regardless of its nature, has an elucidating effect on a young mind softened by the king of beers, for in the midst of this threat the desperate bleacher drunk reached 'a milestone in deductive reasoning. "Marshall!" he screamed, red-faced. "You're a homosexual . . . And if we don't win this game, that proves it!"

Martinez flied to left, and the Cubs were off to San Francisco.

They were out of town for nearly two weeks. I left when they did, and when I got back my apartment had been broken into. It was either a kid or a Cub fan who did it: they didn't touch my computer, but they took my bleacher tickets. I had them for all the toughest dates the rest of the year, and they were stuck into the Bible on my dresser. They also took a tape recorder and a tape player. They left my Dvorak and Sam Cooke tapes. The computer was more valuable than everything else in the apartment, but the Cub tickets were harder to replace. A lot of the weekend series were sellouts already—in the bleachers, anyway. The bleachers always sold out before everything else. People would trade box seats worth ten-fifty for a four-dollar bleacher ticket. Once I saw a guy trade a box seat *and* ten dollars for a bleacher ticket.

The first day back was a Tuesday, May 19, and there would normally have been tickets available on a May Tuesday, but this was the day Harry Caray was coming back. The governor of Illinois had proclaimed it Harry Caray Day. It seemed like people would want to stay home and watch Harry on television on the day he came back, but, no, they wanted to be at the ballpark to sing with him during the seventh-inning stretch. The whole time he was gone, the Cubs played a tape recording of Harry and his beautifully awful rendition of "Take Me Out to the Ballgame" in the middle of the seventh, but what everybody missed was Harry leaning out of the booth and waving his arms.

At Wilcox Realty on Clark Street, there was a huge computer printout in the window that said WELCOME BACK HARRY. On the Sheffield Avenue sidewalk were footprints

and the words HARRY IS COMING. Actually, the latter referred to a movie that was coming to Chicago, but the coincidence was fortuitous; no other movie was ever advertised on
the Sheffield Avenue sidewalk. "You'd think Harry Caray was
pitching," said Becker. He and Jeweler Joe, like me, had to
find somebody selling a ticket. That wasn't hard if you
wanted to pay ten dollars. I decided I'd pay five dollars. Actually, I'd pay whatever I had to, but I wanted to pay five
dollars.

Spuds MacKenzie rode by in a convertible and looked
straight at a girl wearing a Spuds MacKenzie T-shirt.

All over, there were guys asking ten or fifteen dollars for
bleacher tickets. "It got bad when they started selling
bleacher tickets in advance," said Joe. "They should have
never done that." The Wrigleys had only sold bleacher tickets
on the days of the games. That was how bleacher people got
to be good friends, waiting together in line for tickets. But the
Tribune started offering bleacher tickets in advance in 1985.
The reason given was that the crowded lines were becoming
rowdy. The system had its merits, but it changed the bleachers. Scalpers bought large blocks of tickets, creating an artificial shortage. The old guys who used to get in at the pass gate
for nothing got discouraged. The spontaneity was gone; people couldn't leave their offices for lunch and decide on the
spur of the moment to chuck it and spend the afternoon in the
bleachers. Bill Veeck had boycotted the ballpark when the
Tribune started selling in advance. He said it would be the
ruination of the bleachers as they had been known.

Nobody was having any luck finding a ticket for less than
ten dollars. "I'm going home," Becker said. "Fifteen more
minutes and I'm going home."

"Aah, he always says that," said Joe as Becker walked off
in search of a ticket. "Becker will worm his way in. He always
does."

Two tanned girls in shorts were standing near the bleacher
gate, looking around for tickets. Two guys walked up and sold
them a pair for face value. Finally, a guy from Wisconsin with
an extra ticket offered it to me for face value. I went inside. A
few minutes later, Becker and Joe were there, too.

The Cubs were playing the Reds, but the magnificent Eric Davis was not available. Davis had won the Player of the Week the week before, despite Dawson's amazing heroics, and was leading the National League in nearly every offensive category. He had injured himself making a diving catch in St. Louis, where the Reds had been swept by the Cardinals. Cincinnati was still in first place, though, tied in the National League West with the Giants. And the Cubs were tied in the East with St. Louis. Sutcliffe and Smith had pitched a shutout in Los Angeles, Maddux and Smith pitched a three-hitter in Houston, Durham hit two homers one night in San Diego, Dayett did the same in the Astrodome, and the Cubs were 16–5 on the road, best in the league. They were eight games over .500 and they were playing well. They needed only to start winning at home.

It would be a six-game homestand, with Sutcliffe pitching the first against the Reds' Tom Browning. Sutcliffe was already the winningest pitcher in the league, and he was staked to a three-run lead on Tuesday when Dawson, Davis, and Moreland drove in runs in the first. The inning had begun when Dernier reached on an error leading off, a play that Harry Caray missed because he was on the telephone with Dutch Reagan, an old Cub broadcaster himself on WHO radio in Des Moines.

Sutcliffe showed no predisposition to have an easy game, allowing two of the first three batters to reach base against him. This brought Becker out of his seat. "He's been 3 and 1 on every batter!" he said. "Every batter!" Then Sutcliffe made that obligatory pickoff move we've all seen too many times: with Tracy Jones on third base and Kal Daniels on first, he faked a throw to third and then whirled to see if he could catch the runner off first. Becker stood again. "Did you ever see that play work?" he asked. Seconds later, Sutcliffe picked Daniels off first.

He pitched well thereafter, and the Cubs scored three runs in the fifth and three more in the sixth to lead 9–1. Jeweler Joe turned to me with a serious look and said, "Is Sutcliffe back?"

He was, at any rate, headed toward his seventh victory, a

fact so convincingly imminent that in the left-field bleachers, a fan in a Reds cap stood, spread his arms and cried out, "I want to be saved!" The Bleacher Preacher was quick to attend to him.

The rout being on, one fan threw his plastic tankard mug—it was Tankard Mug Day—onto the playing field behind Reds centerfielder Tracy Jones. Other fans screamed at Jones and pointed, but he didn't understand. Finally he spotted the priceless mug and tossed it hastily into the empty center-field section, where it shattered. This brought a cloudburst of tankard mugs onto the field, at which point Reds manager Pete Rose directed his players to return to the dugout. The game was stopped for six minutes while the ground crew added to its tankard mug collection.

A tiny blonde in front of me muttered, "Assholes."

"It's getting so they shouldn't let anybody under forty into the game," said one of the bleacher veterans, Jack Lindenberg. "They get a couple beers in them and they can't control themselves. They're not here for the game. You've got girls out here, they come out here to stand up and do their nails and pick up guys."

The seventh-inning stretch and musical rite, on the other hand, commanded everybody's attention. With two outs in the top of the seventh on Harry Caray Day, the fans began chanting, "Harry! Harry!" It was a gala event. The Cubs even came out of their dugout to join in, and there was white-haired Harry in his wide black glasses, leaning out of his booth and waving his arms, and the fans swaying back and forth with their arms around each other. There were people who attended Cubs games for the specific purpose of singing "Take Me Out to the Ballgame" with Harry Caray. It was a quaint, odd piece of Americana. The timing was so bad between Harry and the chorus of thousands that the song was practically sung in rounds. And everybody—*everybody*—sang the very same words as Harry, which weren't the words I grew up with. Harry sings, "Take me out to the crowd." Didn't anybody else learn it, "Take me out *with* the crowd"? Harry sings, "I don't care if I ever get back." Isn't it, "I don't care if I *never* get back"? Whatever. At Wrigley Field, it wasn't the lyrics that mattered; it was the experience.

The merchandising of Andre Dawson had begun. He had played six weeks and hit twelve home runs in a Cub uniform, and on Wednesday, May 20, they were selling Andre's Army T-shirts at Wrigley Field. It was also Umbrella Day.

Because of the mug-throwing the day before, on Wednesday the Cubs cut off beer sales in the bleachers until the third inning, which is longer than it sounds. Beer drinkers tend to take advantage of the two idle hours between the times that the gate opens and the game begins. Wednesday's crowd, consequently, was gentler than Tuesday's.

A man in a khaki suit said that he'd seen the Great Wall of China but this was the first time he'd seen the ivy wall of Wrigley Field. In left field, a hefty young guy called out to one of the Reds players running before the game, mistaking him for Tony Perez. "Hey, Tony! My old friend Tony!" I had to tell him that Perez was retired, and that he was yelling at Dave Concepcion. He shrugged. "Hey, Davey! My old friend Davey!"

A woman told another woman she had seen a car outside with Illinois license plate NY METS. "I said to the guy, 'What kind of human being are you?' "

And in right-center, an intense, narrow-eyed, black-haired man named Howard looked around for some of the old gamblers. On other days, Howard sold Frosty Malts at the ballpark, but what brought him there was betting. Although younger than the other gamblers, he had bet with the Runyonesque bleacher characters for decades, and not with notable success. For a while, he had worked as a waiter for Amtrak, on the road six days straight, and would come back with big wads of cash that he waved around in the bleachers and often lost. But he always came back. He didn't bet for financial gain, but for the way of life. "You should have been here ten, fifteen years ago," he told me. "What is there now? There's nothing now. There's nothing anymore. It's all gone." To him, if the bleachers didn't have men gambling, they didn't have anything.

Occasionally Howard could still get a bet from one of the old-timers, but it was harder to get a *good* bet. The old-timers knew that Howard had a greater desire to bet than they did, which gave them an advantage. "You're chiseling," Howard would say. "You're chiseling the odds because nobody else is here. You're chiseling and you've been chiseling all day."

Wednesday was not a good day to bet on the Cubs, anyway. The Reds hit three home runs, two of them against starter Greg Maddux, and Dawson left the game in the fourth inning with a mild hamstring pull. In the seventh inning, the bleacher fans waved their Umbrella Day umbrellas during "Take Me Out to the Ballgame"—nobody else did, just the bleacher fans. In the ninth, with the Reds ahead 6–2, Howard seemed to be in trouble. "I need a hit," he said. "I need a hit."

"You need a doctor," said one of the old-timers.

Howard left to pace around. Somebody offered six-to-five he would make another bet before the game was over. It ended 6–2.

The next day was the kind on which bets on the Cubs paid off. For the first time all spring, the air was warm even without sunshine. The weather had arrived from the south, and in its haste made Ernie Banks's flag stand perpendicular to its pole in left field. The Cubs would be without Dawson for the day, but in this wind, they would most likely score often. It was the kind of day for which they were made.

The Reds' Tracy Jones was the first batter against the Cubs' Jamie Moyer. He hit the first pitch in an arc to left field. Jerry Mumphrey took a step back, then another, then several, and then the ball was several rows into the seats. In the bottom of the inning, Mumphrey, a switch hitter batting left-handed against Cincinnati's Ted Power, swung softly and hit a fly ball into the same wind tunnel that Jones's had taken. The game was tied. In the second, the Reds' Bo Diaz pulled up on his swing and homered to left.

In the third, after Moyer walked two batters—a very unwise thing on such a day, but understandable, given the regularity with which strikes were being converted into home runs—Eric Davis came to bat. Davis had missed the first two games of the series with a shoulder injury, but this was a day he couldn't miss. A sleek 170 pounds, Davis didn't hit with his shoulder, anyway; he hit with fast, steely wrists, which on this occasion he snapped into a fastball from Moyer, sending it over the back fence in left field.

Noles replaced Moyer, and in the fourth he encountered the

amazing Davis with the bases loaded. It shaped up as an overkill, a shotgun pointed between the eyes of the Easter bunny, but Davis hit the ball on a bounce to Dunston for a double play. The score was still 5–1, and nobody was leaving. In the bottom of the inning, Power walked two batters and Dunston hit a pop-fly three-run homer to pull the Cubs within a run. Sandberg tied the game in the fifth with a line-drive homer to center that, unlike most of the other five, would have left the park without meteorological assistance. There had been ten runs in five innings, all driven in by home runs.

With greater frequency than the home runs—with no relevance to the game whatsoever, actually—a girl in front of me with spiked blonde hair and rock-star sunglasses was grabbing her boyfriend by the hair and kissing him repeatedly.

The Cubs scored twice without a home run in the seventh inning and entrusted that advantage to Lee Smith in the eighth. Smith was an enigmatic relief pitcher, a powerful Louisiana man whose career statistics suggested enormous success and disputed the visual testimony. It seemed as though he was forever blowing leads, and yet he had averaged more than thirty-one saves in the four seasons previous to 1987. It seemed as though he always hit hard, yet his career earned-run average was less than three per game and his hits-per-inning ratio was exemplary. His strikeouts far more than doubled his walks. Why wasn't this man trusted? As he took his two-run lead into the eighth, I believed that the Cubs would win the game—they seldom lost games that Smith appeared in—but that the Reds would first tie the score. I was not alone in this presumption.

Smith blew Cincinnati down in the eighth and retired the first two batters in the ninth, thanks in part to a stunning backhanded stop and throw by Sandberg. It looked as though the numbers were right about Smith and everybody in the bleachers was wrong. Then Jones singled. Barry Larkin singled. Davis came up.

"Save us from Davis!" yelled Jerry Pritikin in the left-field bleachers.

It was a flaming line drive that Davis hit down the left-field line, both runners scoring easily. Buddy Bell popped up and the game went to the bottom of the ninth inning.

Cincinnati's pitcher in the ninth was a bantam left-hander named John Franco who was Smith's peer statistically but his opposite stylistically. Where Smith depended on force and intimidation, Franco used courage and a screwball. Franco had not been scored upon all season, and he retired Dunston and Dayett forthwith. This brought Dernier to the plate, the operative hope being that he could steal second base if he reached first.

And then, strange as it seemed, Eric Davis was retreating in center field, going farther back until, from the left-field bleachers, I could see him no more. But there was no mistaking what had incredibly happened. An immense and merry noise welled up from every part of the ballpark, and Dernier was fairly leaping around the bases. The first pitch of the game had been a home run, and also the last. This was Wrigley Field at its quintessential finest.

The ramps reverberated again. Outside, to the pounding sound of "Louie Louie," guys danced with girls on their shoulders.

In the visiting clubhouse, Power, the Cincinnati pitcher, said, "I only have one fucking statement. I hope this fucking place burns down tomorrow."

The steel from which light towers were to be made had already been delivered to Wrigley Field, and the work was to begin on December 8, 1941. On December seventh, the Japanese bombed Pearl Harbor, and the next day the materials that were to be used to illuminate the Cubs' park were instead sent to American shipyards for the war effort.

Within five years, meanwhile, lights were up at every other major-league stadium. Given the choice of being stubborn or last, P. K. Wrigley decided that day baseball was the best thing. For the rest of his life, he insisted that night games would be a disturbance to the neighborhood surrounding the ballpark, and this notion was accepted as a basic fact of Cubness until the Tribune Company bought the team late in 1981. The Tribune made it immediately clear that Wrigley's good-neighbor policy was no longer practical in modern-day baseball, and from that moment the issue of candlepower towered over Wrigley Field. Now, with the Cubs pushing into first place, there was an urgency about it. The Cubs and their fans were thinking about the playoffs.

Two years before, having been moved into action by the Cubs' playoff appearance against San Diego, baseball commissioner Peter Ueberroth had issued a statement that future postseason games involving the Cubs might not be played at Wrigley Field if they could not be played there at night. The reason, of course, was national television. Ueberroth had told the Cubs that their home games might not even be played in Chicago; might, in fact, be played in *St. Louis*, of all places.

Actually, this had been good news to the Cubs' organization, in a way. Ueberroth's statement provided it with leverage in its attempt to overturn city and state ordinances that prohibited night games in residential neighborhoods. Hoping that public empathy for their plight would overshadow the resistance to lights from the neighborhood groups, the Lake View Neighborhood Task Force and Citizens United For Baseball in the Sunshine (cleverly, C.U.B.S.), the Cubs had determined in 1985 that the climate was right for a legal challenge. They filed a suit declaring, in effect, that the legislation restricted their right to conduct business. But their petition was greeted with light-hearted disdain by circuit court judge Richard Curry, who wrote:

> The scheme which has major-league baseball trashing a residential community and tinkering with the quality-of-life aspirations of countless households so that television royalties might more easily flow into the coffers of twenty-five distant sports moguls is . . . repugnant to common decency. . . . Justice is a southpaw and the Cubs just don't hit lefties.

Two years later, indications were that the Cubs might be able to get the ordinances suspended for postseason games, but that wasn't what they wanted. They wanted a partial schedule—eighteen dates, they said—of night games, in order to justify the cost of installing lights. Opponents argued that they could use temporary lights at far less expense, but the Cubs didn't want to talk about temporary lights. They wanted real lights, like every other major-league baseball team had used since 1946—ironically or not, the first year of the Cubs' protracted pennantless period. The Cubs had begun to suggest that if they could not erect permanent lights— soon—they would have to consider the option of moving the team from Wrigley Field.

By late May, it was obvious that if the Cubs were to have permanent lights in time for postseason play in 1987, the way would have to be cleared immediately. National League president A. Bartlett Giamatti had been in town to talk to the Cubs about the problem. Ueberroth reiterated that the television networks had the right to request that all league championship and World Series games be played at night, and therefore had the right to make the Cubs play theirs away from Wrigley Field. Pressing for a quick resolution, the Cubs asked Mayor Washington to lift the local laws so that they could begin the installation of lights. They also said that if they were permitted to have eighteen regular-season night games, they would embark on a Wrigley Field renovation that would include plush skyboxes and ten thousand additional seats in the upper deck of the grandstand.

One of the compromises the Cubs were willing to make in the interest of lights was to reduce the number of 3:05 games, which they had steadily increased over the previous few years. The neighbors didn't like 3:05 games because on those days they very possibly might have no place to park when they got home from work. The players hated the later starts, saying the shadows of the late afternoon impaired visibility and could even make it dangerous to bat. But the Cubs said that the extra hour and forty-five minutes enabled more business people to get to the park, and in 1987 there were twenty-eight late starts on the schedule.

Every Friday game from May through August was scheduled for 3:05, and on May twenty-second the opponent was the Atlanta Braves. Their superstar, Dale Murphy, was aware that seven home runs had been hit in Wrigley Field the day before, but he was trying not to be *too* aware of it. "If you start thinking about it and trying to get the ball in the air," he said, "you won't make contact."

In the bleachers, I recognized a beer vendor out of uniform. Vendors pretty much have the run of the ballpark, but the good ones stake out a territory, and before long a fan can recognize not only their faces but their voices. This was a young vendor named Howard—not to be confused with the Howard of small bets and Frosty Malts—and I remembered him as the one who had educated the working woman to the misfortunes of Larry Bowa. He had a camera. A student at Columbia College in Chicago, he was compiling pictorial profiles of Cub fans for a photography project. The photos would be accompanied by a questionnaire he asked his subjects to fill out. He had given the questions to Jerry Pritikin, and Pritikin had a difficult time answering the one about his favorite player. It was between Stan Musial and Hank Greenberg. "Musial stood up at the plate like a Rodin sculpture," the Bleacher Preacher said admiringly. But, of course, Greenberg was Jewish, and Pritikin once got his autograph. "Ever since then, I've been making my *r*'s and *e*'s the way he did." It was evident that, by the depth of his affinity for the game, Pritikin was a member of the minority in even that tabernacle of baseball reverence, the Wrigley Field bleachers. Howard said the player most often listed as the fans' favorite was Dawson, the Cub of seven weeks.

Murphy homered down the right-field line in the fourth. In the fifth, he homered to left. That one made it 6–0.

In the right-field bleachers, three working women had arrived late and sat on the end of the row. They were, more or less, the fans that the Cubs had in mind with the 3:05 Friday starts: professional people getting an early start on the weekend. The woman on the end paid a vendor for a beer and told him to deliver it to a handsome, dark-haired man in a red jacket about six rows behind her. "Which one?" the vendor asked. "You know, the cute one," she said. Then she wouldn't turn around. Her friends told her the guy was with a girl. An inning later, the man in the red jacket squeezed in next to her on the end of the row and stayed a few minutes.

Gerald Perry hit the Braves' fourth home run of the day to make it 9–0. Sanderson and a new left-hander from the Texas Rangers, Mike Mason, had both failed. Durham hit his eleventh homer for the Cubs in the sixth to make it 9–2, and when Jody Davis followed with a single, a guy in the front row yelled, "Extra innings! Extra innings!" The Cubs scored another run, and with two outs and two runners on, Walker flied out easily to left field. At that, a guy got up disgustedly and went for a beer. "Damn it, Chico Walker," he muttered as he headed up the aisle.

It ended 9–5. Afterward, the crowd was small around the black band at Sheffield and Waveland. Down at Sheffield and Addison, a few kids breakdanced to a bongo drummer who played alone. Two winos slept on a bench behind him.

Scalpers had bought up a lot of tickets for Saturday's game, but it was cold and they were selling them off early for six dollars. The veteran bleacherites, Elsie, Al, and Marv, sat in front of the concession stand again. Near them, strangers helped three blind men to their seats.

The Cubs' situation looked good. They had fallen a game behind the Cardinals but were comparatively trouble free. Their biggest problem spot, left field, happened to be the position played by their best prospect, Rafael Palmeiro. Sutcliffe and Smith were throwing well, and the young pitchers had been promising if inconsistent. Durham was having his best start. Dunston, though not hitting as expected, was playing shortstop sensationally and even reliably. Davis was producing, and Moreland would surely begin to. Martinez was a pro in the field, at the least. Dawson and Sandberg were superstars.

Marv chewed on his cigar and said he still thought the Mets would win the division, but nobody in the bleachers agreed with him. "Definitely not the Mets," said Mark Wilmot, the schoolteacher. "They don't have the heads for it. I see the Cubs and the Cardinals." A friend of Mark's, Norb Kudele, liked the Cubs' chances. The Bleacher Preacher believed that it would be Chicago and St. Louis all the way to the final week of the season.

Dawson was back in the lineup Saturday, and he tipped his cap to the heartily cheering fans as he took his place in right field. In two weeks with the Cubs, Dawson had received more ovations and achieved greater celebrity than he had in ten years in Canada, and his reaction to it was graciously awkward. He was obviously flattered, a little self-conscious, and was trying hard not to get carried away with it all. He would tip his cap but wouldn't smile. It was as though the spell would be broken by the briefest moment of emotional indulgence.

The Braves, with vulnerable veteran Rick Mahler pitching, took a 4–0 lead against the Cubs, for whom vulnerable veteran Ed Lynch was pitching. A string of singles—something unusual—brought Chicago three runs in the fifth. Neither team scored in the sixth, and in right-center the bleacher people exchanged opinions on the strange case of Milt Pappas's wife, who had disappeared for several years and finally turned up in a car at the bottom of a pond. Pappas had once pitched a no-hitter for the Cubs, but Elsie had another memory of him. "One day Pappas was exercising in the outfield before the game, and it was the day after he'd had a bad outing," said Elsie, who, as usual, was wearing a scarf over short hair that had never lost its redness. "I yelled out, 'That's right, Pappas. Maybe if you exercise, you'll pitch better.' He turned around and said to me, 'Up your ass, lady.' Well, about three weeks later, some other woman is getting on him about something, and he yells up, 'Lady, you and the redhead can both go to hell!' "

In the eighth, with the Cubs down, 5–3, Dunston batted with one out and Durham on third. Marv said, "Watch Dunston swing at the first pitch." He did.

"Watch him lunge at the ball," said Elsie. "Come on, hotdog! He'll *have* to learn to wait for that ball to come in."

Somebody said that Dunston was still young, and that he tried hard. "Aw," Elsie said, "he's been a rookie out here for three years. He'll never learn." He hit a fly ball to bring in

Durham and make the score, Braves 5, Cubs 4.

The Braves scored against Noles in the ninth, and the Cubs trailed by two when they faced Gene Garber in the bottom of the inning. Trillo lined out to second baseman Ken Oberkfell, who made a diving catch, and Sandberg batted with one out. One of the blind guys, Bobby, made a strange, whooping sound: "Ryno, woo! Ryno, woo! Ryno, woo-woo-woo-woo!" It was his imitation of the legendary Ronnie Wickers.

Wickers, a snaggletoothed, perambulating black man, had been showing up faithfully in the Wrigley Field bleachers for nearly twenty years. He had no apparent means to purchase tickets—it was said he slept on a cardboard box in an alley—but had often received them from generous players like Billy Williams. Ronnie was a fixture in the bleachers, a friendly, visible figure in unclean clothes, a populist hero to some and a worthless annoyance to others. Elsie hated him. The old gamblers used to throw things at him. None of the regulars thought much of him, really—he was more of a tourist attraction—but they had nonetheless become concerned about him. He hadn't shown up at the ballpark all year, and there were rumors. One was that the Cubs had made him unwelcome. The most recent rumor was that he had been killed on the streets over the winter.

Sandberg, who had been moved into the leadoff spot—Chico Walker apparently having been judged a failure by Michael and the Cubs—grounded out, and Jerry Mumphrey batted with two outs in the ninth. Although few believed that the thirty-four-year-old switch hitter was a serious candidate for the left-field job, he had been filling in against right-handed pitchers while Walker floundered and Palmeiro remained in the minors. The significance of Mumphrey's appearance in the lineup seemed to be that Dayett, despite his earlier start against a right-hander, would not be given the opportunity to win the job full time.

Mumphrey doubled, his third hit of the day, and extended the game long enough to give Dawson another chance. Dawson represented the tying run, but the circumstances seemed to conspire against the possibility of a home run. Garber, the man best known for stopping Pete Rose's hitting streak at forty-four games in 1978, was a clever junk-ball pitcher who would not throw into Dawson's power. And the wind was blowing in; there hadn't been a home run all day. Garber quickly got ahead in the count, and with two strikes he came in with a low pitch that Dawson lashed at. It was not a home-run pitch when it was thrown—only when it was hit. Dawson had lifted the ball off the plate and somehow sent it speeding through the wind. It landed amidst astonished bleacher fans sitting a few rows over the 368-foot marker in left-center.

Mark Wilmot nearly dropped his White-Out. "I don't believe it," he said. It wasn't just Dawson that was so richly remarkable; it was Cubness.

Dawson's home run reminded Mark of the time Pete La-Cock—known mainly for being the son of Peter Marshall, former host of "Hollywood Squares"—had done the same thing. He smiled in reluctant respect for what he had just seen and shook his head; it was the second time in a week that the Cubs had won or tied a game on a home run with two outs in the ninth. "Since Dallas Green has been here, I don't *want* to like the Cubs," Mark said. "But when you're here, you just can't help it. I find myself pulling for them anyway. There *is* something magic about them. Win or lose, they'll play with your heart."

Mike Mason and Ron Davis pitched scorelessly in the tenth and eleventh, with Dunston running all over the field in inspired defense. In the bottom of the eleventh Dawson came up with two outs against Jeff Dedmon. It was still cold, and the crowd had thinned considerably, but those who remained stood in tribute; the real tribute was not in the ovation they accorded Dawson, but in the fact that they were moved to their feet in anticipation merely because he was at bat.

"If he does it again," said Mark, "the Cubs will win the pennant."

Dawson flied to right. Mark sat back. "I guess there's still only one God." At Wrigley Field, God has worn number 23 ever since Ryne Sandberg twice tied a network television game with home runs against the Cardinals' Bruce Sutter in 1984.

Davis pitched unexpectedly well into the twelfth, when he

left with a sore elbow, upon which Michael had to summon Jamie Moyer for his first relief appearance of the year. In the thirteenth, Moyer put two runners on base and the Braves' Gerald Perry hit a dangerous-looking line drive to left-center field. It was headed hastily for the wall, but so was Martinez. Just when it seemed that the ball would get there first, the young centerfielder left the ground in an elegant, deerlike leap, and caught the ball just as his blue and white uniform pressed into the ivy. Then Moyer got Murphy on a bouncer back to the mound.

In the middle of the fourteenth, Harry Caray led the crowd again in song, the second seventh-inning stretch of the day. The Cubs didn't score and Moyer pitched on. By the bottom of the sixteenth it was getting dark, the kind of faded light in which Gabby Hartnett, old Tomato Face, delivered his famous "Homer in the Gloamin' " against the Pirates in 1938. Sandberg led off and singled against Jim Acker. Then Mumphrey hit the ball into left field, as he nearly always did, and it eluded the desperate reach of Ken Griffey. It was his fourth hit, Sandberg scored, and the game was finally won.

In the clubhouse, Mumphrey said that Dawson made everybody on the team play at a higher level, and Martinez said he had always dreamed of catching a ball in the ivy.

It was well past the dinner hour, and on the way home I turned into Ricky's Restaurant at Broadway and Belmont and ordered Swedish meatballs. Leonard Becker, the gray and goateed bleacher man, walked in, sat down with me and had a cinnamon roll. Since it was Saturday and the crowd was large, he hadn't gone to the game, but he had watched it at home. He watched ballgames all the time at home, and when there weren't any more on television, he would find one on the radio, sometimes listening until one or two in the morning. Being retired, he didn't have to get up early to go anywhere. If the Cubs were out of town or he didn't feel like going to the ballpark, he'd go downtown to the courthouse and sit in on the trials. There was a crowd of regulars at the courthouse, just like in the bleachers.

"Why wasn't the leftfielder playing Mumphrey closer to

the line?" Becker asked. "He's a dead left-field hitter. Everybody knows that. And tell me this. I was watching the Sox game and Bannister had a no-hitter going and that ball falls in front of Redus in left field. Why was Redus still in the game? The Sox had a big lead and Redus is bad defensively.

"I know everybody says they can manage better than these guys, but," he smiled, aware of how he sounded, "I *know* I can manage better than these guys. They don't think. Why do you have Redus in there with a big lead and a guy working on a no-hitter? For his ego? Aach."

The meatballs were good. I asked Becker what he thought of Martinez.

"You know what I like?" he said. "Guys who make it look easy. Joe DiMaggio looked like he wasn't doing anything out there. I don't know all these young guys' names, but I look at the way they go after a ball and I can tell if they're a ballplayer."

"Instinct," I said.

He rapped his fist lightly on the table and nodded. "Instinct. That's what it is."

On Sunday, the Cubs were being single-handedly beaten by an unimposing journeyman pitcher for the Braves named Charlie Puleo. Home runs had been departing major-league parks at a record pace in 1987, and while various theories suggested that the balls were being wound tighter or the bats were bouncier, many thoughtful observers believed that baseball had simply been hit with an epidemic of wretched pitching. Support for this school of thought was provided by the disproportionate number of Charlie Puleos on major-league pitching staffs.

And yet, here were the slugging Chicago Cubs, a game out of first place in the National League East, and there, on the same grassy field, was Charlie Puleo, shutting them out through seven innings. Not only that, but the Braves led 1–0, on the first home run of Puleo's career, a high, deep drive against Sutcliffe that glanced off the glove of a left-field bleacher fan and fell onto the sidewalk outside.

The only Chicago batter to hit the ball with any conviction against Puleo was Sandberg—he had two doubles—and in the eighth inning he came up with no outs, Martinez on second, and Dernier on first. In this important situation, however, God was called upon to sacrifice. He bunted the ball in front of home plate, where Atlanta's catcher, Ozzie Virgil, fielded it and threw to first. Sandberg apparently beat the play there, and with home plate left uncovered, Martinez came all the way around to cross it, apparently tying the score. But home plate umpire Frank Pulli called Sandberg out for leaving the baseline, and both runners had to return. Just like that, the game was taken from one team's grip and placed in the other's.

For this twist of justice and dashing of design, a tanned man in his thirties, wearing a blue-jean jacket and standing behind the bleachers in right-center, was angry at the world. "They just wasted Sandberg!" he screamed. "They just wasted him! Mister Golden Boy, he does nothing wrong, does he? He just lost the game. Mister Golden Boy didn't know the rules. . . . And look at this Pulli! I hate this home plate umpire. He's the worst. . . . What's wrong with Michael, anyway? How can you bunt with Sandberg?"

"Hey, I'm sorry," his friend said, "but the play worked. Sandberg just screwed it up going out of the baseline."

"Aw, come on. We've got the worst manager in baseball."

There were still more baserunners than outs, and the Braves brought in a left-hander, Paul Assenmacher. Dayett batted for Mumphrey and brazenly doubled down the line in left, driving in both runners to give the Cubs a 2–1 lead and lightening the emotional state of the man in the blue-jean jacket.

"How 'bout that Dayett?" he said. "Isn't he something? He's got a magic wand. That Dayett, I like that son of a bitch."

The Cubs took their 2–1 lead into the ninth, with Sutcliffe standing to get his eighth victory, most in the league. Dernier had pinch hit for him in the eighth, however, and the ninth, per usual, was Smith's.

Murphy led off for the Braves. "Oh, God," said Marv, shifting his cigar. "Jeez." Smith fanned Murphy. Then it was Simmons. "Oh, God," said Marv again. "This guy hits the long ball, too." There were no long balls, but with two outs, Atlanta rallied and tied the game against Smith with a single by Virgil. It was extra innings for the second day in a row.

While Marv mutilated the end of his cigar, Norb wasn't worried. A former Indiana basketball player and labor mediator who lived across the Indiana line in Munster, Norb had come upon some free time and was spending a lot of it in the bleachers. Years before, he and his friends used to help the guys who sold bottled beer out of a stand behind the back row of seats. One of his friends, Mike the Armenian, got angry when they removed the bottled beer stand and hadn't come back to the ballpark since. "The Cubs are going to win," Norb said. "It's just the way they're going. I can tell."

Smith worked through the tenth, and Dickie Noles did the same in the eleventh, in which Dunston turned another athletic double play. "I wish I was in that dugout now," said the guy in the jean jacket. "I'd tell Michael what I think. I'd love to manage this team. They'd be in first place."

In the bottom of the eleventh, Dunston came to bat with no outs and runners on first and second—almost the identical situation in which Sandberg had batted in the eighth, the only difference being that then the Cubs trailed by a run and both baserunners were important. This time, one run would win the game. Dunston did not attempt to bunt. The guy in the jean jacket who had been so livid when Sandberg *did* bunt said, "What, you don't bunt?" Dunston hit into a double play. "My God! First and second and you don't bunt? Of course you bunt! Our manager's an idiot!"

The Cubs won the game in the twelfth when Dernier singled against Jeff Dedmon, stole second, and scored on a two-out single by Dawson. The bleacher fans bowed in deference to number eight, their serious, slim-waisted hero, and the team left for Cincinnati ten games over .500.

Living near Cincinnati as I did, I'd been to countless games at Riverfront Stadium, but on Monday, Memorial Day, the

Reds' stadium seemed different to me than it ever had before.
I'd just spent two months in Wrigley Field, where Babe Ruth
pointed to the center-field bleachers and then homered there
in the 1932 World Series against Charlie Root; where there
were old stone apartment buildings across the street; where
fans threw back home runs hit by the other team; where the
field had to be mowed; where ground balls went from Tinker
to Evers to Chance, and also from Terwilliger to Smalley to
Addison, the latter being a street. Riverfront was built the
year after Neil Armstrong walked on the moon, when the
prevailing stadium architecture was Classical Insipid, the creative inspiration of a publicly funded research team from the
Beltway Community College of Cement and Symmetry.
There was no parking problem at Riverfront; the stadium
itself sits in the middle of one of the largest parking garages in
the Midwest. There were no street people gathered around the
ballpark; it is not encompassed by streets but by plazas and
elevated walkways.

The first thing I noticed inside was how nicely everyone
was dressed. There was no black or leather, there were no
funny T-shirts or tight shorts or even jams; the crowd was
dressed for dinner at Red Lobster. The people came not in
party groups of six and eight but in families of four, the
youngest wearing the ballgloves. The ushers were not scowl-
ing young men with their sleeves rolled up to the tops of their
beefy arms; they were kindly older gentlemen in red ties.
Early in the game, one of them walked over and informed us
that we would be welcome to move over into another section
if we wished to have a better view of the new Jumbotron
scoreboard. The loudest person in our midst was a Cub fan
named Marty from Rockford, who yelled out, "Hey, why
don't you get some real grass?" He said he had been kicked
out of the Wrigley Field bleachers twice. An Illinois woman
wore a T-shirt that said: CHICAGO CUBS—IF IT TAKES FOR-
EVER.

When the usher opened up a section of seats in the shade,
the people in the front rows scrambled there to get out of the
sun. How strange—at Wrigley, it was the other way around.

Nobody talked to anybody they didn't already know.

In the ninth, with the Cubs trailing 5–4, Dayett hit a ball against the top of the fence in right-center. At Wrigley, it would have been up by the concession stand. The Cubs lost the game when, with the bases loaded, Trillo sent a grounder to Ron Oester's right, Oester spun and threw to shortstop Barry Larkin, Larkin made the phantom force at second and relayed to first, and Nick Esasky picked the ball out of the dirt for the double play. It wouldn't have happened that way at Wrigley Field. No reason—it just wouldn't. The Cubs would have won that game at Wrigley Field.

In Atlanta, the Cubs lost twice in extra innings. Just the week before, they had twice beaten the Braves in extra innings. But at Fulton County Stadium, they had runners at third base with no outs in the ninth, tenth, and eleventh innings one night, and all three were thrown out. The game had been tied on a two-out homer in the ninth by Virgil, the very way Dawson had tied the Braves in Chicago.

Apparently, the traveling secretary had forgotten to pack the magic.

June

IN THE HEADY early days of May, Keith Moreland had said that the first of June would reveal whether the Cubs were legitimate contenders in the National League East. May was over, and they were 28–20. Despite the difficult trip just concluded, the Cubs were in second place, two games behind the Cardinals. June first, bless its optimistic heart, was saying yes.

But, really, shouldn't people have known better? Weren't the Cubs just toying with their great fans again, teasing them, raising their imprudent expectations? With any regard for history at all, or any slight perception of inevitability, shouldn't the fans have realized that it wouldn't last, that there would be the same old swoon in June and good-bye in July? Item: 1977. The Cubs were eight-and-a-half games in front at one time in 1977—twenty-five games over .500—and they ended up 81–81, in fourth place, *twenty* games behind the Phillies. Item: 1969. We should like to spare Cub fans yet another haunting reminder of 1969, but it is pertinent here to recall that in 1969 the Cubs were nine-and-a-half games in front of the New York Mets in *the middle of August* and lost the pennant by eight games.

Were people going to believe four decades of history, or the morning paper on June first? Fate, or Keith Moreland?

Then again, this Andre Dawson was really something, wasn't he? And 1984 wasn't that long ago—they *did* win the division in '84. Sutcliffe was looking like the pitcher he was then. And what about 1935? What, was everybody just supposed to *ignore* 1935? Let it not be forgotten that in 1935 the Chicago Cubs won twenty-one straight games in September to overtake the St. Louis Cardinals and storm the National League pennant. And those were the Dizzy Dean Gashouse Gang Cardinals, not the Punch-and-Judy disabled-list Cardinals that were but two little games ahead of the slugging Andre Dawson–Rick Sutcliffe Cubs in 1987.

That's how it works in Chicago. There is always reason to believe, and as long as there is, Cub fans will. On the first day of June 1987, hope was so real that it raised Ronnie Woo-Woo from the dead.

It turned out, actually, that Ronnie hadn't been dead at all, as the rumors had him, but was working at a pizza joint. There was still plenty of room for juicy speculation—a little pepperoni and some extra cheese didn't seem to be enough to keep a guy like him away from Wrigley Field for two months—but as the warm breeze blew from the south and the Cubs prepared to play eighteen home games in the first twenty-two days of June, Ronnie Wickers was back at the ballpark, slapping hands as he squeezed down the rows, putting his arms around the girls, and making that shrill, grating, awful, famous noise that over the past two decades had become the primal scream of the bleachers. "Woo!" he screamed. "Cubs! Woo! Cubs! Woo! Woo-woo-woo-woo-woo-woo-woo!" The last part could have led a tribe of braves charging down the hill on horseback.

Ronnie's reappearance was a media event. One of the local television stations called him Chicago's most famous street person. A camera crew followed him around the bleachers. He wore a blue shirt with his name on the back: RONNIE WOO-WOO.

And by the bottom of the first inning of Monday's game

with the Houston Astros, Ronnie was woo-wooing in deference to Andre Dawson, who lined a pitch from Danny Darwin over the heads of the kids wearing ballgloves at Waveland
and Kenmore. Strangely, though—the wind was blowing
out—the Cubs otherwise were little trouble for Darwin, who
retired fourteen of them consecutively and led 2–1 after six
innings. Moyer was pitching well for Chicago, but despite the
presence of Ronnie and the wind, the afternoon was not shaping up as a classic one at Wrigley Field.

It was also hot and humid, and my wife, who is not a fan of
the game but had come up with me for a Chicago weekend,
walked out to the ramp to break the boredom and cool off in
the breeze. Mark Wilmot's wife, Laurie, went home early to
clean the house. "This is a bad game to make a baseball
convert," said Mark. He and Laurie had just been married
two days before, and it was important to him that she would
come to appreciate at least a few of baseball's multifarious
virtues. He knew that he had Wrigley Field working in his
favor, but it had failed him against the undistinguished
Danny Darwin. "I'll work on her this weekend," he said
hopefully. They and another couple were planning to tailgate
at a Brewers game. "She likes Milwaukee and she likes tail-
gating, so she'll put up with the ballgame."

Houston's Kevin Bass hit a monstrous three-run homer
against a yellow-brick house on Waveland in the top of the
seventh, and a short while later an apparently intoxicated
young fellow noticed me keeping score. (The bleachers had
become such an all-purpose place that a person drew attention to himself merely by keeping score of the game. I kept
my homemade scoresheet in a notebook holder, which
prompted numerous inquiries as to whether I was a scout.)

"What'd Sutcliffe do?" the guy asked.

"Sutcliffe?"

"Yeah, what'd Sutcliffe do?"

"You mean Moyer?"

"Yeah, Moyer."

"Well, he pitched pretty well until he got hurt with that
three-run homer."

"Yeah, I think it's bad. He gave up that three-run shutout. I think it's bad."

At that, I figured it was time to take my wife to the airport. It was 5–1 and she needed to get back home to the kids, and I reasoned that if I waited until after the Cubs batted in the eighth, the streets would be crammed with people leaving. As we got into the car, Trillo was coming up against Julio Solano with runners at second and third. The radio announcers— Dewayne Staats, Jim Frey, and Lou Boudreau—noted how nice it would be if Trillo could get on and at least give Dawson a chance with the bases loaded. We were headed west on Addison as Trillo walked to load the bases and Dawson came up as the tying run. Then suddenly there was this terrific shouting coming over the radio, the ball drifting deeper and deeper into left-center field, and as we came to the intersection of Addison and Western, the score was tied. I shook my head. Horns honked.

Mumphrey made a weaving catch to save the game in the ninth, and we watched from a television in an airport lounge as Houston's Jose Cruz hit a fly ball to left in the tenth inning and the wind blew it into the seats. In the bottom of the tenth, Dave Smith struck out Dawson with the tying run in scoring position and the Astros won 6–5.

It didn't seem right. They had passed out visors with ANDRE'S ARMY written on them that day, and the man had hit two home runs, one of them a grand slam, to tie the blasted game, and all to what avail? Why? How could such a stirring performance not have mattered? A baseball fan needs answers to these things. Baseball is too poetic for its lyric verses to bear no significance. Dawson's day had to mean something.

Maybe it meant that Dawson, great as he was, would not be sufficient to provide victory for the Chicago Cubs; no single player would be. In fairness to the team, Durham had missed the game with a shoulder injury and Sandberg had been given the day off, but the metaphor was conspicuous nonetheless. Dawson, alone, would not be enough to make the Cubs win in 1987—but he would be enough to make them interesting. He had been heroic even in defeat, and that valorous quality was a Cub-crossed characteristic all the way back to Hank Sauer and Ernie Banks and Billy Williams. Cubness was being perpetuated here. There had been defeat, but with heroism, with drama, with moment.

Whatever the first of June foretold, the Cubs, win or lose the pennant, would have their hero.

The fans in the right-field bleachers gave Dawson a standing ovation Tuesday as he came out to take his position in the first inning. Jerry Pritikin said he was thinking about moving from left field to right.

Nolan Ryan, the great forty-year-old fastballer, was pitching for the Astros, but a middle-aged woman who sold real estate in the suburb of Schaumburg told me that the Cubs usually hit Ryan pretty well. They scored one against him in the first (driven in by Dawson) another in the second (*not* driven in by Dawson), and then Dawson came up in the third with Sandberg on first base. Suddenly, the wind shifted and began to blow in circles. The sky lost its color. Lightning flashed behind the grandstand as Dawson leaned his shoulders over home plate. "Just like a scene from *The Natural*," said Pritikin. The homer was by Hobbs, but Dawson touched all the bases.

Then Mumphrey walked and the rain came. In the unprotected bleachers, fans scrambled to get under the scoreboard or the concession stand or on the ramp, where the wind blistered through and the water rushed past sneakers and deck shoes. The vendors sold beer on the ramp. Meanwhile, the rain made pools in the outfield. In left, the entire warning track was submerged. The dugouts were deluged. Thousands of people left for their cars and the neighborhood bars, and others would have if it weren't raining so hard. It rained without relief for half an hour, an hour, an hour and a half. In what would have been about the middle of the seventh inning, the crowd at the bottom of the ramp sang "Take Me Out to the Ballgame."

Leonard Becker sat on a step, huddled against the concrete

wall of the ramp, and he said they would finish the game. People chuckled and pointed at the field, or what could be seen of it. Jerry Pritikin said if they got the game in, the Cubs would win the pennant. I told Becker no way they would play.

"I've seen this for fifty years," he said. "When I was your age, I thought they'd never be able to get a game in when it was like this, but they do."

"If they continue this game," I said, "I'll respect your opinion for the rest of the year."

"You should respect my opinion anyway."

The delay was two hours and forty-six minutes, and then they played baseball. The water had drained completely from the outfield. It was playable. It was amazing.

It was also one of the most pleasant ballgame afternoons of the season. It was like the early sixties must have been. I counted one hundred thirty people in the bleachers. You could sit wherever you wanted. You could watch the game without the sideshow. The bleachers in their brimming, boisterous, beery, brawling, good-time glory were a fun and famously fascinating place, but this was another great way to watch baseball; a greater way to really *watch* baseball.

Countless people had tried to get back into the bleachers after the rain stopped, but pass-outs were not permitted at Wrigley Field. Outside the park, security boys were involved in five separate fights with angry fans who couldn't get back in. One guard nearly had his finger bitten off. The Bleacher Preacher said he was about to leave—in fact, he was halfway out the gate—when he decided he couldn't and turned around. He hadn't missed an inning all year and didn't want to chance it.

It was nearly dinnertime when the game resumed, and they closed the concession stand in the bleachers. "We wait in the rain for three hours and they screw us," a guy grumbled. Some of us thought about ordering out for pizza. Those who remained, though, were a hardy few with appetites for baseball. There was a middle-aged, businesslike man with a tidy wife who looked like someone who wouldn't get wet. My guess was they were from out of town and were going to stay around to see what they came to see. There was a mother and

son, Ruth and Anthony Steinmiller, both dressed in Cub uniforms. There was Steve, a broad and deeply tanned right-
center regular who always sat in the back row. There was
Mary Ellen, another regular who seldom sat at all. There was
a man and his four-year-old boy. There were two women who
didn't look like the types to wait through nearly three hours
of rain. I would have presumed them to be girlfriends or
wives of ballplayers, except that they wouldn't have been sitting in the bleachers if they were. There was Mike Roche, an
advertising account executive who had taken ten days of vacation because the Cardinals and Mets were coming in after
the Astros. His son's name was Mickey, as in Mantle—there
was a picture of the Yankee slugger over the boy's crib—and
Mike carried around a copy of the birth announcement,
which was made up like a baseball card. "I'm sick," he said,
smiling.

The fellow sitting next to me, a sociable man named Terry
Hemstreet who worked for the railroad, said he was the ulti-
mate Cub fan, and in a way he was. There was a general
difference, however, between Wrigley Field's Cub fans and
baseball fans, though the two might and often did overlap.
The Cub fans watched the Cubs, followed the Cubs, loved the
Cubs, loved Harry Caray, loved Wrigley Field, loved going
there, didn't like the Cardinals, hated the Mets, dressed in
Cub colors, drank coffee out of Cub mugs, and had only a
fifty-fifty chance of correctly guessing which arm Mark Eich-
horn of Toronto threw with. The baseball fans knew the other
league. They cared about the Cubs, but not to the extent of
throwing back the other team's home runs. Mike Roche, for
instance, furtively brought an old beat-up ball with him to the
bleachers so that, if he caught a home run, he could throw
back the beat-up ball and keep the real one. He was a baseball
fan.

Terry Hemstreet, on the other hand, hadn't realized that a
future Hall of Famer had started the game for the Houston
Astros, and he wasn't familiar with the Cub pitcher, who had
recently come over from the Texas Rangers. "Who is this
pitcher," he asked, "Nick Mason?"

"Mike Mason."

"Oh, yeah. Nick Mason is the drummer for Pink Floyd."

But his dedication to the Cubs was unimpeachable. He came to as many games as he could, and taped all of them—even the ones he attended. "I can't get enough," he said. "I just can't get enough." He would fast-forward the tapes when the other team batted. Sometimes he screamed at the television and the neighbors thought he was strangling his sister. Like so many who were hopeless Cub fans, his dad had been one. His dad told him that the Cubs would win a pennant in his lifetime. "He died in '83," Terry said. "At the end, I'd tell him the Cubs were winning, and that would perk him up."

When the game resumed, the Cubs did as well. Dawson tripled in two more runs in the fifth—giving him five RBIs for the day—and Mason was having an easy time of it. The pitcher later said he had relaxed during the long delay by putting his feet up in the clubhouse and watching the water roll by.

In the sixth, Dawson banged into the brick wall in foul territory catching a fly ball from Glenn Davis, and in the seventh, with the Cubs ahead 11–1, he dove to catch a line drive by Chuck Jackson. In the bottom of the seventh, he came to bat with a man on base and a chance to hit for the cycle for the second time in the season. He needed a double. Aurelio Lopez was the pitcher, and Dawson, by golly, sent a rapid line drive right toward the ivy wall in left-center field. It would have been a double, too, except that he was in one of those ruts where he just couldn't seem to keep the ball in the park. It failed to stop at the fence; just went right on over for his second home run of the day and eighteenth of the season. The Steinmillers, in their Cub outfits, captured the ball after it bounced around the empty bleachers.

The score was 13–1; it seemed like Dawson's home run was the only one he had hit all year that didn't tie or win a game or at least have a profound influence on its outcome. It was as though he had reached the point of extravagance; watching him touch the bases was almost to be embarrassed for him. In the dugout before he batted, Billy Williams had told Dawson that if the ball went out, he should deliberately miss third base, thereby being credited with only the double he needed. But it was no use. The man just couldn't help himself. In two days, he had hit four homers and driven in twelve runs. He had passed Eric Davis for the league lead in RBIs.

"I'm tickled to death," said Terry Hemstreet. "I'm tickled to death."

Jerry Pritikin said he was moving to right field for sure.

Elsie was sitting over by the ramp on June third. Her scarf was off. Summer must have arrived.

Beautiful warm weather had blown in after the storm the day before, and the wind was westerly, which meant that it favored balls hit to right field. When Dawson assumed his position there, the bleacher fans stood up and bowed to him in their reverent way. "I think it's so cute the way they do that," said Elsie. Sutcliffe walked the first batter, Billy Hatcher; the second, Bill Doran, hit a home run to—of course—right field.

"Dumbbell!" Elsie shouted at the National League's winningest pitcher. "You know better than to get the ball up in this wind!"

However, Houston's Bob Knepper, a pitcher educated in the classics, was even dumber. He walked two of the first four batters, Dawson singled, and then he threw a pitch up and away to Brian Dayett, who was happy not to pull the ball to left field but instead to send it over the wind-shortened fence in right. Moreland followed with another homer, and when Sandberg batted for the second time in the inning, he hit the Cubs' third home run. Dawson finally made the last out after nine runs had scored.

It was 11–2 by the top of the third, at which point a girl in a bathing suit walked to the concession stand and the boys above in center field hooted hotly at her. At about the same time, the 195-pound Dawson and the 165-pound Dernier were running toward each other in pursuit of the same fly ball. "Watch it!" screamed Elsie. "Don't run into Dawson!"

Dawson hit his nineteenth homer in the third, and the inning ended 13–2. One of the five nurses in front of me, a

Kentucky woman with five Cub buttons on her cap, yelled out, "I hope you're watching, St. Louis!" Meanwhile, the man to my left, dressed in a safari-style suit complete with a wide-brimmed hat, was reading in the *Wall Street Journal* about Alan Greenspan's appointment as chairman of the Federal Reserve Board. He also had the earplug in from his little transistor AM radio, one of which WGN had handed out to everybody before the game. (When I got home that evening, I found that I could not turn mine off.)

Hatcher hit a grand slam for Houston in the fourth to make it 13-6, and a guy in right-center waved a Texas flag. A peanut fight ensued, resulting in the ejection of the fan with the flag. The girl in the bathing suit walked to the concession stand again. Leonard Becker said, "This game isn't over yet, my friend."

With the bases loaded in the sixth, Moreland hit a drive to right-center that dropped into the seats for the third grand slam of the game, setting a National League record and tying the major-league record set by Texas and Baltimore in 1986. By this time, John Vukovich, the Cubs' third-base coach, wasn't even giving signs to the batters; he was just folding his arms and gazing off toward the outfield. On such days at Wrigley Field, it seems as though there will never be a normal game again as long as the wind blows out. It looks so ridiculously easy—almost inevitable—for the big leaguers to turn their bats and pop the ball out of the park. Perspective is lost. Was this the Cubs, or nature, or the Twilight Zone? What was real here?

It was 20-7, and already the Cubs had scored more runs than any team ever had against Houston. Leave it to Wrigley Field. The major-league record for runs scored in a game happened, not surprisingly, at Wrigley Field in 1922, the Cubs beating the Phillies, 26-23. It was ironic, wasn't it—though probably not coincidental—that the highest-scoring game and the only double no-hitter in major-league history happened in the same ballpark? More recently, there was the memorable game of May 18, 1979, when the Phillies beat the Cubs, 23-22.

The girl in the bathing suit made one more trip to the concession stand, and the Cubs scored two more runs. The runs came on Davis's home run in the seventh—the Cubs' sixth homer of the day. The final score was 22–7.

As he left the ballpark, one chubby fan said he hoped he would die on the way home.

The Sports Corner bar at Addison and Sheffield had a little lunch counter on the Addison Street side, next to the el station, and on June fourth a middle-aged, blue-collar baseball fan walked in and reminded the waitress that he'd eaten a Polish sausage sandwich in there the day before. "That's the reason they scored twenty-two runs," he said. "Give me that Polish sausage again."

But the wind had shifted once more, and it was very possible that the Cubs would not score even two runs against Danny Cox and the St. Louis Cardinals, who were in town for the four most important games of the year so far. The likelihood of a low-scoring game became increasingly and bitterly real when Sandberg hit into a double play in the first and another in the third. In the fifth, with St. Louis leading 2–1 and Dunston and Martinez both running with the pitch, he cracked a line drive that Vince Coleman caught in left field and turned into yet another double play.

It was peculiar: some of the best players in the National League were coming together for four games that would determine first place in their division (St. Louis led by just a game going in), and the single most important factor in the outcome would probably be the wind. If the wind blew out, the leggy Cardinals would be overmatched by the Cubs' home-run men. If the wind blew in, however, it would play right into manager Whitey Herzog's game of speed and strategy.

Ironically, the Cardinals had taken the lead when Jack Clark hit a two-run homer against Greg Maddux in the first, but the two runs seemed as big as a baker's dozen from the day before. The Cardinals still led 3–1 in the eighth, when the shadows covered home plate and Todd Worrell, their big relief pitcher, delivered mist out of the sunshine. Dawson struck out for the third time. In the ninth, Davis batted with the tying run on base. A man behind me badmouthed Davis because the Cubs' catcher was always complaining about the shadows in the 3:05 games, which this was. The man lived in Springfield, and a friend of his in the state building there had once given him the license plate of former Cub Jose Cardenal: CUB 1. He had a piece of newspaper on his nose to protect it from the sun. Davis struck out. "That's all right, Jody," he shouted sarcastically. "The shadows are bad.

"Piss on him. Play Sundberg."

Moreland also struck out in the shadows, and St. Louis was two games up.

The next day, Red Schoendienst, the former Cardinal manager and player, stood around the batting cage and said that there had always been something about Wrigley Field that made it difficult to play in. He pointed to the center-field section that was now velvety green, a perfect background for hitters. "That sumbitch out there," he said. "We'd play doubleheaders, and by that second game, between the people sitting up there and the shadows, it was tough to see. And I think the crosswind used to blow harder than it does now. I remember a lot of times Bill Nicholson would hit towering flies that would start out in right-center and land foul. Hell, this is a strange park."

Over by the Cub on-deck circle, photographers were taking pictures of Andre Dawson and Jack Clark, two of the early Most Valuable Player favorites. Clark's home run in the first game of the series was due him, because just before coming to Chicago he had twice been deprived of homers in Cincinnati when the other leading MVP candidate, Eric Davis, leaped to catch balls that were already over the center-field fence. All three men were enormously deserving, but there is an innate, unwitting prejudice that develops when one watches a great player often. He becomes the top of the curve. Davis and Clark were having magnificent years, but after watching Dawson for two months, it was impossible for me to believe that anybody could be doing more. Those who had watched

Davis and Clark every day could probably say the same about them.

As 3:05 approached Friday, the wind turned on the Cubs. If the game had begun at 1:20, the stiff breeze would have been in their favor, but it began to reverse itself about the time the bleachers filled up—mostly with men. It seemed that ninety percent of the bleacher people on this June Friday were men between the ages of about twenty-two and thirty-six. It was a stag party. A good-looking young woman wandered into the right-field bleachers in search of a seat, and a man pointed to his lap. Another woman sat down and a fellow called attention to the hair on her thighs. A chant was taken up: "Shave your legs! Shave your legs!"

The pitchers were Scott Sanderson and Greg Mathews, and it was a tight, Cardinal kind of game, 1–1 through five innings. The Houston series—thirty-five runs in two games—seemed as fresh and pertinent as one day's picnic is to the next day's growling stomach. The Cubs had been on a team-record pace for home runs. They had been on the verge of first place. And the way they were going now, it would take three weeks to score as many runs as they had on the single day before St. Louis arrived.

The Cardinals went ahead in the sixth, and in the eighth, the Cubs' young reliever, Drew Hall, couldn't throw strikes. A guy next to me named Jim, who worked at a place that made teeth and was wearing a Beatles T-shirt and narrow reflecting eyeglasses, screamed at Gene Michael for not removing the kid. Then he addressed the numerous Cardinal fans in the vicinity. "You guys win the battle of managers," he conceded. "Ours sucks. He's an American League manager; he doesn't know what to do with pitchers. These fucking American League managers don't know how to manage in the National League."

The Cardinals scored three runs that inning to go ahead 5–1. A Cub fan threw a beer onto the field from the back of the right-field bleachers. A Cardinal fan in right field stood up and made sweeping motions, alluding to what the Cardinals would do to the Cubs in the series.

In the bottom of the inning, St. Louis inserted Tito Landrum in right field, and several cognizant Cub fans made a point to remind a noticeably loud White Sox patron in their midst that Landrum was the otherwise obscure player who hit the dramatic home run for Baltimore to beat the Sox in the 1983 playoffs. Herzog also replaced Mathews that inning with Worrell, despite the fact that the Cubs had managed but two hits. "Look how fast Whitey pulls his pitchers," Jim said pointedly. "See that, Michael, you asshole?"

He lowered his voice. "I'd better save my throat," he said. "I won't have anything left for tomorrow."

Early Saturday, I walked to the top of the upper deck of the grandstand and watched the crowd mill below, Cardinal red and Cub blue mixing colorfully with the bright umbrellas of the Friendly Confines Cafe. To the east, I could see the sailboats on Lake Michigan, and the gale that moved them along tunneled formidably through the chain-link fence high above the baselines of Wrigley Field, nearly forcing me backward.

My friend Randy, a Cardinal fan from birth, had come in from Denver for the series, and when he got to the ballpark Saturday and saw the flags pointing at the streets, he said, "Oh, shit, Bob Forsch is pitching." Randy was with a buddy named Cisco whom he had met through the Cardinal Fan Club in Denver. Cisco was a first-rate fan, owing in no small part to his job as a repairman of business telephones, a duty that called for him to park his van in an advantageous place and wait diligently for service calls, with only box scores and *Baseball America* for company. In their perambulations around Division Street the previous evening, Randy and Cisco had encountered countless other Cardinal fans. One in particular stood out. They had noticed that he wore a Cardinal hat with a condom taped to it. An hour later, they saw the same fellow again, wearing the hat but no condom.

Saturday's crowd, more than thirty-nine thousand people, was the biggest at Wrigley Field since August 1984—not at all surprising, considering the weather, the standings, and the rivalry. In front of the park, Cardinal fans were selling brooms for five dollars. There was give-and-take between them and Cub fans, but nothing confrontational. Cisco was from New York originally, and he said that if a fan wore a Cardinal or Cub hat at Shea Stadium, it would be yanked off without delay. Of course, to Cisco, Wrigleyville was practically Iowa. He grew up in a neighorbood, he said, where it was absolutely essential to get in a fight on the way home from school. The only times he didn't get in a fight after school were when he was detained at school for fighting. When he got home, his mother would beat him up for getting his shirt ripped. Somehow, Cisco got through it all and became a Cardinal fan, and in this regard he and Randy were only in a moderate minority Saturday. The elements, however, were in the Cubs' favor for the first time in the series. A run pool was taken in a small section of the bleachers, and the lowest guess was thirteen.

More than half that many were scored in the first two innings, the Cubs getting three in the first against Forsch and the Cardinals four in the second against Jamie Moyer. Moreland homered and the Cubs regained the lead in the fourth, but then the game slowed down and the diversions took over. A guy in right field had his head wrapped to look as though it were shaved, and he held up a sign identifying his group as THE ANDRE WORSHIPPERS OF THE HARRY CARAYSHNA FAITH. Another baseball cultist had a T-shirt bearing a crest and the name of his order, SONS OF THE BLEACHERS. Ronnie Woo-Woo walked through slapping hands and posing for pictures. Cardinal fans, in deference to their amazing shortstop, called out, "Ozzie! Ozzie!" Cub fans answered, "Harriet! Harriet!"

The Cubs led 6–4 in the top of the seventh inning, and Forsch was due to bat for St. Louis. Moyer was still pitching for the Cubs. "Steve Lake will hit," said Cisco. He wasn't even looking at the field. "I don't have to look, because he's the only right-handed hitter left." Moyer got Lake and finished the seventh, then yielded to Lee Smith.

The eighth was the last inning for beer sales, and Howard,

the vendor/photographer, said the day had been one of the top five he'd had in nine years of working the ballpark. That meant he would make close to two hundred dollars for the afternoon, money he would use to buy film. The Cardinals went down in the eighth, and a bleacher regular named Steve Schanker (who, it was said, could sing the national anthem backward) shouted from the back aisle: "Wrigley Field! Sunshine! Beating the Cardinals! What could be better?!" It was the happy sort of baseball afternoon that had become virtually extinct everywhere but on the North Side of Chicago.

"This is great," gushed Randy, unbowed by the score. "This is great. This place is a shrine. The trouble is, I'm afraid that after being here, I'll never be able to watch a game anywhere else."

Of course, it got interesting in the ninth with Smith on the scene. The Cardinals scored once and had two men on when he persuaded the other Smith—Ozzie—to pop up as the whole ballpark stood. Then the whole ballpark repaired to the streets of Wrigleyville for a premature Oktoberfest. People on the roofs of the apartments on Waveland Avenue threw beer at Cardinal fans as they walked by. One Cardinal fan wished he had a cup so he could dodge around catching it. It was harmless fun, mostly, but on Sheffield, a guy lay bleeding under the Redtop Parking sign.

In front of Gate N, a Cub fan stood with a piece of broken bleacher in his hand, seat numbers 110 and 111. He claimed he found it. He saw by Cisco's hat that he was a Cardinal fan, and said, "You couldn't have this in St. Louis with those *plastic* seats."

Cisco and Randy seemed to think that it would be the Mets, not the Cubs, who ultimately would challenge the Cardinals. Of course, they hadn't been at Wrigley Field when Dernier beat the Reds with a two-out home run in the ninth, or when Dawson tied the Braves with two outs in the ninth one day and beat them with two outs in the twelfth the next. I believed that Cub fans were optimists beyond the point of calculated reason, but after being in Wrigley Field for two months, I also believed that Chicago would take St. Louis down to the wire in 1987.

Mike Mason, who had offered such hope in his first start with the Cubs, wasn't up to the task in his second, and after the top of the fourth, the Cardinals led 9–0. "Well, this looks like the first bad game here in a while," Randy said. Just as he did, the Cubs scored seven. In this Bermuda Triangle of ballparks, anything was possible. The rally was concluded by Dawson's twentieth home run—twenty, you might recall, being the approximate number of home runs Herzog had predicted Dawson would hit for the season.

I looked down our row and noticed that not a single leg was covered at the knee. Along the right-field fence, a fan held up a sheet on which he had spray-painted: DEATH TO RONNIE WOO-WOO. The Cardinals scored two more in the fifth, and in the center-field bleachers, some guys displayed a sign that said: WE'RE STILL MARLA MEN. Attached was a blowup of the *Playboy* photo spread that had prompted the controversial firing of Marla Collins as the Cubs' ballgirl in 1986.

St. Louis added another run in the sixth, the Cubs scored two, and a mannerly young man next to me drank another beer. The custom was a beer an inning. He had no concern about driving home. "The el is right there," he said, pointing across Sheffield. In front of us, a flight attendant originally from the St. Louis suburb of Ladue—the stew from Ladue— testified that she hadn't much cared for Chicago when she moved here over the winter, but loved it in the spring. "The metamorphosis I've seen in Chicago in the last two months is incredible," she said. She kissed her boyfriend, and a guy in front of her turned around and said, "Come on. This is a ballpark, not a goddamn hotel."

It was five o'clock when the Cubs batted in the ninth with the score 13–9. They say that because of the way the shadows fall, the team ahead at five o'clock always wins at Wrigley Field. When it ended, the Cubs were three games behind the Cardinals.

Randy and Cisco caught the Clark bus back to their hotel, noting that it was number 22, just like the Cardinals' cleanup hitter.

Losing three out of four to St. Louis did nothing to quiet the issue over lights. In fact, one of the staunch opponents of lights, state representative John Cullerton, announced that he was going to propose legislation that would permit the Cubs to light Wrigley Field for postseason games. Taking it further, Cullerton said he and local alderman Bernard Hansen of the 44th Ward would clear the way for the Cubs to get the permits they required to add new seats and skyboxes—*if* they would agree to use the lights for postseason games only and cease in their efforts to play regular-season night games.

It was, of course, entirely politics. Postseason baseball would naturally be lucrative to the city as well as the Cubs, and it was in Chicago's best interest to ensure that Cub playoff or World Series games not be exported. Also, by eliminating the obstacles to postseason night games, the legislators would have disarmed the Cubs of the soft sword they swung in the name of sympathy. If, at the same time, they could preclude the immediate possibility of regular-season night games, all points would have been won by the neighborhood.

But the Cubs weren't buying it. Their spokesman, Don Grenesko, told the *Chicago Sun-Times*, "Until we can play regular-season night games, we're not going to do anything with the stadium." Grenesko reiterated that temporary lights were out of the question and said that permanent lights would cost five million dollars, an expense that had to be defrayed through revenue from regular-season night games. To the Cubs, the direct financial benefits would be twofold: Although their attendance was consistently exemplary considering that they had the smallest ballpark in the National League, they would nonetheless be able to attract bigger crowds for some of the mundane weekday games—particularly those early and late in the season. Also, at night they would be able to charge prime-time advertising rates for their television and radio broadcasts, a benefit that was doubly lucrative to the Tribune Company, which owned the team and both stations.

The Cubs sensed that public sentiment was shifting their way in light of concurrent movements to develop new playing sites for the White Sox and the Bears, replacing Comiskey

Park (the oldest stadium in the major leagues) and venerable Soldier Field. Those old parks were landmarks, but Wrigley was a precious artifact. The Cubs knew if they convinced the city that leaving Wrigley Field was an advancing possibility—perhaps an inevitability—politics would be on their side. "If they tried to tear down Wrigley Field, fans would be fifty deep holding hands around it," said Mike Murphy, the Bleacher Bum from way back. "Hey, would you want to be mayor of Chicago when the Cubs left Wrigley Field and moved to a dome in the suburbs?"

In the meantime, though, the Cubs still had a losing record for the year in their precious old park, and having failed against the Cardinals, they were confronted by the New York Mets for the first time at Wrigley Field in 1987. The Mets had struggled through the first third of the season but had reason to believe that first the Cubs and then the Cardinals would be eminently catchable. Dwight Gooden had returned from his drug rehabilitation, winning his first start impressively, and reliever Roger McDowell was back from his injury. Moreland, among others, maintained that the Mets were still the team of reckoning in the National League East.

It was June eighth—a date on which, two years before, the Cubs still led the division—and more than twenty-eight thousand people were at the ballpark on a working Monday afternoon. Bill Veeck once said that the Cubs are for everybody who ever said no to their boss. Even in his circuit court opinion concerning the right to lights, Judge Curry had alluded to the great Chicago tradition of long baseball lunches. "The real litmus test for Cub loyalty," he wrote, "is the willingness to blow off the job and flirt with unemployment to attend a game starting in the early afternoon." Actually, this game started in the late afternoon—3:05—but the spirit of the thing was intact. Two professional women, dressed forbiddingly in business suits, arrived slightly tardy and found seats in the back row next to two men. Of course, not all of the crowd had come directly from the office. Nearby was a woman wearing a penguin hat for reasons unknown, Ron Cey being in Oakland.

Durham, back in the lineup for the first time after his shoulder injury, hit a fly ball to right field in the first inning, and from left field it was plain to see that the swirling wind pressed against the flight of the drive, dropping it benignly into the glove of Darryl Strawberry. It wasn't a deep fly at all, but on a more generous day it might have meant three runs for Chicago. Moreland managed a home run in the second inning against Ron Darling, and a bleacher fan in left-center informed centerfielder Len Dykstra that he sucked. Hearing their favorite word, those around him immediately took up the old "Right field sucks" routine, which entirely interrupted the fellow's train of criticism. "No!" he screamed. "*Dykstra* sucks, you dumb assholes!"

Given its encompassing applications, "sucks" had no serious competition as the preeminent bleacher word. No one has ever satisfactorily explained why this charge represents the particular character flaw that most disgraces a ballplayer or a section of bleachers, but it had enlisted a broad class of plaintiffs at Wrigley Field. The fellow next to me on Monday, a University of Illinois sportswriter named Phil Favorite, said that in a game he had attended several years ago, Pittsburgh's John Milner had trapped a ball that the umpires gave him credit for catching, at which Milner turned and smiled at the hooting bleachers crowd. Phil was not surprised to hear a couple of voices call out "Milner sucks"—until he noticed that the accusers were a couple of gray-haired grandmothers.

With the Mets in town, the designated suckers were Dykstra and Strawberry, a Mutt-and-Jeff pair of outfielders who shared only their unappealing gray, blue, and orange road uniform and the conspicuous cockiness that went inside. Dykstra was an especial favorite of the women who sat behind him in center field, and Strawberry seemed to bring out the recessive redneck in the male bleacher species. "Dar-ryl" was also a pleasing sort of sound to make in a loud, sing-songy manner.

The two businesswomen removed their jackets in the third, and Mumphrey, who had tripled, scored on a double by Dawson. Sutcliffe, meanwhile, was performing like a pitcher in the pay range in which he was, and he took the Cubs into the five o'clock shadows with a 2–1 lead. By this time, the businesswomen were sitting on the rail behind their seats with the two men between them.

Lee Smith relieved Sutcliffe in the seventh and got out of a tight spot, but he was still pitching in the ninth and apparently tiring. He threw a pitch to Kevin McReynolds that was obviously lackluster, and McReynolds lashed a single. Then Smith walked Howard Johnson. It was plain that the big reliever didn't have it; he was pitching longer than he normally did, and he was losing it. Everybody knew it. But there was nobody warming up in the Cubs' bullpen. Barry Lyons doubled to tie the game. Smith was in the process of walking Mookie Wilson intentionally when Jody Davis happened to notice Lyons gawking into the Mets' dugout, and picked him off second. But an apparent victory had been at least detained, and the Bleacher Preacher came storming by, miffed that Sutcliffe once again had been statistically deprived by failing relief. Pritikin had been a defender of Lee Smith in the past, but had come to the end of his patience. "I'd trade him right now for Frazier and Fontenot," he said, invoking the names of the two pitchers whose failings had been the most flagrant in recent Cub seasons.

"He worked pretty long," I said futilely. "I think he just got kind of tired."

"Lee Smith wakes up tired," he said. "He's the only player on the Cubs that I can't stand."

It was 2–2 going into the bottom of the ninth, and one of the businesswomen was wearing a Cub hat that belonged to one of the guys. Doug Sisk was pitching for the Mets, and with two outs Martinez singled. It was apparently no big deal. Manny Trillo, the old utility infielder, batted for Sutcliffe. Being the veteran that he was, Trillo usually let the first pitch go by, but with extra innings being just an out away, he decided, what the heck, to go up swinging. Sisk, not expecting this and not respectful of Trillo's inconsiderable power, threw a fastball that started out for the middle of the plate and ended up four rows into the left-field bleachers.

The ramp thundered again, people screaming and leaping and pounding each other on the back. One girl held a radio to her ear, and with her eyes closed tight, screamed, "Cubs win! Cubs win!"

The two businesswomen went on over to Murphy's with the two guys.

Where I live near Cincinnati is not the country, exactly—I can be at Riverfront Stadium in twenty minutes—but the mailbox is about a hundred yards away. If I walked a hundred yards from my building in Chicago, I would pass the homes of about four hundred people. In the twenty-five minutes it took me to walk up Broadway or Clark to Wrigley Field, I was in the immediate vicinity of more ethnic restaurants, more bars, more bookstores, more neon, more courtyards, more fire escapes, more double locks, more arched doorways, more panhandlers, more black pants, more bagels, more Polish sausage, more Asians, more gays, more prostitutes, more young professionals, and more funny hair than in my entire Ohio county of Clermont.

On Tuesday, June 9, as I walked under the el tracks and past the Mongolian House restaurant on Clark Street, a Mercedes Benz drove by packed with more people—eleven—than I was likely to encounter in a trip to the post office back home. They were college kids, and they were sitting on top of the seatbacks, hanging out the windows, crammed against the ceiling. I wondered if they knew what they had—youth, friends, privilege, and baseball in the afternoon.

It turned out that the college boys actually got to Wrigley Field earlier than Darryl Strawberry that day. Strawberry had stayed out late at a night spot called The Limelight, overslept, and didn't make it to the ballpark until quarter past noon. New York's manager, Davey Johnson, fined and benched the big slugger for his tardiness. The other Mets, though punctual, proceeded to play as if they had kept the same evening hours. By the fourth inning they had committed five errors, all of them on the infield.

The only New York infielder without an error, third baseman Howard Johnson, hit a home run in the second, and two batters later the fans in left field were still yelling for a guy in right to throw the ball back. When that modern Wrigley custom began, bleacher fans would take up a collection and pay somebody forty or fifty dollars to toss the ball down; but the philanthropy soon passed, and now the throw-back was considered a Cub fan's moral obligation. When the man in right refused to comply, the left-field fans expressed their collective opinion that right field sucked. "That's enough," said a disapproving fan in left, bringing his considerable weight to his feet, "I'm going over *there*."

Dunston and Durham homered in the fourth and fifth, and the Mets' Tim Teufel did the same in the seventh, tying the game with a drive to straightaway center that dropped into the basket put up at the top of the outfield fence in 1970 to prevent fans from interfering with fly balls and from jumping onto the field. As Teufel's home-run ball lay temptingly in front of the section of closed-off bleacher seats, an agile guy in right-center swiftly hopped over there and claimed it. Despite the vociferous urging of the crowd, he wouldn't throw it back. Even the usher was yelling at him to throw the ball back. The guy's real problem, though, was that he had violated not only Wrigley Field custom, but also Wrigley Field rules: he had ventured into forbidden center field, and a burly Crowd Control guard escorted him out of the park. As the maverick fan was being taken up the aisle, a well-dressed young businessman said to him, "Get outta here, you faggot."

Sandberg, who theretofore had not played anything like the infallible deity that he was reputed to be, broke the tie with a two-out single off pitcher McDowell's leg that drove in two runs in the eighth, and Lee Smith came in to pitch the ninth. I couldn't see Jerry Pritikin anywhere. Smith got the first two batters, and as the crowd rose in anticipation of the final out, Mookie Wilson homered to right field against the wind. With the crowd still standing, Dykstra singled, and the Mets sent for a tall pinch hitter. "That's got to be Strawberry," said a dark-haired fan as number 18 loosened up. "He's the biggest baboon they got." Smith struck out Strawberry to end the game.

I thought about the Strawberry remark again the next day,

when there was an item in the news about a twenty-three-year-old black woman who had moved into a house in the South Side Irish neighborhood of Bridgeport to be with her white boyfriend. Bridgeport, like so many other old ethnic Chicago communities, was a homogeneous and self-preserving place, and the white neighbors didn't conceal the fact that they wanted her out. Ostensibly, the neighbors were trying to protect the ethnic integrity of their small world, but would their reaction have been the same if the woman had been Swedish or Italian? The fact was that racial intolerance had a long history in Chicago, and it wasn't over. Two Sundays before, my wife and I had walked along the beach for a little over a mile, and were surprised to find that as we passed a pier we crossed from a pure white beach to a pure black one; past another pier was an Hispanic beach.

There was no wanton racism in the bleachers of Wrigley Field, but a subtle bigotry still asserted itself randomly. One of the bleacher ethics held that nothing was off limits in the harassment of an opposing player, and race being a handy subject, occasionally there were overtly distasteful remarks such as the one concerning Strawberry. The same applied to Chicago's black players. If one batted or pitched his way into disfavor with the fans—as Lee Smith had done in 1987, despite his fine numbers—it was not uncommon for the criticism to take on racial overtones. On the other hand, black Cub heroes such as Ernie Banks, Billy Williams, Ferguson Jenkins, Gary Matthews, and now Andre Dawson, were among the best-loved men ever to wear the uniform.

More significant than any passive prejudice in the bleachers, though, was the conspicuous scarcity of black fans. In other ballparks black fans have traditionally followed baseball from the inexpensive bleacher seats—in St. Louis, for instance, there are still old black bleacher men wise in the ways of the game. At Wrigley Field, they are a conspicuous minority. The racial imbalance in the bleachers was particularly notable in light of the raging issue of discrimination in baseball management following the unfortunate early-season remarks of Dodger executive Al Campanis, who said on national television that blacks "don't have the necessities" to be major-league managers.

Anyway, Strawberry was out of the lineup again Wednesday, but Dwight Gooden was in it. Security guards confiscated all drug-related signs that fans tried to get into the ballpark, although one made it through: JUST SAY NO.

No, in fact, was precisely what Gooden said to the Cubs on Wednesday. Sandberg, who had assumed the leadoff spot against right-handed pitchers, hit his first pitch high in the air to Strawberry's replacement in right field, Mookie Wilson, but the wind kept the ball in the park and it was a while before the Cubs came as close again to scoring.

Dykstra was New York's first batter, and after he grounded out to Sandberg, a guy in front of me wrote down the abbreviation *G.O.* on his neatly printed scorecard. A nurse in the next row, wearing a Cub shirt and listening to the radio, straightened him out in terms of scorekeeping protocol. "Four-three, buddy," she said. "Four-three." For whatever reason, Wednesday seemed to bring out the best of the baseball women. Another woman nearby wore my favorite of all the countless Cubs T-shirts. It was simple and gray, with quiet red and blue lettering that said: CHICAGO CUBS . . . WORLD CHAMPIONS 1908.

On this day I also got a peek at the most creative implementation of the ubiquitous Cub logo. It was a tattoo, and it appeared quite high, indeed, on the thigh of a thirty-two-year-old Indiana waitress whose friends called her Tidbit. Tidbit had grown up in St. Louis, but when she was eight years old her Uncle Jack made her a Cub fan. "The Cubs are my summer," she said succinctly. She sat always in the same spot in the first row of the upper center-field section, on an unpainted piece of bleacher board that was identified by the graffiti "Tidbit's Seat." One day the WGN camera caught her smoking a cigar in the bleachers. Tidbit did not fancy herself a general expert on baseball, but she knew what she had to know. "Yo, Dykstra!" she yelled in a loud, deep voice. She had no insult for New York's centerfielder—just a "yo."

The Mets scored three runs in the second against Scott

Sanderson and rallied again in the third. Sanderson was due to bat in the bottom of the third and Michael wanted him to finish out the inning so he could use a pinch hitter, but it was painfully apparent that the pitcher would have a hard time getting three outs. The Mets scored twice and Sanderson worked on. "Let him give up some more runs, you asshole," shouted a fan in right-center. Sanderson was getting hit so squarely that Michael's strategy—one that was widely practiced—seemed patently inappropriate. The bleacher logic was this: by using a pinch hitter, a manager improves his offense for one batter; but for every opposing batter who comes up against a pitcher who has nothing, he hurts his defense. While the fans clamored for a change on the mound, Sanderson faced three more batters. They all scored on Tim Teufel's home run. Mike Mason came in to pitch, and Michael didn't get to use his pinch hitter after all.

In the sixth inning Keith Hernandez, who had shaved his mustache to change his luck, hit his second home run of the day. The Bleacher Preacher caught it, his first ball of the year. Naturally, he threw it back, although he said it hurt his voodoo elbow.

The Mets had a dozen runs before the Cubs could score a couple, so I left to get an early start on the drive back to Ohio. The final score was 13–2, and after the game WGN radio was publicizing a fantasy baseball camp with the 1969 Cubs, the most popular Chicago team since World War II. There was a free enrollment to be won, and a lady called up and said there would be nobody more deserving than her friend who played 6-9-C-U-B-S in the lottery every week.

The Cubs were on the road for only three games, but the games were in St. Louis and they lost them all. They were six games behind the Cardinals when they got back home. What was worse, Sandberg had torn ligaments in his ankle running out an infield single in the Saturday game, and would be out of the lineup for as long as six weeks. It seemed early for the Cubs to start their collapse, but this was the date—June fifteenth—that they lost their lead in 1985. Within a week that year, they were in fourth place; their losing streak reached thirteen. All the signs were in order for another year just like the other ones.

"The problem," said Jerry Pritikin, "is that they get your hopes up, and then, boom."

Jeweler Joe waved his hand in resignation and said, "They're through. They were playing lucky anyway."

"Sure they're through," said Norb Kudele. "But that doesn't matter."

The Phillies were in town for four games, with the Cubs' Greg Maddux pitching the first against Bruce Ruffin. Paul Noce had been called up from Iowa to take Sandberg's place at second base, and early in the game he started a slick double play in which Dunston leaped over a charging baserunner and threw authoritatively to first. "He's the only shortstop in the league who makes that play," said the fellow next to me, a journalist named Jeff Cox who was a great admirer of Dunston, and also of Bill James, the eminent if somewhat arcane baseball analyst. It struck me as noteworthy that he quoted Bill James to me without first inquiring if I were familiar with James's work. For all the extracurriculars that had crashed upon the bleachers in recent years, where else could one move without formality or precedent into a discussion of Bill James?

With Sandberg out of action, Dunston would have to mature quickly as the leader of the Cubs' infield if they were to make anything of 1987. Despite all of the unpromising signals, there was still hope if the young pitchers could perform as Maddux did Monday. He left in the seventh with a 2–1 lead.

Against Smith in the eighth, the Phillies tied the game and appeared to take the lead when Juan Samuel came around from first base on a double by Von Hayes. But as Samuel returned to the Philadelphia dugout, about fifty box-seat fans screamed for Jody Davis to step on home plate. He did, and umpire Greg Bonin verified that Samuel had not touched it, calling him out.

In the ninth, though, Glenn Wilson scored the lead run for

the Phillies when Smith stepped in a hole and threw a wild pitch. In the Cub half of the inning, Dunston led off with a single against Steve Bedrosian (who would set a league record if he could get his ninth straight save) and then stole second. But he jammed his right hand into the base and broke it. The pinch runner, Mike Mason, was left at second when Bedrosian retired Dayett and Mumphrey.

If pennant prospects had been thin before the game, by the end of the day they were anorexic. With Dunston's injury following Sandberg's, the stellar middle of the Cubs' infield would be missing for nearly two months. Even worse were the poetic symbols, which had been so propitious just a few weeks before when Dawson and Dernier and Trillo were hitting heroic home runs. As omens went, Monday's defeat was bad. It seemed that if destiny were to attend the 1987 Cubs, they would at least have won the game that their great fans had tried so conscientiously to save. When even that was insufficient to rally the boys, it appeared that they were spent.

Attempting to subdue desperation with youth, the Cubs called up Rafael Palmeiro. Palmeiro was regarded as the Cubs' best hitting prospect, a college graduate and left-handed batter so mature that when he came up to the major leagues late in the 1986 season, he went to the plate twenty-nine times before he swung and missed a pitch. He had been the favorite to win the starting left-field job in spring training, but had been reluctant to, and the Cubs had still not resolved the position. Chico Walker had been sent back to the minors. Mumphrey had been hitting well in his platoon role, but they knew he was not a long-term solution. Palmeiro was the man of the future, and he started Tuesday's game in left, with Mumphrey in right to give Dawson a rest. Another minor leaguer, Mike Brumley, had been called up to replace Dunston, and he and Noce were the double-play combination. Trout, who had missed six weeks with a thigh bruise—remember, this was the man who once went on the disabled list after falling off his bicycle—was back and pitching.

It was Beach Towel Day, but only kids got them. I was with two friends, Peter and David, who had come in from New

York. David paid a kid four dollars for his beach towel. The kid said he was going to use the money to buy a batting glove. A few minutes later, we saw him with two batting gloves and wristbands.

It was a blisteringly hot afternoon and we sat in left field behind a family of four from Fort Wayne named the Ehrsams who said that the day would cost them one hundred fifty dollars. They came often. "If they close this place," said the mother, Darlene, "I'll never watch another baseball game." Her husband, Steve, nodded and said, "You've never been to a game until you've sat in the bleachers at Wrigley Field."

Mumphrey, apparently having trod upon Dawson's magic grass in right field, homered in the first. When he returned to his position, the right-field bleacher fans bowed to him as they did to Dawson. It was unlike anything that had ever happened to a journeyman such as Mumphrey, and he couldn't resist turning his head slightly to peek from under the cap he always pulled down hard over his forehead. Palmeiro tripled home a run in the third and Durham brought him in with a double. Noce was inspired at second base, and Trout was rolling. In the center-field bleachers, a construction worker said that the Cubs could get hot at home and be right back in the race. He also said that he used to like the White Sox, but he hated them now because they were on pay-TV.

Martinez homered in the sixth and the Cubs scored three times to go ahead 7–1. The next inning, I found myself in my first bleacher argument. I had brought a nylon bag to the game to carry some things for my friends to read. I realized it was unwise to bring something to the ballpark that I wasn't willing to get wet or dirty, so I hadn't said anything twice before when people behind me spilled beers onto the bag. But in the seventh, I looked down and the thing was drenched. I stood up, turned around, and said something to the effect that it was the third time it had happened and enough was enough.

The guy behind me said, "Aw, three times. Isn't that too bad?" And so I proceeded to engage angrily in a mindless argument with a guy who was drunk and had one tooth missing and another one chipped—obvious testimony that he was a miscreant of long standing. David had gone for a beer or something, and as he returned, here I was exchanging loud and stupid sentences with the drunk behind me. Finally the guy zinged me with the ringing clincher: "I bet you don't even smoke reefer, do you?"

Not five minutes later, the same guy bolted out of his seat and raced up and across the aisle. A fellow up there had been squirting beer out of a spray bottle, and he had apparently wetted my opponent. He had also apparently wetted my friend Peter, who is a large person with a voice that could carry from Cleveland to first place. Peter was shouting epithets at the guy with the bottle, incensed that the Crowd Control usher was standing by with his arms folded. How do we get into these things?

Peter thought it would be sensible to move, but I wasn't in the mood for sensible. So we stayed put and watched Trout put two runners on in the ninth with two outs and a 7–1 lead. Michael had Smith and Lynch in the bullpen. I couldn't understand it. He had let Smith get pounded in a close game, with nobody else warming up, and Trout was trying to go the distance with a six-run lead and he had two guys throwing. He brought in Lynch to pitch to Glenn Wilson, and Wilson singled in a run. Lynch walked Greg Gross to fill the bases, and then Michael called in Smith.

At that, Jerry Pritikin left the ballpark. The day before, when Smith had lost the game with a wild pitch, the Bleacher Preacher had sworn that he would walk out in protest the next time Smith came in. He took a picture of the park to prove it. "My heart was pounding in fear that they'd tie the game," he said.

Von Hayes grounded out and Smith had his sixteenth save.

The commissioner had said the wrong thing to the Economic Club of Southwest Michigan. Speaking to a group of businessmen in Benton Harbor, Peter Ueberroth let slip that the Cubs would probably be allowed to play their league championship games in the daytime at Wrigley Field if they made the playoffs.

For the Cubs, this news was much too good to be acceptable. How could they enlist sympathy if the commissioner was going to reverse himself and let the team play postseason games at home? Alerted quickly to the downside of such restrictive freedom, Ueberroth showed up at Beautiful Wrigley Field the next day and took it all back.

And as if it wasn't tough enough having friends like the commissioner, the Cubs' leverage was also being undermined in Springfield, where Cullerton had sponsored legislation that passed unanimously and lifted the state's opposition to postseason night games. The state representative acknowledged that his bill was intended to call the Cubs' bluff and make them admit that the issue wasn't the postseason prohibition.

The issue over postseason lights would be a moot one, though—at least for 1987—unless the Cubs could do something quickly about the pennant race, such as beating the Phillies a couple more times. To that end, they sent Jamie Moyer out to pitch Wednesday against Philadelphia's Shane Rawley. After a moment of silence for Dick Howser, the Cubs scored two runs in the first. Dawson had three straight hits, and Moyer did a capable job of holding the lead. He and Maddux had now each pitched strongly in their last outing. Hope had not left the hallowed premises.

Smith came on in the ninth to hold a 5–3 lead. "God, I hate him," said a woman nearby. It was an otherwise uneventful inning.

The next morning was more eventful, the Phillies naming Lee Elia to be their manager. This brought back all sorts of mixed memories to Wrigley Field, where Elia had managed in 1982 and 1983. With the Cubs, he was a respected baseball man and a popular manager with the players, whom he had defended profoundly and, unfortunately, profanely. His Chicago legacy will always be the head-spinning diatribe he delivered in April 1983, when the Cubs were 5–14 and Elia was incensed at the Wrigley Field fans for their criticism of his players. After a 4–3 loss to the Dodgers (in which Lee Smith let in the winning run on a wild pitch) he cut loose with an outburst that featured forty-six expletives. Included was the memorable appraisal of Cub fans' employment status: "They oughta go out and get a fuckin' job and find out what it's like to go out and earn a fuckin' living," he said. "Eighty-five percent of the fuckin' world is working. The other fifteen percent come out here. A fuckin' playground for the cocksuckers."

Elia's comments were directed at the general Wrigley crowd in theory, but at the bleacher crowd in reality. The rest of Wrigley Field was not like the bleachers. Everywhere else, the seats were reserved, and in many instances they were covered, logistically precluding two of the principal features of the bleachers, sociability and sunshine, to which Budweiser and Old Style together represented a companionable third party.

For seven innings on June eighteenth I sat in the grandstand. An older man walked up one of the aisles with his friends and said, "This is where I was when I 'bout got killed in '34 when that ball came up here and I didn't see it." The beer vendors, who carried two cases in the bleachers, carried one in the reserved sections. I found a private seat along the right-field line, but I could have sat almost anywhere. Space was at a premium only in the bleachers; the rest of the park was wide open.

It was quiet in the grandstand. It was so quiet, actually—so detached—that I had trouble concentrating on the game. I found it difficult to concentrate on the game in the bleachers, too, but only because of all the distractions. It made me think of and envy Arnold Hano, who in 1954 wrote a book about a single day in the bleachers at the Polo Grounds. The game he wrote about happened to be the great World Series game between the Giants and Indians when Willie Mays made the famous catch of Vic Wertz's long fly ball. It was an intense, important game that naturally commanded attention, but I was nonetheless impressed by Hano's acute perception of what was happening on the field—the shifting of the fielders, the timing of the baserunners, the tactics of the pitchers. I wondered if he could follow a game with such vigilance at Wrigley Field in 1987.

The grandstand was comfortable. I put my feet on the

empty seat in front of me and watched passively as four runners were thrown out at home in the first inning and a half—four of the nine outs in the game. Martinez threw out a runner from center field and singled his first three times up. He was leading off now, with Sandberg hurt, and his offense was rapidly catching up with his fetching defense. Palmeiro was also hitting encouragingly, but when he was at third base in the first inning with one out, he tagged up on Durham's fly ball to fairly deep right field and was rather amazingly thrown out by Glenn Wilson. It was curious how such an otherwise ordinary player like Wilson could have such a spectacular throwing arm.

Wilson was also an engaging outfielder who, unlike grimmer players around the league, enjoyed the give-and-take with the Cub crowd. Wednesday, he had picked up a foul ball and heaved it over the bleacher fence onto Sheffield Avenue. I asked him why he had done that. "The day before," he said, "I picked up a foul ball and tossed it into the stands, and they said, 'We still hate you, Wilson.' So I thought I'd do something different. I always have fun with the people out there."

Palmeiro and Moreland both hit two-run homers in the third against the Phillies' rookie, Mike Jackson, and the Cubs were in good shape behind Sutcliffe until the seventh. Then, with Chicago ahead 6–2 with two on and two out, Sutcliffe faced Mike Schmidt. I had watched by the batting cage earlier in the day as Schmidt, a man with 511 home runs, had stood off to the side and swung his bat over a facsimile of home plate that he had drawn in the dirt. He was businesslike about what he was doing, and also a little preoccupied. He had been one of the critics of the manager who had just been fired, John Felske, whom he nonetheless regarded as a good man; I wondered if he might have been feeling a little responsibility for Felske's dismissal. Maybe he had a headache. Maybe he felt rotten for no good reason. In the first inning, he had grounded out on a half-swing and been exceedingly irritated. It certainly seemed as if something was bothering him; if so, he had to get rid of it, because he faced Rick

Sutcliffe in the seventh inning with the game on the line.

The game was on the line, really, only because he was Mike Schmidt. It was 6–2, but the pitchers stopped throwing in both bullpens to watch. The crowd was quiet, intent. The count went to three and two, and Schmidt rolled a ball to Moreland's right. The third baseman's throw hopped twice and arrived late at first. Schmidt had not struck the big blow, but Sutcliffe had not retired him either, and so DiPino came in to pitch. Hayes singled, and then Wilson doubled against Ed Lynch. It was 6–5.

Across the aisle from me, a blonde woman in designer blue jeans was eating an apple, was not drinking beer, and did not stand for the seventh inning stretch and song. There was nobody like her in the bleachers.

When I moved from the grandstand to the cheap seats in the bottom of the seventh, my first impression was how vast and pretty the greensward looked. The outfield was like the most verdant thing in the world, and only from behind it, in the bleachers, did one get the full effect. Former Cub second baseman Glenn Beckert, after his long playing career was over, went out to the bleachers in right-center one day, spread his arms, and said, "I can't believe the view you get from here. Now I understand why fans keep coming out here." My second impression was how lively and friendly the bleachers seemed after the grandstand.

In the eighth, the remarkable Jerry Mumphrey, in his first appearance since slightly pulling a muscle on the day he subbed for Dawson in right field, hit a long three-run homer to left. Later in the inning, Dawson batted, and a guy suggested that everybody stand and bow. "I don't bow to anybody," snarled a fan in the back row. "And besides, Dawson hasn't done anything in four days."

The Phillies scored two in the eighth against Ron Davis to make it 9–7. Smith came in, gave up a hit, and got the last out. The Cubs had won three in a row.

Down on the sidewalk, as people danced to "Tequila," I talked with a sharp young woman named Patty who was a graduate student in sociology at the University of Chicago and whom I'd met over two innings in the bleachers. She was interested in the sociology of the bleachers—in fact, she said she was inspired by it and wanted to spend her summer writing a paper on the subject—and we tried to hash out why the bleachers were the unique contemporary cultural phenomenon that they were.

We tried out a lot of theories and decided that the best one was beer.

Just when everybody was willing to write off the season, the Cubs had gone and beaten the Phillies three straight. That was how it always worked with them. Now the Pirates were coming into town, and they weren't much. This thing wasn't over; the boys of Wrigley were still soliciting contributions of faith and fidelity for 1987. On their way to the ballpark Friday, a family walked past an old man sitting on a doorstep near Sheffield and Cornelia with three Cub buttons on his shirt, and the old man said to the young boy, "Don't let 'em beat the Cubs, now." At the souvenir stand by the el station on Addison, a father bought Cub hats for his two small sons and beamed as they put them on.

The Pirates were in last place, and the previous night they had lost in the tenth inning at St. Louis when Jack Clark hit a home run against Don Robinson. A guy in the left-field bleachers before the game Friday held a ball in his hand and yelled out, "Hey, Robinson! I caught this last night from Clark!" Robinson chuckled. A Cub fan wearing a Cardinal hat walked past Jerry Pritikin, and Pritikin asked him where he got the hat. He had lost a bet on the Cubs last week, he said, and now he had to wear the hat until July fifth. The Bleacher Preacher gave him a Cubs sticker to put over the Cardinal logo.

Dickie Noles, who was successfully rehabilitating from an alcohol problem, made his first start of the season for the Cubs, and gave up four runs in the first four innings. A fan hollered, "I wish you'd go back to drinking, Noles." A guy gave a dollar to a beer vendor and asked him to deliver a condom to a girl a few rows back. Otherwise, it was hot and dull. Pittsburgh's pitcher, Brian Fisher, had just cut his hair like Arnold Schwarzenegger's in the movie *Predator*, and when the day was over, his new look was unscored upon: he had shut out Chicago on six hits. The optimism that had supplied the Cub fans with so much energy just three hours before had been melted down by mid-summer reality. The crowd yawned, stretched, and left.

I walked home on Broadway, and fell in with two guys and a woman who took off at noon every Friday when the Cubs were in town. "The Cubs," the girl said, shaking her head, "I don't know."

Across the street I saw Leonard Becker on his bicycle. He asked if any of his old buddies had been at the game. It had been a Friday 3:05 start, which meant a big crowd. They hadn't.

Saturday's was a big crowd, too, and another listless one. It was the hottest day of the year so far, and the fans and Cubs both seemed to be sapped. Were the fans that way because the Cubs were, or the Cubs because the fans were? Was it because the Cubs had played all day games but one for the past three weeks? Was it just the heat? Or was it just the Pirates' pitching?

The game began with Barry Bonds hitting a home run to left field against Greg Maddux. Mike Dunne, one of the three players the Pirates obtained from St. Louis in the trade for Tony Pena, allowed a triple in the first to Martinez leading off; Martinez scored, but the Cubs were practically done for the day. "I thought yesterday's game was the dullest one I'd seen here in years, but this one isn't much better," said Steve Schanker, who worked nights at a Super America station and often went without sleeping when the Cubs were in town.

One of the blind guys said he smelled marijuana. Fans in right-center took turns squirting themselves with water from a spray bottle that a woman had brought. Maddux struggled to keep the Cubs in the game, and DiPino relieved him in the seventh with the score 4–1. "I hate DiPino," said a guy with a crewcut who was holding two beers. "I used to go drinking with Guy Hoffman and they sent Hoffman down when they traded for DiPino."

A little rain cooled off the ballpark later in the day, and the Pirates hit three home runs in the ninth against Ron Davis. A man standing under the shelter of the concession stand bellowed out, "Ron Davis, my hero!"

"What is this guy doing in the major leagues?" shouted another.

"Get him out of there!"

"No, let him finish. This is his last major-league performance."

"You call this a major-league performance?"

Durham homered in the ninth, but before that the Cubs had sent twenty-nine straight batters to the plate without one scoring. Friday, it had been thirty-five.

I stopped for dinner at the Monterey on Broadway, an earthy little kitchen-style restaurant where you could get soup, salad, bread, entree, vegetable, drink, and dessert for less than five dollars. The people who came in while I was there were two older men in worn-out clothes; a black woman with her young child; a softball player with a shaved head; a neatly casual man in his fifties; a kid who borrowed two bucks; and three young people outfitted in black, one of them a guy with very long black hair, a large earring, and a studded belt slung low. The restaurant had a big window on the neighborhood, and past it walked men and women of countless social types, among them slow-moving people wearing Chicago Cubs baseball caps.

It hadn't occurred to me, but Mary Ellen, a bleacher regular who was Steve Schanker's friend and had gone with him and others to the Cubs' playoff games in San Diego in 1984, pointed out on June twenty-first that the Cubs were actually as close to last place as they were to first. Veteran Cub fans keep an eye out for such things. Mary Ellen also said it was just a slump, no big deal. Of course, she was one to hold out hope to the end. Regarding San Diego, for instance, she said she was still waiting patiently for the San Andreas Fault to kick in.

It was Father's Day, and in the left-field bleachers a father was with his two daughters, about twelve and sixteen. College boys behind them flirted with the older daughter, and the father bought the boys beers. He was a family man letting his hair down in the bleachers, and he was enjoying every minute of it. The Pirates scored a run in the first against Trout, and the Cubs rallied against Doug Drabek in their half. Behind me, a guy and a girl were arguing. "What do you mean?" he said. "You called me a fucking idiot." She started to answer, but he cut her off. "Wait a minute. I gotta watch Dawson and Durham. They're my two favorites."

The Cubs scored three. Back on the rail behind the right-field bleachers, a guy named Vic punched holes in a wad of All-Star ballots. He had a short mustache and wore an old Cub jersey that didn't have a number on the back. "I'd be Banks or the guy who drove in all those runs," he said. The guy who drove in the runs was Hack Wilson, with one hundred ninety in 1930; we decided that Wilson wouldn't have had a number when he was with the Cubs. "Okay, then, that's whose number it is."

Vic must have had a hundred All-Star ballots there, and he was voting for Sandberg, Dawson and Jody Davis on every one. He also voted for Jack Clark, and a guy next to him said, "Do you think anybody in St. Louis is voting for Sandberg?" Vic said he had been in St. Louis, and they were. He had seen more people voting at Busch Stadium than he did at Wrigley Field, so Vic was sort of the self-appointed distributor for his section of the right-field bleachers. If somebody wanted a ballot, he said, "Here, take some of these—as long as you don't vote for Strawberry or anybody who plays in a dome." He thought teams in domes should have their own league.

Trout held the lead, but he was working slowly, getting behind the hitters. He walked the pitcher. A gray-haired regular bleacher fan next to me said softly, "Come on, Trout." I wondered how many times in his life the man had spoken of Steve Trout under his breath—how many times he had said, "Come on, Trout." And how many others had said the same thing, people whom Steve Trout would never meet? The impact that the left-handed pitcher and the gray-haired fan had on each other's lives represented a phenomenal disparity that was unlike the common one between a celebrity and a fan. Fans don't have stakes in the successes of rock and movie stars like they do baseball players. When Rambo takes on the bad guy, nobody says, "Come on, Stallone."

On this day, the sentiment of the gray-haired man regarding Trout was shared by many. Trout was working so slowly that it was difficult to maintain concentration on the game. Friday's game would take more than three and a half hours to complete, and it brought attention to a problem within the sport that was beginning to become significant. For numerous reasons—television commercials, speedy baserunners who attracted countless pickoff throws, fidgety batters, tentative pitchers, small strike zones—in fewer than ten years, the average length of games had gone from less than two hours and twenty-five minutes to more than two hours and forty-five minutes. It was to the point that even good fans were getting bored. Baseball has never appealed to people intent upon fast action in their spectator sports, but it seemed on the verge of losing some of those who had been willing to tolerate a reasonable lack of it.

Trout *was* pitching effectively, though. In the fifth, he came to bat with a 3–2 lead and a runner on base. On top of a house on Waveland Avenue, a sign went up: BUNT. He did. Martinez was the next batter, and a new sign went up: HIT US. Instead, he singled home a run. Earlier in the season, Martinez had repeatedly failed in important RBI situations, but he was beginning to do all the things that a good player does. Such was the accelerating popularity of the dark, handsome New Yorker, that a banner had unfurled in the bleachers a few days before: DAVE MARTINEZ—MARRY ME.

Jerry Pritikin spotted two fans in Pittsburgh caps. Also noting the Pittsburgh television cameras, he said, "If you two are here, why are they beaming the game back to Pittsburgh?"

In left field, a recent graduate of Indiana University leaned against the back fence and reflected on what it had been like when his school won the NCAA basketball championship a few months before. "That was so much fun," he said. "I felt like I was a part of all that. All those tickets I bought, all those games I went to over four years . . . I really felt like that was part of me out there. When it was over, I ran naked through a field by my dorm." He was a Cub fan, too, but they had never made him run naked through a field.

Lee Smith inherited a 6–3 lead in the ninth. With two outs and one man on, the crowd stood. "This is vintage Lee Smith," said Steve Schanker, who almost never sat down during a ballgame. "I guarantee that with everybody standing up, he'll let this guy get on." Sid Bream singled. As R. J. Reynolds came to the plate, another guy in the back of the bleachers yelled at Smith, "If you throw a slider, you son of a bitch, I'll kill you! Throw that damn fastball up and in!" Whatever it was he threw, Smith struck out Reynolds.

That night, my father, who had a satellite dish, called from Missouri and said that baseball games were taking so long he was losing interest in them.

Monday's was quicker, though, because Rick Reuschel pitched for Pittsburgh and Jamie Moyer didn't fool around, either. Martinez tripled in the third and scored on a single by Palmeiro, and that was the only run of the game for seven innings. Despite the absence of hitting, it was nonetheless an enjoyable afternoon; the efficient pitchers didn't permit it to drag.

I also found the company good. I sat in center field, and on my left was a high school guidance counselor named Ron who was in two baseball fantasy leagues and had traded for Moyer in one of them (Moyer and Oddibe McDowell for Rob Deer and Mike Flanagan). He was consequently encouraged by what he was seeing. Ron was a quiet fan, but when a Pittsburgh runner reached first against Moyer, he said, "Get two," knowing full well that the infielders couldn't hear him and were already aware of the double-play possibilities, anyway. It was just an urge. Being at ballgames has a way of making our urges audible; it's a communication intended not to impart advice, but to express a will that is presumably shared by others nearby. Of course, when Ron started coming to the bleachers, the players probably *could* pick up on what people said in the cheap seats. "I remember sitting in the left-field bleachers in '68 and hearing Durocher chew out Adolfo Phillips in the dugout for swinging at a bad pitch," he said.

Ron was encouraged not only by Moyer, but by the fact that the Cub farm system was finally starting to produce some legitimate major leaguers. Since the sixties group that included Williams, Santo, Hundley, Beckert, Kessinger, Brock, and Jenkins, the Cubs had received only paltry benefits from the players they raised themselves—particularly in their batting order. Some of the most accomplished ones, such as Joe Carter, Mike Krukow, and Willie Hernandez, prospered only after leaving Chicago. Ironically, the most productive men the organization had developed in the past two decades—Rick Reuschel, Bruce Sutter, and Lee Smith— were all pitchers. It seemed hard to believe, but when Dunston became the regular shortstop in 1986, he was the first product of the team's farm system to win a full-time place in the Cubs' lineup—the only one to come to the plate enough times to qualify for the batting title—since Kessinger in 1966. Now, though, Ron could see a future in young players such as Moyer and Maddux and Martinez and Palmeiro and some of the good kids still in the minors.

On my other side was a blonde bartender whose friends called her Dancing Annie and who had been a Cub fan as long as she had been a baseball fan, which was since 1969. She was eleven then. "I played on a softball team with my next-door neighbor," she said. "Her mother was the coach, and to get us to really play hard, she convinced everybody on the team that we were the '69 Cubs, position by position. Can you imagine getting nine-to-twelve-year-old girls interested in softball? But I mean, this woman had us believing we were the '69 Cubs. Bridgette, my neighbor, played third base and she was Santo. I was Hundley, and man, I blocked that plate so nobody could get in there against me."

Noticing that she was keeping score, I asked Dancing Annie if her dad had taught her. "He doesn't know how to keep score," she said. "He's a White Sox fan. I learned from an old guy I used to sit next to in the bleachers." As sort of a family rite, and despite their conflicting loyalties, she had filled out her All-Star ballot at her father's house on Father's Day. She voted for Dawson, Sandberg, and Moreland. "Of course, I question Moreland," she said as she put down her beer to mark Noce's single in the fourth. "But I love the way he always puts his shoulder into it whenever there's a fight."

Martinez saved two runs with a running catch against the fence in the fifth, and in the seventh Dancing Annie went to the ticket office outside the park to stock up for the next homestand. While she was gone, Durham hit a huge drive onto Sheffield Avenue, which excited the crowd until it passed on the wrong side of the foul pole. Minutes later, Annie's boyfriend and I saw her down on Sheffield, talking to a man on a motorcycle. Somehow she was readmitted to the ballpark and returned to her seat in the proud possession of a scuffed National League baseball. I had been keeping up her scorecard while she was gone, and when she took it back she looked and said, "Where's the home run?" We told her it was a foul ball. She couldn't believe it; she had heard the crowd roar. "Do you mean to tell me I paid five bucks for a foul ball?" We looked outside; the man on the motorcycle was gone.

Moyer had been pitching out of trouble all day, as was his wont, but in the eighth he walked Mike Diaz, and then Andy Van Slyke—another acquired from the Cardinals in the Pena deal—hit a two-run homer to put the Pirates ahead. The skillful Reuschel took his 2–1 lead into the bottom of the ninth, which Durham began with a single. Moreland was next, and Ron and I discussed whether he should bunt. He squared around to do so on the first pitch, but took it for a ball. Then he homered into the left-field bleachers to win the game. Dancing Annie stood up and screamed, "My hero!" I felt beer on my back and saw a cup flying toward the field. Then I saw beer raining all over the bleachers, and cups all over the field.

The Cubs left for New York, and for the first time all year, they left with a winning record at Wrigley Field.

Moreland said later he had missed the bunt sign.

July

IT WAS HOT and crowded on Friday, July 3. At the bleacher gate, the guards confiscated plastic spray bottles that people had intended to fill with water so they could cool off in the searing sun; the guards said that drunks started fights with spray bottles. On Sheffield and Waveland, the rooftops were teeming with holiday-weekend parties. The bleachers were so full that people had to hold their beers over their heads to walk through the back aisle. Clusters of shirtless men formed around the vendors.

The Cubs had lost five in a row in New York and Pittsburgh .before they won two out of three in Montreal. Now they had ten games at home, starting with the Giants, and Wrigley Field was within five hundred people of its capacity of 38,143. People had either bought their tickets ahead of time or felt the way Steve Schanker did. "I was just about to give up on them," said Steve, standing in front of the center-field steps with his shirt stuffed into the back pocket of his cutoffs. "Then they won a couple of games and sucked me in again."

To the right of the right-field bleachers, in a private section of eight-dollar seats reserved for large groups, were nearly a hundred happy men in their thirties, forties, and fifties, some with their wives, some without, some of them familiar faces over the last few years, some of them not. Steve watched them for a minute, smiled, and said, "Those are the guys I looked up to when I was a kid."

It had been more than fifteen years since some of the men over there had seen each other. A lot of them had taken professional jobs in other cities. Others still came to Wrigley Field and sat with their families in the grandstand. But in the summer of 1969, they had all sat shoulder-to-shoulder, back-to-knee, and beer-to-beer, if they were old enough, in the fraternal federation of the left-field bleachers—young, rowdy, and famous beyond all intention.

Mike Murphy, who had been one of the youngest of them back then and blew the bugle when they needed a musical charge, had decided during the winter to try to get the old Bleacher Bums together over the Fourth of July weekend, and bought out the 107 seats in the private section. He bought the tickets first and then spread the word, because the Bums prided themselves on being spontaneous. They had never planned any of it—the yellow helmets, the songs, the beer baths, the media. In fact, when celebrity status arrived and the left-field bleachers filled up with people wearing yellow helmets, the original Bums were the first to evacuate.

Like the other authentic Bums, Murphy was a bleachers guy back when they were just for baseball fans. He found the bleachers, really, by accident. "I remember the first game I ever went to," he said. "It was 1958, and I was seven years old. I kept badgering my parents to take me to a game, and finally they said okay. They weren't big fans, and they didn't realize that the game we picked was like the biggest draw in years. The Cubs were playing the Milwaukee Braves, and they were both up there around first place. We got here and it was standing room only. But then they announce, almost like an addendum, that there are also seats available in the bleachers. People are standing in the ramps in the grandstand and shunning the bleachers. That's when the bleachers was a sixty-cent ticket, and it was like the dregs. I remember we sat way up under the scoreboard and the Cubs won 5–4. There were four home runs—Ernie Banks, Hank Aaron, Joe Adcock, and then my favorite Cub, Moose Moryn, won it with a two-run homer."

When he was old enough, Murphy's mother would drop him off at the park or he would take the el there. They said that Wrigley Field was the world's biggest daycare center. Kids who couldn't afford a ticket would get into the ballpark by sliding down the beer chute or falling in step with one of the church groups. The ones who could afford it afforded the bleachers. The bleachers were for gamblers, old men, and kids. It was intimate. They would make fun of Warren Spahn's nose and the mink-lined shoes of Willie Mays's wife. The players got to know their faces and voices.

One of the kids, Steve Friedman, took special pride in making life miserable for a mediocre Cub outfielder named Don Landrum. "He was an especial bum," said Friedman, "because he was a bum who came from somewhere else. It's one thing to grow our own bums, but we didn't need to bring them in from other teams." One day, Landrum confronted Friedman and asked why he hated him so much. They talked. Landrum began giving Friedman gifts. Friedman became Landrum's biggest fan, if not his only one.

As the Cubs got better in the late sixties, the Bleacher Bums became more audible, visible, and outlandish. They threw frogs at Cleon Jones, white mice at Lou Brock, hot dog buns at Willie Stargell. They called Pete Rose a fairy. They tossed a softball around, and they threw their beers up in the air when the Cubs hit a home run. All of it was natural to them because they had grown up together laughing and cursing in the bleachers. They had grown up together as kids who cared about something, and not because it was on TV; as an open frontier back then, the cheap seats were not as photogenic as they would later become. The bleacher boys cared about baseball for one reason only: because they did. They were kids with passion, independence, and wherewithal— heady kids on their way to being actors, authors, producers,

mailmen, businessmen. One or two became scalpers. Friedman became the producer of NBC's "Today" show. They
were cross-culture kids with little in common, really, except
an ardor for baseball that gave rise to the lively, indigenous
consciousness of the seats beyond Wrigley Field's ivy walls.

The Bums made it a point not to tell the press about their
reunion. They wanted July third to be like 1969 again. When
Paul Noce hit a home run, they threw their beers in the air
and let them fall on their balding heads and sagging bare
chests, just like they did eighteen years before, when their hair
was thicker, their bodies thinner, and Noce was nine. At one
point, they broke into their old song, "You Better Stop Kicking My Dog Around," except Dick Selma wasn't there with
his towel to lead the chorus from the bullpen. The unofficial
leader of the Bums, Ron Grousl, wasn't there, either, because
none of the Bums knew his whereabouts. They couldn't dance
on the top of the wall anymore. The players didn't talk to
them. Things had changed a lot.

From their private place next to the bleachers, the Bums
could look over and see what they had indirectly and uninten-
tionally wrought. 'Eighty-four had a lot to do with it, too, but
bleacher culture had been dilating since '69. Groups came in
BMWs from downtown offices and in buses from out of
town. People stood with beers in their hands, backs to the
ball field, and chatted with those behind them as batters dug
for third. Guys got girls' phone numbers. Just down the aisle
from the Bums' reunion on July third, a television crew inter-
viewed a fan wearing a blue wig. It was ironic—a hundred
originals from 1969 were a few feet away, and the camera
crew was interviewing a guy in a blue wig.

In the Bums' old haunt, left field, a new group of regulars
held forth. They saved seats for each other and scrambled
after home runs and yelled at the other team's leftfielder. The
best at yelling at the leftfielder was Steve Herzberg, the curly-
haired fellow who wore tie-dyed shirts and blew bubbles and
worked in the freezer of a meat warehouse and came to the
ballpark every home weekend with his wife. Herzberg frequently brought *The Sporting News* to the game, because, as

he said, "information is ammo." In the most recent edition, there had been an item about the Giants' leftfielder, Jeffrey Leonard, and his unfortunate financial dealings. "Hey, Leonard!" Steve shouted. "Way to blow that four hundred fifty thousand, buddy!"

Leonard had stolen home in the first inning Friday when Jamie Moyer tried to pick another runner off first base. After that, Moyer struck out seven straight San Francisco batters—a team record—and a guy in the right-field bleachers was worried about his two hundred dollar bet on the Giants. But their parimutuel pitcher, Kelly Downs, gave nothing more than Noce's homer in the seventh, and the Giants won the game 3–1.

It was at this point eighteen years before that the Bleacher Bums would have made the rounds of the bars. They called it a grand slam if somebody got around to the watering holes on each of the four corners encompassing the ballpark. Their favorite place, though, was Ray's Bleachers. It was owned by Ray Meyer, who was not the DePaul basketball coach, but was the father of one of the Bleacher Bums who also had the same name. When Meyer ran it, the bar was less popular but more provincially piquant than it became after he sold to Jim Murphy, who effectively gentrified the place, capitalizing on the upscale trend of both the neighborhood and the bleachers. Ray had a pool table in the middle of the floor, and before a ballgame he would put a big piece of plywood over the pool table and stack it with relish and peppers and onions. The bars and little restaurants around Wrigley Field became known for their dress-your-own hot dogs, but the concept came from Ray's. After the games, Ray would clear the peppers and people would dance on the pool table. Once, after the Cubs lost, a relief pitcher named Roberto Rodriguez danced on the pool table, and the next day there was a picture of it in the *Tribune*. Rodriguez was speedily released.

A lot of the ballplayers drank with the fans at Ray's back then—Santo, Beckert, Selma, Pepitone, Jenkins. They didn't do that in 1987, of course. Nothing was the same. With Ray's gone, most of the Bums preferred to take their postgame refreshment at Bernie's on the corner of Clark and Waveland. "It's still the old-fashioned place, grease on the walls," said Mike Murphy. "That's where the real Cub fans go."

The Bums went over to Bernie's after Friday's game, and a crowd gathered around Murphy's, as usual.

The Cubs were in a slump, and in keeping with the holiday spirit, Dallas Green tried to light some Roman candles in the players' pants. He said that some of the guys in the middle of the lineup—Jody Davis, in particular—were trying to hit home runs all the time, which is the way big, slow guys have traditionally tried to hit. He said that Scott Sanderson was being sent to the bullpen so he wouldn't mess up the pitching staff so much if he got hurt again. And he had more sorry words for the Sarge. "I just can't cut a deal," Green told the *Tribune.* "We've done all we can for him. He certainly knows where he is on this team. Gene Michael is not going to play him."

And then, on the Fourth of July, Michael put Matthews batting fourth in the Cubs' lineup, with Durham, Davis, and Dayett (hitting .329) on the bench. Seeing Matthews in his old place, Jerry Pritikin went straight to left field and yelled, "Who's in charge?" The fans were supposed to answer back, "Sarge!"—but nobody did. Pritikin couldn't believe how much the bleachers had changed in just three years. It was disillusioning to the Bleacher Preacher that the magic of '84 had disappeared so abruptly, as if under a magician's handkerchief.

In other ways, though, the Cub spectacle ripped right along. To tourists, Wrigley Field was like a natural wonder; sometimes there would be as many as a hundred buses lined up along the sidewalks and crowded streets. More people watched the Cubs on television than any other team; their market share was several times that of some. There were more than ninety thousand members in the Die-Hard Cub Fan Club. Cub merchandise sold as well as any in the major leagues.

And there was certainly no evidence of beer sales flagging.

Many of the vendors were putting themselves through school, and if there were many more days like those of the Fourth of July weekend, they would have money left over for pizza, clothes, and a new wing on the Arts and Sciences Building. Friday, a few of the hustlingest beer-carriers in the bleachers had made two hundred dollars.

To sell as much as they could and reduce their down time, most of the vendors carried two cases of twenty-four tall cans, the total weighing about fifty pounds. They started selling an hour or more before the game but had to quit after the eighth inning; on a normal day, they sold beer for about four hours. A beer cost $2.50, and their 16.5 percent commission gave them just more than forty-one cents a beer. It came to $9.90 a case for the vendors—plus a little bit in tips, minus the cost of beers that were spilled before they reached the customer. A two hundred dollar day meant that they had to sell more than twenty cases of beer, which meant ten trips trips down to the commissary for restocking. To do it in four hours meant that they had to sell five cases an hour, a case every twelve minutes, a beer every half minute—and that was counting the time it took to restock. What it meant was that in the first days of July, individual vendors in the bleachers were selling a beer about every twenty-five seconds.

The bunting was out for the Fourth of July. Bill Veeck was the great practitioner of American ingenuity as pertained to baseball, and I honored America by sitting where he used to sit. So did a fellow from Minneapolis named Mike Flaherty, who worked in a paper mill and was visiting Wrigley Field for the first time. "Oh, it's more beautiful than I thought it would be," said Mike. "I can't believe that grass. They must have a great hybrid."

Mike was with his wife and a friend from Chicago named Mary O'Grady, a director of nursing who maintained one of the best scorecards I'd seen all season. It was neat, concise, informative, lacking only one thing that it would have needed to compete for Scorecard of the Year: margin notes. For example, I went with my friend Peter to a game in Milwaukee, and as the vendor came around selling, of all the darn things, wine coolers, Peter dutifully marked down "wine coolers" in the margin of his scorecard. The best scorecards are the ones that, years later, allow a person to best remember the occasion. But Mary O'Grady's was awfully good. She said her mother taught her. She and her mother were Cub fans; her father and her brother, White Sox fans. Aye, the fightin' O'Gradys.

On my other side was a group of sorority girls, some of them graduated. Wendy Florio was wearing her Kansas Jayhawk wristwatch. Although she had been raised in the North suburbs, her family was devoted to the White Sox. Wendy had taken a job in advertising at a radio station, however, and in her line of work, the White Sox wouldn't do. "I feel like I've got to learn about the Cubs to be able to bring clients out here," she said. "I've also got to learn how to play golf." The Cubs were golf; the White Sox were bowling.

Mike Flaherty of Minneapolis stood to sing happily during the seventh-inning stretch, by which time all the scoring had been completed at 5–3, Cubs. Michael's experimental lineup produced three runs in the first three innings against Atlee Hammaker, and Sutcliffe pitched well with the lead. Matthews didn't get a hit, but Manny Trillo, playing first base instead of Durham against the left-hander, drove in two runs, suggesting that the move would be worth making again.

In the eighth, a fraternity guy who was one of Wendy's friends had to lock his arms around a drunk who was trying in vain to punch him. They tumbled down a few rows of bleachers. "God, we've got to leave," Wendy said. Uncharacteristically, the crowd in general was leaving early—holiday barbecues, perhaps. Mike and his group stayed to the end, though. He watched Smith get the last three outs in the shadows, gazed winsomely at the playing field, and said, "This game will never die. This game will never die.

"At least not in my lifetime, and that's all I care about."

The next day, the last of the Giants series, Steve Herzberg took his position in the aisle behind the seats in left field and apologized to Jeffrey Leonard for all the mean things he had said the previous two days. Nearby, a comptroller named Ken from Santa Cruz wore a Giants hat and a T-shirt with the words THERE'S NO PLACE LIKE WRIGLEY FIELD. I thought the combination begged for an explanation, and he said, "It means I'm a baseball fan." He proved this when he looked over across the field, noticed number 35 for San Francisco leaning against a fence, and, realizing that 35 had been the number of Chris Brown, who had been traded the night before in a big deal with the Padres, deduced that the guys from San Diego must have already arrived. He was right. Kevin Mitchell hit two home runs in his first game as a Giant.

Dawson also hit his first homer in four weeks, and after three innings, the Cubs led 5–2, generally pounding baseballs that Gene Michael claimed had been scuffed by the Giants' Mike Krukow. Despite his team's success against San Francisco's pitcher, in the third inning Michael approached home plate umpire Terry Tata with half a dozen baseballs in his hands, all of which, he said, had been noticeably scuffed by Krukow. When Tata was unsympathetic and ejected Michael from the game, Stick fired the six balls to the ground in an impressively angry visual display that was practically volcanic for the mild manager. From the time Green had publicly criticized the players, though, Michael had been performing his duties with a little extra flare in the nostrils. Unfortunately, this had no apparent influence upon the bleacher people, few of whom were eager to see Stick stick. After he had repaired to the clubhouse Sunday, a firecracker went off. "Hey," said a fan in left field, "maybe Michael shot himself."

The Cubs never scored again after Krukow left in the third, and the Giants won 7–5, rallying against Cubs rookie Lester Lancaster. It wasn't a very good day for anybody on Chicago's side. One bleacher fan in right field was suddenly startled out of his seat, and when his friends asked what was wrong, he said, "A bird shit on my head."

Dawson's second home run against the Padres Monday bounced on the street and landed in the second-floor porch of the house at 1038 Waveland. A twelve-year-old boy caught it, then gave the ball to his sister for a minute as he went inside to watch the replay. As he looked at the television, he saw his sister jumping up and down with the baseball in her hand.

When Dawson returned to his position in right, the fans took up a new chant: "Raise his pay! Raise his pay!" For the first time all year, Dawson turned and smiled.

He drove in four of the Cubs' seven runs, and San Diego didn't get any against Trout. Trout had been pitching well, and on July sixth, while shutting out San Diego 7–0, he also pitched quickly. It was wonderful; the game was over in two hours and eleven minutes—about half an hour quicker than the normal game. That meant that the twenty thousand people at Wrigley Field had an extra half-hour each on their hands—a total man-hour windfall of ten thousand. On the other hand, think of all the games that go half an hour longer than they should or really have to. For every half hour lost to a crowd of twenty thousand, the loss of man-hours is equivalent to two hundred fifty work weeks—five years on the job. Imagine it: if pitchers were made to work more quickly, and batters didn't groom after every pitch, and umpires moved the game along, and if somehow major-league baseball cut ten minutes off every one of its regular-season games, the savings in time for the more than forty-six million fans over the course of a season would be the equivalent of a full calendar year for nearly nine hundred people. That takes no account for those watching or listening to the games at home.

Then again, is there anything that nine hundred baseball fans would prefer to do with an extra year?

The Dawson phenomenon being at a peak, I started Tuesday in the first row of the right-field bleachers, which put me next to Marv Rich, a tan man with short gray hair who had been sitting there since 1943. "The bleachers are the same as always," he said, "except on weekends, when all the yuppies come and drink beer and talk about their jobs and don't pay attention to what's going on." Marv usually didn't make it to weekday games because he worked in the warehouse of a furniture store, but he had taken a week of vacation while the

Cubs were in town. The rest of his vacation he had reserved for October, as usual, in the event that the Cubs were in the World Series. He had gotten to know October in Bermuda.

Eric Show was pitching for San Diego, and Dawson hit his twenty-fourth home run in the first inning, giving him four homers and nine RBIs in his last ten times at bat. With that, the Bleacher Preacher had a chance to display his newest sign. It was in the shape of a check, written out to ANDRE DAW-$00000N.

Noce hit a home run leading off the third, and the Cubs were ahead 4–2 when Dawson came up again. Given the way he had been battering San Diego pitchers, most of the people in the ballpark expected some sort of a brushback pitch from Show, a standard sort of reminder that the pitcher was not going to passively accept the batter's blatant disrespect. The first two pitches were a ball and a strike, and then, with Dawson leaning over the plate in his customary manner, Show's fastball came directly at his exposed left shoulder. With frightful suddenness, Dawson was flat on the dirt. He had turned his shoulder to get it out of the way, and the pitch caught him flush in the face. It was a chilling sight as he lay perfectly still, face down, blood on the ground. The Cubs' trainer, John Fierro, bolted out to attend to the great star, but for several moments he was the only one in the ballpark who moved.

Then, from the Cubs' dugout, Rick Sutcliffe dashed across the frozen frame, headed directly for Show. John Kruk, San Diego's first baseman, intercepted Chicago's pitching ace, but the mesmerism had been broken and the infield became a frenzy of ineffective fighting. That quickly ceased, as if both sides suddenly realized that there was a man lying motionless at home plate. Then the Cubs began slowly advancing on the Padres, moving inexorably as a front, the Padres retreating at the same pace. Finally, after three minutes on the ground, Dawson sat up, and then, reflexively and to startling effect, sprinted to the mound in pursuit of Show. Teammates interceded and led their pitcher hastily through a storm of ice cubes to the dugout. Dawson, meanwhile, momentarily broke free of the hands that held him and made several purposeful strides toward the exiting pitcher. He was then taken to the hospital, where he received twenty-four stitches in his left cheek.

Dawson's fortune was that the beanball had not struck him in the eye or broken any bones in his face. He would be back playing in a few days—actually, sooner than Show, who didn't return to the game. The Padres said he had hurt his foot in the fight, but Show had decided to leave the ballpark for his own safety. He was escorted by security guards. Later, he issued an apology in which he stated that he had not intentionally thrown at Dawson and would regret the incident the rest of his life. The apology was accepted neither by Dawson nor Chicago.

When the game resumed, Dawson and Sutcliffe had been ejected for fighting. The Cubs' pitcher, Greg Maddux, was ejected in the next inning, when he hit Benito Santiago in the back. Michael and Trillo were booted at the same time— Michael automatically, since both teams had been warned about beanballs, and Trillo for tossing sunglasses onto the field. In the fifth, Scott Sanderson threw three straight pitches ridiculously inside to the Padres' star hitter, Tony Gwynn. "Today was the first time in my life that I've been scared to go to the plate," Gwynn said. In the eighth, Sanderson and coach Johnny Oates—the acting manager—were ejected when Sanderson threw behind Chris Brown, who was just back from a month on the disabled list after having his jaw broken by a pitch. The total of ejected Cubs was seven, one of whom would spend the next several days holding an ice pack to his face. They won anyway, 7–5, and Dawson had the game-winning RBI.

There were death threats reported the next morning at the Padres' hotel. At Wrigley Field, Jerry Pritikin dressed up his voodoo doll like Eric Show, a fan wore one of the PUCK FADRES T-shirts left over from the '84 playoffs, and the Cubs got their pound of flesh, although not before San Diego had established a 7–0 lead against Jamie Moyer.

It was 8–4 when Mark Wilmot decided to go home at the end of the seventh. The question of whether to leave in lop-sided games is always a difficult one at Wrigley Field. Mark had seen plenty of comebacks in the little ballpark, but this one had been 7–0 at one point. He collected second and third opinions on the likelihood of the Cubs at least tying the score, and finally decided, nah, the odds were prohibitive. They scored eight in the eighth.

The first four, which tied the game, came on an unlikely grand slam by Jim Sundberg, the former American Leaguer who had followed the Cubs while growing up in Galesburg, Illinois, and was eating sunflower seeds in the dugout when Michael told him to pinch hit. Then Bob Dernier batted with two on and one out. The fellow next to me, a junior high school teacher from Elgin, Illinois, said that numerous girls in his school were infatuated with the Cubs at large and par-ticularly taken with the curly-haired centerfielder. "When the Cubs are on the West Coast," he said, "they'll go to bed for a couple of hours after dinner so they can stay up and watch the ballgame. They love Dernier. One time I told a girl that the Cubs had traded Dernier, and she broke down crying." Dern-ier singled and the Cubs led. Then Moreland doubled and Davis tripled—a stunning accomplishment for a man of his speed—and Chicago had hit for the cycle in the eighth. The final was 12–8. It was the Cubs' biggest comeback since 1982.

Dawson had an appointment scheduled later that day at a souvenir shop on Michigan Avenue. He kept it.

On July ninth, the Wrigley Field bleachers turned fifty years old. The park itself was seventy-three, having been built in 1914 by Lucky Charlie Weeghman, who owned fifteen din-ers and the Chicago franchise of the Federal League. Needing a place for his team to play, Weeghman leased vacant land in a busy residential district at Clark and Addison streets and hired an architect named Zachary Taylor Davis to build a baseball facility that would cost about a quarter of a million dollars and be an "edifice of beauty," as Lucky Charlie called it. He picked the right man for the job. Four years before,

Davis had built Comiskey Park on the South Side of town. If there were a wing at the Hall of Fame for designers of stadiums, Davis would be prominent within, for, three-quarters of a century later, the ballparks that he built in Chicago remained, along with Fenway Park in Boston, as the oldest in America and still among the best in many important respects that elude the imaginations of contemporary designers.

Weeghman Park accommodated twenty thousand customers when it was built, two thousand of whom could sit for ten cents in the bleachers erected in right field. Even more economical were the relatively unobstructed views from the windows and rooftops of the apartment buildings on Waveland, and from the platform of the el station a half-block behind center field. There were no bleachers in left, but on a particularly crowded day, fans could perch on top of the fence out there. There wasn't room for left-field bleachers when the park was built. The fence was only 310 feet from home plate, and it stood only a few feet away from the porch of a house on Waveland. When there became some question over the manliness required of a batter to clear the close wall, Weeghman had the porch removed and relocated the fence back against the house. Before the next season, he razed the house and also another, took out the right-field bleachers, and moved them to left.

The Federal League collapsed after the 1915 season, and Weeghman Park might have taken the same route if Lucky Charlie had not bought the Cubs from Charles Taft and Charles Murphy. Instead, Weeghman moved the National Leaguers over from the West Side Grounds in 1916, despite warnings that the Cubs would never make it on the North Side, and they were playing at Clark and Addison when William Wrigley took ownership three years later. Wrigley and his son Phillip tinkered with the outfield seats throughout the twenties and thirties, and, finally, in 1937, P.K. decided to elevate the bleachers and renovate them entirely. His notion was to make them summery, but in those days—before air-conditioning, tank tops, and double-digit sun protection factors—people preferred generally to stay out of sweaty weather. For the greater part of their first half-century, the bleachers were just benches without backs, hard wooden accommodations for the lonely lovers of baseball and the occasional crowd that overflowed the grandstand. They were private vantage points from over the shoulders of Augie Galan and Andy Pafko and Hank Sauer and George Altman and Billy Williams, and also Stan Musial and Willie Mays and Hank Aaron and Gino Cimoli. They were for guys with nicknames, and guys with time. Once, the authorities were tipped off that John Dillinger was out there. The bleachers, like a fishing hole, were where a guy could get away. They were cheap seats in the sun.

Then the cameras came out, followed by the people. Selma waved his towel, Santo clicked his heels, Jay Johnstone went up and sold stuff. When the Cubs won the division in '84, Jim Frey, the manager, walked his players around the field so they could tip their caps to the fans in the bleachers. As the 1987 season began, *Esquire* wrote, "Where is the best seat in the best bleachers in the best ball park of them all?" Like "Jeopardy," the answer preceded the question. It was: "Aisle 152, Row 4, Seat 101, when the wind is blowing out." It didn't say Wrigley Field. It didn't have to. Aisle 152 was just behind Jerry Mumphrey.

There was no particular observation of the bleachers' fiftieth birthday. People wondered why the scoreboard hadn't been painted, and also why the Cardinals kept winning. Even while sweeping the Padres, the Cubs had fallen farther behind St. Louis, which won consecutive doubleheaders from the Dodgers and hadn't lost in a week. The season was halfway over, and the Cubs were nine games behind, tied with Montreal and half a game ahead of the Mets.

For their own part, though, the Cubs seemed to have recovered from the bad stretch in June when they won only seven of their last twenty games, and had generally satisfied their kind constituency in the semiseason. Both Chicago newspapers wrote favorably of the job Michael had done, the *Sun-Times* reporting that sixty percent of fans polled believed there should be no managerial change; the bleacher fans, obviously, were more disposed to be critical than the rest. According to the poll, however, fans wished to see Dayett get an opportunity at third base and Palmeiro at first. Nearly half of them wanted Durham, Moreland, Dernier, and Lee Smith to be traded, and the vast majority preferred that the Cubs dispose of Sanderson, Ron Davis, and Matthews. "Love him," wrote one fan regarding Sarge, "but he has to go. No wheels." Another expressed the same coldly sympathetic sentiment: "Thanks for half a pennant, but it's over now."

The Dodgers were in town, and to help celebrate the bleacher anniversary, Mike Marshall was back in right field. He and teammate Pedro Guerrero had engaged in a lively difference of opinion concerning Marshall's frequent injuries, and some of the bleacher fans were clearly aware of this. "Hey, Marshall!" one guy yelled. "Pedro hates you!" It became a chorus.

In defense of the Dodgers—who at times seemed incapable of it themselves—they were undoubtedly exhausted after their ordeal with the rain in St. Louis. Thursday's game with the Cubs was their fifth in less than forty-eight hours, and it showed grossly. Behind Sutcliffe, the Cubs led 9–1 after four innings. When the fifth began, the skies were dark and it appeared that Chicago might only need three more outs to secure the victory. Conspiring with the clouds, Steve Sax and Tom Lasorda, the round manager, wasted some time arguing the call on Sax's strikeout leading off the inning. With two outs, Moreland erred on a grounder by Jeff Hamilton. Sparrows flitted nervously around the right-field fence, and thunder bellowed in the northwest. John Shelby homered, and two extra balls were returned with it to the playing field, delaying the game even longer. Guerrero hit one onto Waveland, and moments later the ball came back over the outside fence. By that time, though, the Dodger slugger was only at about second base; he had remained at home plate admiring the long home run before making his tour, and Sutcliffe let him know he didn't like it. "Run the bases!" he yelled. He and Guerrero had been friends when both were in the Dodger minor-league system; Sutcliffe said he used to let Guerrero borrow his car in Albuquerque, and that was how Guerrero met his wife.

The rain held off one more inning, time enough for three more homers—Franklin Stubbs of the Dodgers, Trillo, and Moreland. Then it came in sheets so thick that the playing field couldn't be seen from the bleachers. When it stopped, the umpires decided it was too dark to continue with the game. Had the field been unplayable, the game would have been over; but because the reason for quitting was darkness, it would be resumed the next day with the Cubs leading 12–5.

The storm hadn't lasted long, but it had been nasty, and there was only one survivor among the National League flags on top of the scoreboard. "It's a bad sign," said Steve Schanker. "All the flags came down except the American flag and the Cardinals'."

Around the time of the fiftieth anniversary of the bleachers, there was a letter in the *Sun-Times* from a longtime Cub fan named Richard Vachula, a public relations man from the Chicago suburb of River Grove.

"In my thirty years of following baseball," he wrote, "the biggest change has been the fans. I remember twenty-five years or even ten years ago, the people who attended games were true baseball fans. They really knew the game. They kept meticulous score of each game and sometimes knew as much about the players as the manager. . . . Many were senior citizens who grew up during the grass roots of baseball. . . . They learned to appreciate watching baseball long before TV made baseball easy to observe.

"Sadly, there are fewer real fans or connoisseurs of baseball now. They have been replaced by loud, obnoxious fans who know nothing about the game and whose main purpose at the game is to drink beer. . . . Anyone who comes to a baseball game to get drunk is no fan of baseball. Have you ever tried to discuss the split-fingered fastball with a fan who has consumed ten beers? Have you ever known a drunken baseball fan to know the correct score of a game?"

I had just started to get accustomed to the drunkenness around me in the bleachers, but it hadn't been easy. Drunks tended to dominate the activity in their immediate vicinity, and it was unnatural for a sober person to catch the same spirit of heedless conviviality. The outfielder would be playing the ball off the wall and the batter rounding second, and the drunk in front would be trying to drink out of two cups at once. People who didn't drink could feel uncomfortable in the bleachers, even resentful, but gradually I'd come to realize that, for many of the harder-working drinkers anyway, their day in the bleachers was important. Vachula was right: the baseball experience wasn't the same as it used to be; it wasn't pure anymore. But, if nothing else, more people were partaking of it.

On Friday, July 10, a young Budweiser vendor named Mark sold twenty-one cases without leaving aisle one hundred fifty in left field. A sizable number of the beers were sold to a group of ten young women who were playing some sort of money game in which dollar bills were passed down the row with each batter, the person holding the pile adding a dollar to it if a Dodger got a hit and pocketing the whole thing if a Cub got a hit. Nobody seemed to understand how it worked except for the woman who was running the thing and seemed to spend most of the day standing up and trying to explain it; naturally, she was accused of cheating by those who didn't win.

It was a long afternoon, starting with the completion of the suspended game from the day before. When Steve Schanker arrived, he pointed up to the flags on the scoreboard and said, "Did you see what the Cardinals did last night?" After the St. Louis flag weathered Thursday's storm, the Cardinals had scored four runs in the bottom of the tenth to beat the Giants. "When I heard how they won, that was the first thing I thought about." Steve worked the night shift, and he hadn't slept since he woke up in the Cubs' eight-run eighth inning two days before.

The suspended game started in the seventh inning, in the middle of which Harry Caray suddenly said, "Hey, we for-

got!" It was the season's weakest rendering of "Take Me Out
to the Ballgame." Although the bleachers were full, the
grandstand was empty for the suspended game. There was no
more scoring.

In left-center field, I sat in front of a retired printer for the
Wall Street Journal named Al Levin, who wore a wide straw
hat and a plaid shirt and said, "I've been coming here through
good and bad." I asked him if he ever got fed up with the
Cubs and their aversion to winning. "Why should I get excited about these guys?" he said. "With the tax breaks these
bastards get?" He was indignant over the fact that owners
were able to depreciate the salaries of their players.

The fellow in front of me had a battery-pack television; the
day before, the game had gone on so long that he missed
Vanna White on "Wheel of Fortune." The guy said he
brought his kid to the game once. After the game he asked the
kid what he learned, and the kid said, "Right field sucks."

The Dodgers held a 3–1 lead after seven innings of the
regularly scheduled game, the Cubs repeatedly being turned
back when centerfielder John Shelby caught long fly balls. A
drunk behind the bleachers in left yelled, "Fuck you, 31,"
suggesting that perhaps there should be a ballpark ordinance
prohibiting fans from cursing players whose names they don't
know. He was an example of a guy who came to the park for
the beer, not the baseball, and it was offensive. When Shelby
tracked down a drive by Dawson in the sixth, he screamed,
"Fuck you, 31, you black beanpole!"

In the eighth, Guerrero homered against Greg Maddux,
this time taking a few steps before watching the ball soar into
the seats, and the Cubs scored twice in the bottom of the
inning against Orel Hershiser. His reliever, Ken Howell, took
a 4–3 lead into the bottom of the ninth, as dark clouds raced
along the first-base line toward Lake Michigan. Sundberg
singled, Trillo walked, and with the winning run on base,
Matthews struck out pinch hitting. Rain began to fall, at
which point Martinez delivered his biggest hit of the year, an
opposite-field fly ball that cleared Tito Landrum's head in
left field and bounced to the wall. Sundberg scored, and Trillo

was circling third on the wet basepath as Landrum picked up the ball and threw it to shortstop Mariano Duncan. Duncan's relay to Mike Scioscia was perfect, it and Trillo arriving at virtually the same time and place, and umpire Bob Engel thumbed the runner out. The instant he did, the clouds released waves of rain upon the ballpark. It was a masterpiece of dramatic timing—the runner, the ball, the rain, and the score all converging at the same heightened moment. Nature had held off until the game was tied and the Cubs took one last slide at the plate.

During the delay, bleacher fans watched replays of the call on which the game had stopped—roaring in outrage as one angle showed that Trillo had beaten the throw, then mumbling quietly as another revealed that he may not have reached the plate—and tried to figure out what would happen if the game were called because of rain. But it wouldn't be. Tied games at Wrigley Field were never called on account of rain when they could be called on account of darkness, which allowed them to be resumed instead of started over. And so, after ninety minutes, the umpires declared that the light was insufficient to continue playing or waiting, and suspended the game until the next day once again. Thirty-six thousand people had seen portions of two games and all of none.

That evening, the Cubs traded Gary Matthews to Seattle for a minor leaguer to be named later.

The people in the bleachers Saturday were happy for Sarge, satisfied that the trade was to his advantage. They weren't so pleased on behalf of Lee Smith, however. Smith had been named to the National League All-Star team, and to his detractors it only underscored the basic problem they had with the big reliever. It wasn't so much that Smith was a *bad* pitcher, but that the Cubs and the rest of baseball seemed to think he was so *good*. It wouldn't have bothered the fans so much when Smith blew leads if the Cubs hadn't myopically entrusted them to him over and over, as if he were the savior of saves and second coming of Bruce Sutter. It seemed that when the fans booed Lee Smith, they were not booing the man on the mound so much as they were venting their frustration with the Cubs' timid unwillingness to do something different. For the manager, though, Smith was the safe move. When the ace of the bullpen blows a lead, the manager can always say, "Hey, I went with my best."

Matt Young, the Dodger pitcher whom a bleacher bum referred to as Egg Foo, struck out Paul Noce to end the ninth inning of the suspended game, and Smith pitched the tenth for Chicago. Sax singled, and the Dodgers took the lead when Duncan tripled into the right-field bullpen. In the bottom of the tenth, Dawson came to bat as a pinch hitter, his first appearance since the beanball, and beat out an infield single. Palmeiro singled, but Moreland ended the game by hitting into a double play. The thundering climax of the previous afternoon had only mocked the Cubs; the completed game ultimately became just another lost day in the middle of summer.

The regularly scheduled game brought both Dawson and Sandberg back to the Cubs' lineup. Sandberg had missed a month because of his ankle injury, and he had attended his father's funeral earlier in the week. In his first at-bat, he homered against the back fence in left field.

It was the Cubs' 115th home run of the season, putting them on a pace well ahead of the team record of 182. The regional Pepsi-Cola distributor was conducting a promotion in which it put numbers on the bottoms of the cans, a large prize being awarded to whomever had the number that matched the Cubs' home run total at the All-Star break, and a friend of Marv Blum named Ralph had a good number, 199. A guy in the bleachers from Danville, Illinois, offered Ralph twenty dollars for the can.

On the aisle next to them, a foursome arrived late and tried to find seats in the crowd of thirty-seven thousand. One of the guys asked Marv to move over. Marv, who was sixty-three years old and packed produce for a living, had been watching baseball in the bleachers since, as he described it, "Charlie Grimm would dance around down there at first base"—the thirties—and he wasn't about to squeeze over for some impolite come-lately. Marv chomped on his cigar and told the guy there wasn't room. The guy disagreed. "Quit jackin' your jaw," Marv said.

Later, the other fellow became engaged in a dialogue with a White Sox fan concerning the merits of the team across town. It went like this:

"The Sox suck."

"No they don't."

"Yes they do."

Trout pitched his second straight shutout, the Cubs won 7–0, and things didn't look so bad. Dawson and Sandberg were back, and with Trout pitching like he was, and the young people—Palmeiro and Martinez and Moyer and Maddux and even Lancaster—things didn't look so bad at all.

I went to dinner that night with Steve Schanker and Norb and Norb's fiancée, Jennifer, and a limo driver named Michael whose friends in the bleachers called him Shadow. The restaurant was a small neighborhood place a mile or so south of the ballpark called Little Bucharest, and it served heavy plates of fowl and goulash and sausage. On this night, there was also Rainbow Trout on the menu; though obviously coincidental, we were willing to suppose that it was in honor of the afternoon's winning pitcher, who had never looked better. There was talk about the Cubs rallying behind their previously unpredictable left-hander.

Sunday's would be the last game before the All-Star break and although the Cubs were still nine games behind St. Louis, nobody believed that the Cardinals would remain so far in front. Nearly thirty-six thousand showed up again at Wrigley Field despite dark, windy conditions that brought on another thunderstorm just after the national anthem. It stopped in ten minutes, the organist played "Blue Skies," and the Dodgers jumped all over Lester Lancaster in the middle innings.

Shelby started the scoring with a home run in the third. A guy in left field caught the baseball and presented it proudly to his girlfriend, who promptly threw it back. The Dodgers scored ten runs in the next three innings and won 12–0 behind

Bob Welch, putting a quick finish to the theory that the Cubs, inspired by Trout, were about to make their run.

I got in my car to drive back to Ohio, and about the time I passed Comiskey Park going south on the Dan Ryan Expressway, it was announced that the Cubs had traded Trout to the Yankees for the undistinguished Bob Tewksbury and two minor-league pitchers.

They talked about the trade on "The Sportswriters" show on WGN radio, and none of the sportswriters seemed to think it was any big thing. But I reflected on how pleased Steve Schanker had been about Trout at Little Bucharest two nights before, and I imagined how many people had repeated the pitching rotation over and over in their minds that night and had begun to like the sound of it. I thought of all the Cub fans who really believed the team had a chance, and it seemed like the Cubs had rabbit-punched them in the embrace. It seemed like the Cubs had shortchanged the one hundred seventy-three thousand people who had come to Wrigley Field in the past five days. The fans weren't willing to give up on the year at the All-Star break, but it seemed that the Cubs were. It seemed like a raw deal for all the people I saw every day in the bleachers.

One of the ways to look at the lights issue was this: the Cubs were owned by the *Chicago Tribune*, the biggest and most powerful newspaper between the coasts, and the official opposition to lights came from the city and state. The most staunch opposition was actually from the community, but the city and state made the laws that forbade night baseball. The state really didn't care about lights at Wrigley Field, except to the degree that the representatives from Lake View did. The city was another matter. It was operated by Mayor Harold Washington, a black man who had overtaken the white establishment of Democratic politics in Chicago and whose electability, at least in small part, depended on the degree to which his character and competence held up to the scrutiny of the local media, of which the *Tribune* was kingpin. Was it prudent for Washington to dig in against the mightiest of the media for a cause that was championed by only one pocket of constituents? For the mayor, the potential hazards seemed far greater on the side of resistance. What if he lost the Cubs to the suburbs?

And so he tried to win friends in the neighborhood that was causing all the commotion. He set up a committee, headed by urban consultant Nicholas Trkla, to convince the Lake View Neighborhood Task Force that the city and the Cubs were trying to work together to minimize traffic and noise problems that might be brought on by night baseball. Trkla and the task force met several times, with a final review session scheduled for Monday, July 27, at Ann Sather's, a Swedish family-style restaurant on Belmont Avenue. The agenda didn't call for any voting, but the task force was determined to show its support for a resolution it had drawn up, which stated: "The best efforts of the city have failed to demonstrate that night baseball is compatible with the continuation of a reasonable lifestyle in the Lake View neighborhood." Trkla tried several times, by shouting, to adjourn the meeting before the vote was taken, then huffed out of the room in futility. The resolution passed, sixteen to one. The Cubs' representative, Don Grenesko, said there would be no more meetings.

The neighborhood group had presumed that Trkla was brought in to advance a compromise, but was unable to identify one of any consequence. Potential compromises seemed to abound, however. For instance, if the Cubs had reduced their demand from eighteen night games to twelve and also cut back considerably on the 3:05 starting times, perhaps the neighborhood would have been willing to drop its resistance to lights on the basis that there would be no increase in night games for a determined number of years; something on that order, anyway. "Trkla wouldn't budge on the eighteen games," said Michael Quigley, aide to 44th Ward alderman Bernie Hansen. "We had a small subcommittee meeting— Trkla, Grenesko, Mark Atkinson (head of c.u.b.s.), and a few others; all the most important people in this thing, really—and we brought up the idea of going down to twelve games. Grenesko said it was the first time there was any meaningful discussion about it. We had to have something to take back to the community. But Trkla wouldn't even go down to twelve games."

Blindsided on the task force play, Washington brushed himself off and ran laterally. He commissioned a thirty thousand dollar city-wide study to determine the prevailing public disposition toward lights at Wrigley Field. The study—which would be ready after the season—would isolate the attitude of the neighborhood, but it was an essentially new tack to bring the rest of Chicago into the issue. Naturally, support for lights would be dramatically higher outside Lake View than within it, and producing numbers to that effect could give the mayor the mandate he might need to justify abolition of the restrictive ordinance.

The Cubs had been gone for two weeks when they arrived back in town on July twenty-eighth. They were ten-and-a-half games out of first, the scoreboard had been painted, and Lee Smith had pitched three scoreless innings in the All-Star game. "It made me so mad," said Jerry Pritikin concerning the latter development. "Now the whole world thinks Lee Smith is great. That's the curse."

Pritikin had decided not to take the advertising job he had contemplated earlier. The only money he had earned all summer was one time when he carried his voodoo doll and wore a T-shirt bearing the name of a local sports bar. But he had been getting publicity. Eric Show said he heard that Chicago fans had been sticking pins in his effigy; Pritikin wanted to write Show and tell him it was unintentional, like the pitch to Dawson. A Chicago radio man had said something derogatory about the Bleacher Preacher on the air. "He can't criticize me," complained Pritikin. "I'm an institution in the bleachers." He said he was going to send the guy a note with a pin in it, the message being: "One prick deserves another."

The Expos were back in town, and not looking nearly as laughable as they had when Bill Murray made fun of them in

April. In fact, Montreal was in second place, six games behind the Cardinals and four in front of the Cubs, who had fallen behind the Mets into fourth. Without Trout, the Cubs' pitching looked too thin for them to be factors in the pennant race.

"It was a bad trade," said Dancing Annie. "Trout has nice legs." Jeweler Joe had brought his eight-year-old grandson, Zach, to the game, and I asked Zach about the Trout deal. "Tewksbury's terrible," he said, chomping on nachos. "He's oh and two."

Zach was good company at a ballgame, well-read beyond his years and familiar with players going back to Wee Willie Keeler in the nineteenth century. "I have a record book five hundred pages long and another one a thousand pages long," he said as he sipped his Pepsi. "I want to write a record book when I grow up." What a wonderful thing baseball is to an eight-year-old boy: an introduction to the world; something to read about, talk about, care about. Through a studied interest in baseball, a kid learns history and heroism and how to work with numbers. Inevitably, kids who grow up as baseball fans are better with numbers than other kids. Once, in a junior high school math class, the teacher was asking for percentages of fractions like three-sevenths and four-elevenths, and in the back corner of the room, Ray Hartmann and I were answering, ".429 . . . .364," and the other kids couldn't believe it. Ray and I sort of looked at each other and shrugged. They were just fundamental batting averages. It was as if the teacher were asking how many socks we had on.

Martinez led off the Cubs' first with a home run against Bob Sebra. "Okay," said Zach, shoving down a hotdog, "tell me who the nine players are who all play different positions and who won back-to-back MVPs." I got Morgan, Murphy, Mantle, Maris, Banks, and Berra. I should have gotten Schmidt. I couldn't get Foxx, and I would have never gotten Hal Newhouser.

Down in the right-field bleachers, there was a guy in a Cardinal hat. Peanuts were thrown, followed by punches. A jaw was broken.

Sutcliffe, meanwhile, was working toward his fifteenth victory, and a clean-cut eighteen-year-old kid in front of me turned and asked, "Sir"—an ominous beginning—"what was the Reds' lineup on the teams with Bench and those guys?" I named the men of the Big Red Machine teams of the mid-seventies—Griffey, Geronimo, Nolan, Eastwick. . . . He shook his head wistfully in the manner that one might shake his head when thinking about the scores of Rodgers and Hammerstein. "I love those old names," he said. *Old names*? Kids.

It was 3–2 after seven, and Zach was looking ahead. "Do you think Lee Smith can hold a one-run lead?" he asked, nervously scraping the bottom of his ice cream cup. "I don't think the Cubs can hold a one-run lead over three innings."

As it turned out, the Expos tied the game in the seventh, and the Cubs went ahead again with two runs, munificent assistance being provided by Montreal catcher Jeff Reed, who managed to make three errors in the inning. None of them were particularly unsightly, but it was a notable performance, nonetheless. Durham hit a three-run homer in the eighth, and Sutcliffe's fifteenth was secure.

"I saw this hat," said Zach, nibbling on an apple he had brought from home. "It said SOX SUCK. And they do."

At Little Bucharest that evening, I asked Norb and Mark and Steve about the back-to-back MVPs. Nobody got them all, and nobody believed that the catcher wasn't Campanella. Norb said he was going to go home and look it up in the *Baseball Encyclopedia*. I had faith in Zach.

"All right," said Norb, "who was the last catcher to make three errors in an inning?" He had heard the answer on the radio—Andy Seminick. It was the kind of question you could only answer if you had just heard it on the radio. Norb smiled. "How many ballplayers do you think are sitting around right now talking about the last catcher to make three errors in an inning? They're all talking about stocks and bonds and tax write-offs."

The tortes we ordered were awesomely huge and rich, and it was agreed that the new paint job on the scoreboard looked terrific; nobody could recall the last time it had been done. "Thirty years from now," Norb said, "we'll all be sitting around saying, 'Do you remember when they painted the scoreboard in '87?' But the thing is, nobody will be able to agree on the year. We'll have to look it up on Mark's score-card."

On the way to Wednesday's game, I passed two winos passed out on a lawn on Sheffield Avenue. They must have been clairvoyant Cub fans.

In the first inning, the Expos scored on a single by Casey Candaele, a sacrifice, a wild pickoff throw by Jody Davis, and a wild pitch from Greg Maddux. From there, it got worse. "The Cubs are two years away," said Norb.

"That's a new one," said a fellow from South Bend, a college administrator who visited the bleachers often with his wife. "Usually, people say the Cubs are a year away." Hey, it was a young team.

The Expos led 9–0 after a home run by Mitch Webster in the sixth. After Webster's home run, Tim Raines batted, and he made some sort of an out, but I don't know exactly what. Usually, when I missed plays, I caught up by copying Mark's scorecard, but Mark had missed this one, too. He went all the way down the back row of the bleachers looking for some-body keeping score. There were a couple of inveterate score-keepers who often sat in the back row in right field, but they weren't there. Neither was Mark's friend, Judy. Elsie was working. Mark knew most of the people in the area who kept score, but none of them were at the game. Finally, he found a kid who had something written down for Raines: SF. A sacri-fice fly after a home run? Does anybody know what Raines did in the sixth on July twenty-ninth?

What the Cubs did, anyway, was lose 11–3. The guy from South Bend said it would give him something to talk about on the way home.

That night the play *Bleacher Bums* was being performed at the Theatre on the Lake by the Indian Boundary Players. The audience consisted of mostly women, and they stood for the national anthem. Some of them wore Cub T-shirts. The play was about the gamblers who used to sit in right-center, and although most of them weren't around the bleachers anymore, I recognized their prototypes. The wife of one of the gamblers was patterned after Elsie. The bullyragged kid was based on Howard who sold Frosty Malts, only he didn't used to have to sell Frosty Malts. One of the blind guys—probably Craig—was the voice and conscience of the bleachers. The only character whose likeness I couldn't identify was a vigorously energetic woman who unnerved one of the Cardinal outfielders with a trenchant list of thoroughly personal insults.

As the Cubs faded closer to Philadelphia and fifth place, it seemed that one of the lines in the play was standing up to the test of time. The coldest and most successful of the gamblers had said, "Never bet on the Cubs after the Fourth of July."

Jim Murphy led us through a door behind his beer garden and up an old flight of stairs to a rooftop covered in the kind of all-weather carpet that looks like the stuff Andre Dawson hated to play on. The Cubs were taking the field, and we sat down on an old set of high school bleachers just as Tewksbury fanned Candaele to start the game. We saw it clearly; I'd been this far away in the upper deck at Riverfront Stadium. There used to be a sign on the roof of one of the neighboring houses: 495. It seemed about right.

We were at the level of the el tracks and the first row of the second deck of the grandstand. Dawson and Martinez were out of the picture in their outfield positions, but in an encompassing, distanced perspective, the ballpark panorama placed Wrigley Field in a fuller context than one could get from inside. The view was of beer vendors dropping off the crowded plane of the bleachers and hurrying down the vacant stairway to fetch their refills; young couples leaning into each other against the back fence; pot smokers under the scoreboard; the shortstop faking the runner back to second; the band setting up outside; traffic circling; police on patrol; scalpers making their last desperate rounds; the four-six-three double play to end the Expo first.

"Wrigley Field is like an anchor for this neighborhood,"

Murphy said. Murphy made his living from the patrons at Wrigley Field, and he had no patience for those in the neighborhood who thought that the ballpark was dispensable; that lights would be anathema, and if the Cubs had to leave, Wrigleyville would just be the better for it. "Wrigley Field helped stabilize this area. This area was down, and then it came back up. I don't think the West Side of Chicago can make that transition. Wrigley Field definitely brings a higher class of people into here."

From above Sheffield Avenue, Wrigley Field *was* the focal point of the neighborhood. What moved, moved around Wrigley. Other ballparks were built off interstates and riverfronts; Wrigley Field was built off the sidewalk. Wrigley had a periphery, a circumculture that could be viewed from above. That was Chicago down there, hustling. Black kids pitched pennies—actually, quarters—against the ballpark wall. A small group of street people disappeared into the crack between the three-flats. The scalpers talked over business; like so many of Chicago's self-made businessmen, they were a resourceful lot. When police cracked down on scalping for the playoffs in 1984, the scalpers sold Cub buttons for one hundred dollars; with each button purchased, the customer received a ticket to the game.

I'd come to the roof with Mark and Norb, and by the third inning, Mark was in his usual spot—standing behind the bleachers. Norb took pictures of the ballpark where he had spent four or five hundred afternoons. There was also a group from United Airlines on Murphy's roof. One of the guys said he was a third cousin of the Wrigleys. Another bowed when Dawson came up.

Neal Heaton was keeping the Cubs in arrears, meanwhile, and as the game lingered, more bleacher people wandered over to the ramp to cool off and listen to the band below. A lot of them were more interested in music than baseball anyway. From under the big, bowed back of the scoreboard— with the blue pennant and huge white lettering, CHICAGO CUBS—disinterested fans gazed through the fence and watched us watching them.

The final was 6–1, and when it was over we watched the street fill up. Vendors peddled sunglasses and ice cream. White guys danced. Kids played Hacky-Sack in the avenue. It was baseball as urban recreation—baseball as it used to be, when ballparks were in happy European neighborhoods and the fans would adjourn to beer gardens that served steins and sausages.

One of the United Airlines guys was from the South, and as he looked down upon Chicago's spontaneous street fair, he said, "What a city."

I was in a friend's wedding back in Cincinnati over the weekend, so I missed a home run by Dawson in a losing effort against the Phillies Friday and three home runs by Dawson in a winning effort Saturday and no home runs by Dawson in a victory Sunday that went ten innings, 3–2. Manny Trillo had homered with two outs in the ninth to tie Sunday's game—at the age of thirty-six, he was getting to be quite a power hitter with two outs in the ninth—and Sandberg won it with a single in the tenth.

The groom, Tim, was a Yankee fan—which is sort of like saying that Edison tinkered around with electricity. We put on our tuxedos at his house, and while I placed his bride's ring in the outside pocket of my jacket, he placed a 1933 Babe Ruth card in the inside pocket of his. Minutes before we walked out for the ceremony, we were writing the all-time Yankee team on the blackboard of one of the church classrooms down the hall. I had Red Rolfe at third base; he said Nettles. At the reception, he wore a Yankee hat and the band played "Take Me Out to the Ballgame." He had a life-size poster of the Babe propped up in a chair at the head table; he would have preferred a statue in the receiving line, but he couldn't pull it off. His wife, who is not a baseball fan, raised no objections; the marriage will last. He took the microphone and sang to her, "Our Love Is Here to Stay" by that immortal battery, the Gershwins.

The Cubs, meanwhile, finished July two games above .500. Montreal and New York were advancing steadily on St. Louis, but Chicago was in retreat. The Phillies had slipped by the Cubs into fourth place.

How had the season come to this? It had happened so gently, so pleasantly, like being sucked into a chocolate whirlpool. One week, people were leaping down the ramp and toasting Trout and making plans for playoff games, and a few weeks later they were setting down their coffee cups and wondering where the pennant race went. There was one, but the Cubs were not party to it.

If nothing else, though, at least they were keeping their heads above .500. If the Cubs won more games than they lost, it would only be the second time in fifteen years; it would be a good season. Plus, they were still way ahead of the White Sox, not to mention Pittsburgh.

August

AT THE PAN American Games in Indianapolis, a pitcher for the women's softball team from Belize, a tiny, tropical, Central American country just under the toe of Mexico on the Caribbean, told a *Tribune* reporter that in her country, "number one is women's softball, and number two is the Chicago Cubs." The superstation signal was easily picked up and distributed over cable systems in Belize, and the Cubs had become the national team. "Eighty percent of the people in Belize love the Cubs," said the team's manager, Charles Soliz. "People take little televisions into their offices to watch the Cubs during the day. The work stops when the Cubs are on."

While the Pan Am Games were going on, meanwhile, the Cubs were losing three straight to the Phillies in Philadelphia. By the time they returned home on August thirteenth, they had dropped to 57–57. They were fading.

In blatantly disparate ways, these two August developments, taken together, illuminated the very core of Cubness. The Cubs' popularity in Belize and their retreat in the standings were both patently emblematic of the franchise and,

161

deeper than that, they had one basic and fundamentally Cub-
bish thing in common: day baseball.

To a similar degree as Wrigley Field itself, day baseball
defined the Cubs. It was by monopolizing the daytime mar-
ketplace that the Cubs had shepherded their far-flung, immense, and immensely faithful multitude. While the Braves
and Yankees and Mets and others competed on prime-time
cable, the Cubs rode alone into the TV afternoons of Wauke-
gan, Yazoo City, and Belize. The people of Belize were profoundly worried about Harry Caray when he was away.

It was day baseball also that made the Cubs the eccentric
and irresistably whimsical team that they were—in part, the
losing team that they were. Summer sunshine brought out the
best in Beautiful Wrigley Field, of course, but its unrelenting
influence burned an even deeper brand upon the profile of the
Cubs. What distinguished the Cubs on the playing field, more
than anything else, was their modern legacy of defeat, and
after forty-two years, it was getting hard to dismiss the fact
that they had not won a National League pennant since becoming the only team without a lighted home field in 1946.
Their last pennant was the year before that, and the coincidence was too great to ignore: day baseball was a competitive
disadvantage. There was some question about whether the
Cubs would ever win without lights.

It wasn't *impossible* for the Cubs to succeed as things were,
just more difficult than it would otherwise be. They did win
the division title in 1984, of course, but they also lost three
straight playoff games on the road to an inferior team—an
occurrence consistent with the reasons that day baseball has
hurt the Cubs.

It has hurt them on the road, for one thing. Most teams win
less often on the road than they do at home, and in the Cubs'
case it probably has had more to do with the dimensions and
weather conditions at Wrigley Field than with the starting
time of the games; because of the home-run possibilities at
their home park, the Cubs have historically been a sluggish
team. But day games have also contributed to the sluggish-
ness. While Cub fans are excruciatingly familiar with the

legendary late-season surrenders of their team, collapse is not merely a Cub tradition; it's a Cub fact. The numbers show that over the years the Cubs have fatigued to a discernibly greater degree than all other major-league teams.

Numerous experts had theorized along the way that the constant adjustment from day to night, and vice versa, inevitably tired a player, but there was no empirical testimony for this, other than the standings. An Evanston postman named Don Zminda became intrigued by the "body clock" theory, as it was called, so he set about to determine if the data supported it. First, he examined for tangible evidence of fatigue among the teams in the National League from 1969 to 1984, comparing won-loss percentages before and after September first. He found that the Cubs played at a winning pace of .499 before September first and .439 after, a negative difference more than doubling that of all other teams. He carried the study all the way back to 1946 and found the pattern to be persistent.

Zminda discovered also that when the Cubs played night games on the road, they fared noticeably worse than when they played in the daytime—again, showing a greater discrepancy than all other teams. He went so far as to study the batting performances of Santo, Banks, and Williams in the first games of each trip, and found that each suffered a substantial dropoff. Taking all the available data into consideration—even the advantage of having opponents adjust to Wrigley Field—Zminda concluded that late-season weariness was responsible for at least three or four defeats a year for the Cubs.

Skeptics might counter that lethargy has resulted from Chicago's consistent uninvolvement in the pennant race, but the numbers reveal that other losers have not withered in the same way. Another possible explanation has more apparent merit, but it, too, accrues to Wrigley Field: the Cubs' fidelity to home runs has fostered older, heavier teams than others; fatigue being an unsurprising consequence. By July 1987, both Dallas Green and Gene Michael were reproving the Cubs for lack of effort. Was it really that, or was it just the tolls of body clock and sunshine? It had been an unusually hot summer.

There was nothing, however, to bring a National League team to life like a visit from the New York Mets. Thirty-five thousand people were at Wrigley Field on Thursday the thirteenth, which was also Billy Williams Day, the batting coach and former leftfielder being honored for his induction into the Hall of Fame. Williams was a quiet, proud Alabama man who had used the platform at Cooperstown to deliver some timely points about equal opportunity in baseball; the speech was so important to him that he'd had it professionally written. In Chicago, though, Williams was not known for his ideology but for his sweet left-handed swing. "Sweet-swinging" went with Billy Williams the way "Beautiful" went with Wrigley Field. Though he endeavored to be recognized for more than the ability to roll his wrists, as a batting coach Williams used this reputation to gently remind the Cubs of his qualifications. A hitter would send a line drive into the gap during practice, and Williams would say, "Um, um, swingin' that bat like Billy Williams."

On his day at Wrigley Field, Williams was given one of those four-wheel-drive all-purpose vehicles that ballplayers always seem to get when they have a "day." Although Williams may have been an exception—he retired as a player before salaries increased geometrically—isn't it odd that, with ballparks full of working people looking on, the one who always gets the truck is the one who could buy it with two days' pay? They also placed Williams's number 26 on the right-field flagpole, opposite the number 14 of his old roommate in left. It was a nice move, curious only in that Williams played left field and Banks spent half his career at first base. The club's justification was that Williams's home runs went to right and Banks's to left.

The Cubs had been out of town for ten days, and for the bleacher regulars, the time off was sort of a summer vacation. Steve Schanker had met a girl. Norb had rummaged through his basement and found a seven hundred dollar Babe Ruth card. Mark had seen games in Milwaukee, Detroit, and

Toledo, and had also carried forth in the benign attempt to get his wife interested in baseball. "I combed through the *Baseball Register* trying to find a player with the same birthday as Laurie," he said. "I couldn't find one, but I did find out that Steve Lyons and Barry Lyons, though not related, were born on the same day." I had gone home and celebrated my son's first birthday. I was welcomed back to the city on Broadway, where a guy bummed my last Chicken Tender, and on Cornelia, where a crabapple buzzed by my head, hit by a little Hispanic kid with power to the opposite field.

Having reversed the anomalous early-season trend that had them losing at home and winning elsewhere, the Cubs were eager to get back to the Friendly Confines, as their comfortable park was appropriately nicknamed. Their pitching had been wretched on the road. Maddux had been sent to the minors, Ron Davis mercifully released, and Sanderson moved back into the rotation. Mike Mason started against the Mets Thursday and left with a sore elbow after less than an inning with New York already leading 2–0. It was 5–0 after two, with Gooden pitching for the Mets.

For the Cubs, Palmeiro had started at first base instead of Durham, an indication that perhaps Michael, like so many of the bleacher fans, was growing weary of the Bull's aversion to hitting with men on base. In the right-field bleachers, a blonde-haired local television director named Al Yellon pointed out that Dawson had driven in himself more often than his teammates had, a startling statistic that reflected unfavorably upon Durham, who had batted behind Dawson for much of the year. Mark Wilmot had always been quick to bring up Durham's good points—the Bull had rare power and fielded well—but even he had run out of patience. "I'm announcing today that I am no longer a defender of Leon Durham," he said. "I've come to the conclusion, like everybody else, that he has to be traded. But I *am* still a defender of Lee Smith."

Thursday's didn't appear to be a Smith type of ballgame, but at Wrigley Field, things often are not what they appear to be. The Cubs scored three runs in the third, when Martinez homered against Gooden, and two more in the fifth to tie the game. Les Lancaster, Jay Baller, and Frank DiPino kept the Mets scoreless after the second inning; and in the eighth, with the bases loaded and one out against reliever Randy Myers, Davis drove a pitch toward the fence in right field, where Strawberry put his glove on the ball but was unable to hold it. For the bleacher fans, it was quite a windfall—the lead had been taken and Strawberry had come up empty. It got even better when DiPino, a left-hander who had inconspicuously been pitching well, took the 7–5 lead into the ninth and immediately fanned Keith Hernandez and Strawberry. Then, with two outs and no runners, it became a Smithian game.

Kevin McReynolds bunted for a single, Gary Carter singled, and Smith walked Howard Johnson to load the bases. With every batter, the fans would stand, anticipating the finish, then return quietly to their seats as another Met went safely down to first. Strike one, and more would be on their feet. Strike two, and the whole ballpark was standing again. It was like "Simon Says," but the stubborn Simon wouldn't say "go home." By the time Dave Magadan batted with the bases loaded, most of the exasperated fans had decided to just hold their positions, sitting or standing, whatever. "You suck, Michael!" yelled Ray Meyer, son of the Ray of Ray's Bleachers. "Thank God he won't be here next year. This clinches it."

On the field, Durham, who had entered the game in the fifth, berated his buddy Smith for letting an easy save slip away. DiPino left the dugout and watched from the clubhouse. Mark was rethinking his stance on number 46, who then struck out Magadan for his twenty-ninth save.

On the night of August thirteenth, it started to rain. It was still raining in the morning. Chicago had never seen such rain before.

The record for rain in a twenty-four-hour period in Chicago was six and a quarter inches. On Thursday night, it started at about nine o'clock, and the record was already broken by the time people got to work Friday morning, if they got there at all. On the Northwest Side, the Kennedy Expressway and all roads to O'Hare Airport were closed. Kids swam in the interstates and dove off the tops of semitrailers. A woman perished when her car swerved into an eight-foot ditch filled with water.

But the baseball game started on time. The amazing old field had drained. About half the people with tickets—seventeen thousand—made it to the ballpark.

The rain hadn't stopped until almost noon, at which time almost nine and a half inches had fallen; as snow, it would have been nearly eight feet. Naturally, many with baseball tickets called the Cubs' office in the morning to ask whether the game would be played, and dozens of them got Jerry Pritikin instead. Pritikin's phone number had a similar prefix as the Cubs', and, of course, the same last four digits: CUBS. He told the callers they had reached the Bleacher Preacher, but he was gracious enough not to complain about Gene Michael—"Michaels," he called him, as did so many other Cub fans—at whom he was still angry for putting Lee Smith into Thursday's game. "Michaels even pulled Gross at the wrong time," said Pritikin, referring to the August tenth game in Philadelphia, when Michael had the Phillies' pitcher ejected in the fifth inning for sandpapering the baseball, and the Cubs didn't score thereafter.

The Bleacher Preacher was becoming rather cynical, actually, about most things concerning the Cubs, Andre Dawson and Rick Sutcliffe excepted. Against the Mets Friday, Sanderson pitched well through the early innings, and Pritikin said, "Do you think he can last through the fifth without going on the DL?" The Cubs scored four runs in their fifth, Moreland homering with two on, and Sanderson was removed in the interest of the groin pull he had aggravated covering first base. Rookie Drew Hall and Jay Baller finished off splendidly, and I sat up in center field and stretched out over two benches. It was the first time since the three-hour rain-delay game in early June that there had been stretching room in the bleachers.

I had missed stretching out at the ballpark; it seemed like

something that one ought to be able to do. Of course, the ballclub would never be convinced of that, and certainly the swelling popularity of the game was a healthy thing for it. But nonetheless, as I sat alone in center field watching the Cubs beat the Mets 6-1 in a mid-August game of only moderate consequence, I decided it was a shame that the ballpark wasn't like this more often. It had been, once upon a time. Other parks still were. Wrigley Field, make no mistake, was still the best of the ballparks, and the bleachers were the best of Wrigley Field, but the rare privacy on August fourteenth was so quieting as to be almost cathartic.

Even in the still wet afternoon, though, the echo of other days left a ringing reminder: the bleachers had become caricatures of themselves, and in so doing only parodied what they could be. They were celebrated, but for the wrong reasons. It was like a little oceanfront town that was so picturesque and naturally quaint that people began to spend weekends there, and motels were developed, and the people who spent weekends there told other people how picturesque and quaint it was, and then hotels were developed, and people spent entire vacations there, and pretty soon the little town was but a backdrop for all of the restaurants and shops and telemarketing conventions, and then came the miniature golf courses; the ocean and the beach and the herons and even some of the old fishermen were still there, but to get to them you had to go through the windmill and between the legs of the Chinese dragon.

The bleachers had gotten to the point of miniature golf, and for those to whom watching baseball was not unlike watching a heron fish the water's edge at dawn, it was unfortunate. Every baseball game should not be an event, because it isn't. Football games are events; they happen only once a week. Baseball happens every day, and its compelling, addictive, special allure is in the way it plays itself out over a season, unfolding with patient, playful deliberation, nothing meaning everything and everything meaning something. For every game to be a circus is to have baseball's rambling rhapsody drowned out by drums and cymbals. Game by game, it doesn't compare with football, and yet the sum total of a football season is but a box of chocolates next to baseball's pig on the spit.

It seemed the only thing that could keep the circus out of Wrigley Field was rain. And maybe the futility of September. Suddenly, I was eager for September.

It was crowded, almost game time, on August fifteenth, and behind me in the right-field bleachers I heard a man calling down the row: "One more cheek? Got room for one more cheek? All right, all four cheeks are now on the bleachers. Thank you."

It was a sales manager for a textile company, a jocular young man named Gary Grossklaus and his friend Grace, who worked in a nursing home in Peoria. There were a lot of Cub fans in Peoria, and Grace said that several of the residents had their rooms decorated in Cub paraphernalia. "Whenever Lee Smith comes into a game, they go crazy," she said. "They start throwing things. I've never seen so much life come to these people as when Lee Smith comes into a game."

In right field, four girls sat down next to each other, each with a word on her back. The first girl's word was WE; the second, HATE; the third, THE; and the fourth, METS. It was a nice effect when they stood up spontaneously.

Martinez homered in the third, and Jamie Moyer and Gary Grossklaus were both in top form. Gary hadn't been to the park in a while, and he turned to check out the paint job on the scoreboard. "Ah, Picasso must have done it. Or was he a sculptor?" He saw Billy Williams's number hanging in right field, and it reminded him of Ernie Banks. "I got divorced the same day as Banks," he said. "When it was over, I said, 'Hey Ern, great day to play two, huh?' I don't think Ernie was in the mood. He was trying to get custody of the kids and the sofa." He saw Ronnie Woo-Woo. "Can you imagine that guy selling pizza? 'Pepperoni! Woo! Green pepper! Woo!' "

The Cubs routed Terry Leach in the fifth, and I asked Gary if he ever gave up hope for the Cubs. "Hey," he said, "they're usually only one or two plane crashes away. You've got to have religion. No, really, the way I look at it, the Cubs are just three players away—the Father, the Son, and the Holy Ghost." I asked him how he handled the playoff disappointment in '84. "I refer to the fifth game as Black Sunday," he said. "The sun didn't come out for two weeks after that. I had to switch to an electric shaver—I didn't think I could stand having a razor blade in my hand."

It was an apparently easy game for the Cubs, which served to show how tenuous and arbitrary winning can be in baseball. These things happened as Chicago built a 6–3 lead: with two outs and two on in the fourth, Moyer blooped a pop fly in front of Mookie Wilson, who slipped in center field as he reached for the ball; with one out and two on in the top of the seventh and the Cubs up by a run, the Mets' Lee Mazzilli smashed a ball toward third, where Moreland snatched it and started a double play; with two outs in the bottom of the seventh, Sandberg drove in two runs with a soft single just past the infield.

In what had been a one-run game, both teams had sent men to the plate with two-out, two-on opportunities. Both men had gone up trying only to hit the ball hard. New York's had succeeded in doing that; Chicago's hadn't. Yet the effect was a four-run swing for the Cubs. The Moyer hit had been a two-run blow, inasmuch as Martinez followed it with a double. If Moyer's ball had been caught, and if Mazzilli's had gotten past Moreland, and if Sandberg's flare had not found a spot—all of which would have seemed eminently natural— the score would have been 5–2 in favor of the Mets instead of 6–3 Cubs. But for the whimsy of a few arbitrary inches here and there, a victory for the Mets would have come as easily and routinely as it actually did for the Cubs, who won 7–3 after Durham homered against a house in the eighth—he had hit one in Philadelphia that Mike Schmidt said was as long as any homer he had ever seen—and DiPino pitched two hitless innings of relief.

As I walked afterward along Wellington, a peaceful, maple-shaded street between Clark and Broadway, two guys were sitting on the steps of a renovated brick house. Two other guys arrived at the limestone Victorian two-story next door, and as they walked to their door, one of the guys on the steps said, "How 'bout them Cubs?" One of the other guys said, "They're making their move."

They were ten and a half out, in fifth place. I thought of something Gary Grossklaus had said: "Being a Cub fan is like getting married for the second time—hope wins out over experience."

While choosing not to be daunted by experience, Cub fans were altogether cognizant of it nonetheless. The next day, Shadow, the dark, friendly limo driver, brought out a poem to that effect. It said, in part, that since the Cubs' last world championship in 1908, radio and television had been invented; four states had been admitted to the Union; there had been fourteen presidents; Halley's comet had appeared twice; and the world had seen a Polish Pope.

The Mets scored three in the first against Maddux, who was back from the minors but obviously shouldn't have been. The game seemed out of hand early, so Mark, Norb, and I busied ourselves trying to select the dream team of American presidents. We had Lincoln pitching, of course, with JFK as the ace in the pen. Taft, who looked like a catcher, had actually been one. Washington played first base for us and batted fourth. Mark, being a history teacher, happened to know that Zachary Taylor was a good athlete, so we gave him second, across the bag from Truman. We figured Grant for a third baseman with a gun. Andrew Jackson would be a hard-hitting rightfielder, Teddy Roosevelt a centerfielder who covered a lot of ground, and Eisenhower a steady veteran in left. FDR managed, and Nixon made deals in the front office. The announcer, naturally, was Dutch Reagan.

The Mets scored three more in the fourth to make it 7–0, and I thought about leaving early to get started on the drive home to Cincinnati. Then the Cubs came back with five. Included were back-to-back home runs by Davis—a grand slam—and Palmeiro. There were some guys in front of us who had their shirts wrapped around their heads like turbans, and just as Mark commented that they were the sort of fans who wouldn't have been in the bleachers five years before, one of them turned and asked him who had hit the second home run.

"Palmeiro," Mark said.

"Paul Merrill? Did they just bring him up from the minors?"

Since it looked as though the game was going to be worth staying for, I went quickly outside to get some cash from the money machine and a fish sandwich at the McDonald's across the street—the only McDonald's in the world with pictures of Ernie Banks on the walls and a Norman Rockwell print signed by Charlie Grimm. When I returned—I had a pass to get back in—it was 10–5. A woman I knew walked by, we talked for maybe five minutes, and when I looked at the scoreboard it was 16–5. At that point, I decided it was safe to leave. My car was just a few blocks away. When I turned on the radio, it was 20–5. Eight more runs scored as I drove past Soldier Field, McCormick Place, and the projects along the Dan Ryan Expressway. The final, as I pulled onto the Indiana Toll Road, was 23–10. It was one day when experience had kicked the tar out of hope.

The wind was blowing out hard on Friday, August 21. "That's not a good sign," a guy in the bleachers said. "Lynch is pitching today."

A left-hander, Jim DeShaies, started for Houston, and that was a good sign for Brian Dayett, at least. Dayett was still hitting over .300—everybody knew he could hit—but was on pace to bat fewer than two hundred times over the full season, despite solidly winning a job as a platoon leftfielder. A platoon was a proven concept, but that was of little solace to the right-handed member of it. In an idle moment—of which he had plenty—Dayett had counted the left-handed pitchers in the National League. He had found thirty-seven, only seventeen of them starters. He was doomed to be on the bench. This was a man who had been an All-Star at every minor-league level—twice a Most Valuable Player—and by the end of 1987 he would have been playing professional baseball for ten years and still not have a full season's worth of major-league at-bats. For the heck of it, Dayett had also counted left-handers in the American League: there were forty-eight.

The Cubs' right-handed platoon in center field, Bob Dernier, was still hitting over .350, and he began the Chicago first with a home run. The kid next to me gave his dad a high five. Sandberg batted next, and two high school girls across the aisle held up a banner that said: HI HARRY! GO RYNO! The wind ripped the sign apart, and only HARRY! was left. They held that up—what the heck. To them, Harry was the star of this game show, anyway; they were the studio audience. You can take kids away from their televisions, but you can't change their channels.

The Cubs scored four in the third on a bunch of singles and Dawson's thirty-ninth home run, and Lynch was hanging in against the wind until the Astros got three in the fifth. Billy Hatcher, a former Cub prospect who played only briefly in Chicago, doubled in the middle of the rally. Hatcher was having a fine season but was the very type of player who would probably have never had a full opportunity with the Cubs. He played a good outfield and hit singles and stole bases—did everything, really, but deliver home runs. He was an Astro or a Cardinal, not a Cub.

In the fifth, Houston's Bill Doran accounted for the eight thousandth home run in the history of Wrigley Field. In the bottom of the inning, Dawson belted his second of the afternoon—he had also hit two the day before in Atlanta—and for the umpteenth time in the past four months, the clamorously adoring crowd brought him to the top step of the dugout to remove his cap. A guy from Iowa in the left-field bleachers said something appropriate about Dawson's "tater"—referring to his home run—at which point his friend assailed his Hawkeye buddy, alleging that "tater" must be a rural Midwestern word. This produced a great international outpouring in defense of "tater" and the way people talk in Iowa. A guy in front of me said he was from Tennessee and he had heard "tater" all his life. Another guy was from Missouri, and to him a "tater tot" was a little guy who hit the long ball. A man from Manitoba said he'd heard the word in every ballpark in every country he'd been in. It was heartwarming to see such a united front against baseball illiteracy.

Dayett flied out to left in the fifth and left the game when Houston brought in a right-hander.

The final was 7–5, and Smith became the first National League pitcher to achieve thirty saves four years in a row. Dunston had returned to the lineup—regardless of what people thought of him, the Cubs needed his speed and daring— and with Dawson, anything seemed possible. That was all it took for another rush of characteristic Cub optimism. Jerry Pritikin pointed out that the Cubs had six games remaining with the Cardinals and four with the Mets.

I ate with Norb and Mark at the Ethiopian Village on Clark Street, and Norb said that the Cubs could be within six and a half games of the Cardinals by the end of the weekend. He also said, among various ultraconservative points of view and a few Ethiopian beers, that the Ayatollah Khomeini would bomb Washington or Moscow, either one, at the blink of an eye.

"Then why hasn't he done it?" Mark asked.

Norb didn't even pause before he answered. "Why haven't the Cubs won the pennant?"

The year they should have won was 1969. Everybody believed that. But '69 was the year anything could happen. Neil Armstrong walked on the moon and the Mets won the World Series; who could explain '69?

"Sixty-nine was the best of times and the worst of times," said Don Kessinger, who had been a dickens of a shortstop. He and other memorable men of '69 were at Wrigley Field on Saturday, August 22, for the Equitable Old-Timers Game, which ostensibly pitted the National League against the American League but in reality featured the most popular Cub team of the postwar period. Banks was there too, and Williams, Santo, Hundley. Durocher was the manager. Before the game, he walked out and bowed to the bleacher fans in left field. "We all still feel today that we were the best team in baseball," said Kessinger. So then, why did it happen? Do ballplayers believe in fate, like fans do? "You don't believe in fate. What you believe in is momentum."

Ron Santo was still wearing his golf glove from the morning's round, when he had shot eighty. His had been an exceptional career obscured by the wrong things—by the heel-clicking routine he did after victories in 1969; by the argument he got into with Don Young over the fly ball that Young missed that year; by the undignified end to his career, as he tried ineffectually to play second base with the White Sox in his final season. All of that notwithstanding, Santo was almost certainly the best third baseman not in the Hall of Fame, and a player whose soul still fit into the blue-trimmed uniform. People said he just wasn't the same player when he went across town in 1974.

"It broke my heart to leave the Cubs," Santo the Old-Timer said as he sat next to his teen-age daughter in the National League dugout. "I felt it was all over. There's no place you can go in the United States—any city or team—where, if they lose, they still get the support the people give you here. The fans here are the best." He had become one of them, and it had hurt Santo as much as any Cub fan when the pennant was lost in 1984. "I was sure they were going to win it," he said. "But when they won the division, at least, I felt that was a lot of pressure off us." A '69 Cub could never wander far from that hilly stretch of his life. Santo turned back to it once again in his dog-eared memory, and it still looked the same. "There's no doubt in my mind we had the best ballclub. If we'd have had one more relief pitcher. . . ."

Or, better yet, Lou Brock. The great unknown of the Banks-Williams-Santo-Jenkins-Beckert-Kessinger-Hundley Cubs was what would have been if Chicago had not traded Brock to the Cardinals for Ernie Broglio in 1964. It wasn't bad luck, though, that sent Brock away. It was bad thinking—the trade itself, and all that it represented. The Lou Brock who wore St. Louis colors and became the greatest base stealer in the history of the game would not have been the same man in Chicago's striped suit. The Cubs were not capable of producing a player like the one who kick-started the Cardinals when they took three pennants and two World Series in the sixties.

"To this day, the Cubs do not view baseball as a battle of foot soldiers," said Brock, still straight and lean as he stood against the batting cage on August twenty-second. "With the Cubs, a single was just a set-up shot for the home run. We didn't run the bases, didn't steal. Nobody taught base stealing coming up in the Cubs organization. The Cubs might have wanted me to switch to that style, but by the time I learned to be a slap hitter, I was in St. Louis. My last hit in Chicago was a two-run homer to win a game against the Pirates. I was convinced I was a home-run hitter. I got to St. Louis, and the manager, Johnny Keane, said, 'We think you have the ability to steal bases.' I said, 'The what?' He said, 'We want you to steal bases.' I said, 'You've got to be kidding.'

"The Cubs, all they ever needed was a good leadoff man," said Brock. "If I'd been here, the Cubs would have won the pennant in '68 and '69." In 1968, the Cardinals beat the Cubs by thirteen games, but what might the difference have been if Brock's league-leading forty-six doubles, fourteen triples, and sixty-two stolen bases had been taken from one team and given to the other? Brock hit .298 and stole fifty-three bases for the Cardinals as the Cubs yielded unforgettably to the Mets in 1969. In 1970, the Cubs finished five games behind the Pirates; Brock hit .304 and scored 114 runs.

And here were the Cubs two decades later, leading the league in home runs, third in batting average—getting runners on base and hitting the ball out of the park—and yet seventh in the league in runs scored. It was practically mysterious. Somehow—the grand jury of the bleachers was ready to indict a ring of conspirators that included untimely hitting, reluctant running, and invisible strategy—the Cubs were embezzling from their bank of big hitters. It was a gross misuse of resources. They were butchering the fatted calf and getting a few Big Macs. They were planting cabbage and harvesting brussels sprouts; throwing out harpoons and bringing in bluegill. While other teams economized, clipping coupons with their baserunning, the Cubs paid in big denominations and waved off the change. More than two decades after squandering Lou Brock, they still avoided speed like it was a dangerous drug.

But on August twenty-second, Brock was in the dugout once more with Banks and Santo and Billy Williams. Feeling like a Cub again, he drove a ball to the right-field wall against the wind—a deep home run under more favorable conditions—and then attempted to circle the bases on legs eight years retired. The throw came in to Gus Triandos at the plate, and Brock, hopelessly out and too tired to slide, fell down backpedaling. "That was great!" yelled Banks in the dugout, applauding Brock's entertaining effort. Banks cheering Brock—it was a provocative concept. Good grief, how many runs could those two have produced? And Brock and Santo? Brock and Williams?

When Williams batted, Banks spotted Shawon Dunston on the step of the dugout and shouted to him. "Hey, Shawon, watch his wrists! Your attention, please, watch his wrists, his wrists!" Williams popped up and grumbled that he couldn't leave the game oh for one. Banks was due up in the second inning, and as he left the bench, he said, "This game is easy." Ryne Duren promptly smacked him with a soft fastball, but Mister Cub gave no thought to taking first base. Instead, he doubled to the wall in left, then scored the only run of the game on a hit by Randy Hundley. "This game is easy," he said as he returned, grinning, to the dugout. "This game is easy."

At Murphy's one day, I encountered a fellow who was studying a picture taken from the bleachers in the late fifties, with Sheffield Avenue in the background, his particular point of interest being a small tree on Sheffield that had since grown far above the apartment building behind it. He was a former salesman named Paul Locke who had gone back to school and become a social studies and history teacher because he was interested in how things had come to be the way they were. He was especially interested in the Cubs and Wrigley Field in that respect. As others rubbed shoulders and raised beers that afternoon, Locke said, "I look for social implications in everything. I really believe there's something to the fact that this whole Cub thing started with '69. I think if you want to understand Cub fans, you have to see tapes of games from '69. It was that whole period—Vietnam and everything. I'm not sure what the connection is, but there's something there. There was so much emotion and tension out in the bleachers in the late sixties and early seventies. There wasn't a lot of long hair out there, but I remember one game, against Houston I think, early in '68, they played the national anthem and a whole section of people wouldn't stand up; they turned their backs to the flag. A couple of them held their fists up, and the rest of them just sat there and talked. I don't know, there's something there."

There *was* something there—something that may not have been anywhere else in baseball: a sort of spontaneous communion between youthful bohemianism and ballgames in the sunshine. The iconoclasts of the sixties and seventies could go to the bleachers and not feel compromised. The Cubs were anti-establishment, too, in their resistance to lights. They were underdogs. With its natural greenery, Wrigley Field was the closest thing baseball had to a real park. People threw Frisbees. And, in the bleachers, the open seating stood for freedom of movement and choice.

It wasn't just the sixties and seventies that the bleachers embodied. Like a good poem, they seemed to suit the times, whatever they were. Sequential photographs of one wooden seat of the Wrigley Field bleachers would create a montage documenting half a decade of America's social evolution, from the long-sleeved post-Depression working man to the short-haired eighties college kid in jams and sunglasses and a T-shirt advertising something. A certain amount of redundancy would be incorporated, perhaps, inasmuch as the bleachers have tended to attract people with a fondness for the past. There were still a few among the modern masses in 1987, for instance, who missed the more sensitive days of 1969.

On August twenty-second, Nick Wagener stood behind the right-field bleachers with a red bandana over his head, looking like the sixties fan that he had been. As with Mark Wilmot and Norb Kudele and Steve Schanker, there was some sort of preservationist sense that made him reluctant to actually sit down on one of the hard benches and mingle in as an eighties bleacher creature. There was no lingering political theme at work, just a reactionary yearning for the days of higher baseball consciousness. Nick had been a stock-options trader and had quit to work part-time and go to more Cubs games. At Wrigley Field, he tied into the counterculture by being actively sympathetic to Lee Smith.

A few rows in front of him was an example of why Wagener chose to stand instead of cramming in with the crowd. There was a clean-cut young drunk yelling unimaginative profanities at Houston's rightfielder, Kevin Bass. This was in contrast to a fellow in the front row with a bushy beard that looked like it hadn't been trimmed since Woodstock and a tweed cap that might not have been removed since Don Young dropped the fly ball. The fellow in front was dealing specifically with what he and others perceived as Bass's conspicuous lack of good looks, and most around him were amused. The drunk in the back, however, was so dull in his ranting that he put himself to sleep. Then he jerked awake and tried fruitlessly to get up. This pitiful pursuit became a community cause for all of the people in section 144, who stood and yelled, "You can do it! You can do it!" Their encouragement was not sufficient, however, and Crowd Control was called in to assist.

Meanwhile, the Astros and Cubs were playing a good ballgame that had been started by Mike Scott and the rookie Lester Lancaster, who left with a 3–2 lead after seven innings. Lancaster was relieved by another kid pitcher, Drew Hall, who caught none of the rookie spirit, in effect taking up where he had left off in his last Wrigley Field appearance. In that one, against the Mets the Sunday before, he had surrendered ten runs in less than two innings. This time, he gave up two without getting an out, and Houston had a 4–3 lead when Dawson batted in the eighth. "How many times can we ask this guy to do it?" said Pritikin, at which point Dawson homered against Scott and a twenty-five-mile-an-hour wind. Pritikin made a reference to Roy Hobbs being alive, Wagener yelled something about Awesome, and in the right-field grandstand, a shameless band of dilettantes tried to start a wave.

At Wrigley Field, a wave was graffiti. Starting one was like doodling in the family Bible, or sticking bubble gum on the walls of the Louvre. The fans in the right-field bleachers shouted down the louts in the grandstand. They made obscene gestures at them, booed them into disgrace. "The Crowd Control guys should have guns for that," said one bleacher fan. "Like, 'You wanna do a wave? Go ahead. Make my day.' "

The game went extra innings, and in the bottom of the tenth, WGN radio switched over to the Bears' exhibition game with the Steelers. Sandberg singled to lead off the inning, and with Durham up it was suggested that Sandberg should get picked off so that Durham could bat with the bases empty. Durham struck out, Dawson hit into a double play, and Michael sent Frank DiPino out for his third inning of work. In the bleachers, it was agreed that three innings were too many for DiPino. Bass was the second batter, and he homered.

Jerry Mumphrey opened the Cub eleventh with a single, and inasmuch as his thirty-four-year-old feet would carry the potentially tying run, Nick Wagener suggested that Dernier, the team's best base stealer, would be an appropriate substitute. Moreland, even slower than Mumphrey, hit into a force out, and after Davis fanned, Dernier was finally sent in to pinch run. "Michael's got to be the dumbest son of a bitch," Nick said, as Dunston flew to center field to end the game.

August twenty-third was blue and beautiful, Canadian air and the bearded sage, Leonard Becker, both returning to Wrigley Field. Becker hadn't been to the ballpark at all during the middle of the summer, which was the hottest he could remember. The old man who ate nachos in center field hadn't been back either, since the beginning of the season, and I was worried about him. Nobody in the bleachers knew who he was.

Sutcliffe pitched for the Cubs against the remarkable Nolan Ryan, who led the National League in earned run average but was 5–13, and each of the big pitchers responded to the challenge of the other. With one out in the third, Sutcliffe tripled down the right-field line, but Martinez and Sandberg left him there. Houston scored two runs when Hatcher, the former Cub, singled, stole, and scored in the fourth, and then Bill Doran singled, stole, and scored in the sixth. After Ryan left the game with a blister on his hand, the Cubs scored two when Durham came through with a titanic center-field home run that would have approached the scoreboard in a more compliant wind. Ryan would have nothing but the blister to show for his effort.

In left field, a man and woman wore T-shirts with pictures of bear cubs and the wording: WE WILL SURVIVE. On the ramp, a policeman named Escobedo explained to Ronnie Woo-Woo that not everybody in the ballpark was warmed by his little routine. In right-center, I asked Norb, who lived in Indiana, why he wasn't a White Sox fan. "The first time I walked into this place, I just loved it," he said. "This is me."

In the seventh, Billy Hatcher pressed his point a little further—the point being that guys who could hit and run could hit and run in Wrigley Field. He tripled home two men to win the game.

Monday was an off-day, followed by three games with the Braves. All year long, I'd been looking for one series that wouldn't matter much, an obscure little corner to cut in the interest of other pursuits, but it had been hard to come by. Somehow, in a 162-game season, almost all of them seem to take on some importance: win this one and take the series; take the series, and have momentum going into St. Louis; big one here, another loss here would make it hard; all right, just stay within four by Memorial Day; five by the Fourth of July; come on, beat the Mets; got to stay within ten; okay, getting hot, big series; win through the weekend and be within striking distance; got to make up for that tough one Tuesday. . . . It's all positioning. Every game *is* important—almost— simply because it is the only present opportunity a team has to improve its lot. It is the next hill, and a long season is reconnoitered with short-range field glasses. August is too distant to scope out in May.

By August twenty-fifth, though, it could finally be said that there would be nothing whatsoever vital about the three- game series coming up between the Cubs and the Atlanta Braves. The Cubs were 62–62, eleven games behind the Cardi- nals, three-and-a-half behind the fourth-place Phillies, eight- and-a-half ahead of the last-place Pirates. They were going nowhere, and neither were the boring Braves, ten games out in the other division.

I went home, and it rained in Chicago. The biggest rain in Chicago history hadn't stopped the Cubs and Mets two Fri- days before, but on August twenty-fifth, a Tuesday, it was still raining at game time, and the Cubs and Braves were canceled for the day. And the next. One of the games would be made up only if it mattered—it wouldn't—and they played a dou- bleheader on the twenty-seventh. The Braves won the first game, and in the second it got dark in the eighth inning with the Cubs ahead 8–6 on five home runs, including two by Durham—both with a man on base, hallelujah—and Daw- son's forty-second. They never finished the game, but Chi- cago was awarded it, and the day was split.

So was the month. The Cubs played the last four games of August on the road, won three of them, and were 66–64 going into September. Though they had departed quietly from the pennant race, it could be said that they hadn't collapsed. They had held their own in August, winning and losing four- teen. Dawson was Player of the Month in the National League. In the American, Chicago's other team was dismally last at 55–75.

Compared to their usual selves and to their cross-town counterparts, the Cubs were looking pretty good, actually. With a decent September, they could have a nice little season.

September ────────────────

THE FIRST SIGN of September was the 58 on the back of Jeff Treadway, Cincinnati's second baseman—58 being a rookie number generally seen only in spring training and the final month of the season. The second sign was the crowd: only nineteen thousand for a Friday against the Reds, who were just five games out of first place in the other division and had Eric Davis, the most compelling player in the National League.

Wrigley Field was different when September began. Family vacations were over and the Cubs were out of the race—but there was more to it than that. Why would there be thirty-one thousand people for Houston on the last Friday of August and nineteen thousand for Cincinnati on the first Friday of September? Many of the suburban and parochial schools were back in session, but the Chicago city schools weren't scheduled to start until Tuesday (although they wouldn't even then, because of an impending teachers' strike). It was simply September. The Cubs were not a September team.

The temperature was 72 degrees on September fourth, with a light breeze, and those who had come to Wrigley Field for

183

the first home game of the month were rewarded by late-season tranquillity and the big breaking ball of Scott Sanderson, who shut out the Reds on four hits through seven innings. "The Reds look dead," said Jeweler Joe. The Cubs led 3-0 going into the eighth, and Smith relieved Sanderson. Smith struck out Eric Davis and Dave Parker in the eighth, held the lead that inning, and retired the first Cincinnati man in the ninth. The next three singled. "Nothing ends quickly at Wrigley Field," Joe said. Howard Hankin, who had left the more fertile Frosty-Malt territory of the grandstand to spend the last inning with his business buddies of the bleachers, paced nervously and called the umpire a crook. Kal Daniels drove in the Reds' second run with a drive off the wall in left. DiPino relieved Smith, and Dave Concepcion, pinch hitting for number 58, singled off Dunston's glove to tie the game. The Reds took the lead on a sacrifice fly by Parker.

The sharp little lefty, John Franco, pitched the ninth for Cincinnati, no doubt remembering the day in May when Dernier jolted him with a game-winning home run. On this late afternoon, Martinez and Dawson managed infield singles against him, and with two outs, he faced off with Dayett. The muscular right-handed batter had power to right-center field, and that was where he sent a pitch from Franco on a deep, promising arc. From where I sat in the right-center-field bleachers, it was apparent that the ball would not clear the fence but would probably reach it, the principal question being whether Eric Davis would arrive sooner or later. As Davis sprinted back and to his left, out of my view, I couldn't help but think about the several spectacular catches he had made during the season, taking away home runs and doubles and winning games with utterly improbable defense. The drama surrounding Davis and this fly ball was precisely why it was so difficult to explain the magnetism of baseball to anybody who didn't already understand. To someone unfamiliar with the litany of heroics from Eric Davis, this was just a high fly and a guy running for it, neither of them visible. There was nothing to see. It was a play not for the eye, but for the imagination. As the ball descended toward the fence, with the

sleek Davis down there, somewhere, running headlong after
it, the invisibility of the play from where I sat lent a heightened sense of expectation. Could he do it again? How much
magic could there be in one ballplayer? Martinez crossed the
plate, and as Dawson came around too, there was confusion
in the park. And then the Reds and their trainer were running
out toward Davis. He was hurt.

As Davis lay injured out of my sight, it seemed that even
greatness could be futile sometimes. But knowing that he had
crashed full speed into the brick wall, cushioned only by ivy
that was already losing its green, I wondered if maybe, when
ability was insufficient, the great players didn't occasionally
state their greatness with sacrifice instead. Then I turned to
look at the scoreboard, and I saw a zero for the Cubs in the
ninth. I couldn't believe it. I had seen both runners come
around, and the Reds running out after their injured star; I'd
assumed the reason there hadn't been a tremendous cheer at
winning the game was because the fans were silenced by
watching the thin, daring centerfielder crumble at the wall.
But he had caught the ball. The zero was a little blurry when I
looked at it again.

Howard watched the replay and then slammed his fist
down on the counter of the concession stand. "Why did he
have to catch that ball?" he bellowed.

The replay showed that while Davis was on the ground, a
bleacher fan threw a cup of beer at him.

Davis was not in the lineup Saturday, his shoulder banged
up from the game-saving catch. The Reds had another one of
their September call-ups in center field, Leo Garcia, which
brought to attention the relative value of Davis and other
players in the league. I asked Mark for his ideas on the Most
Valuable Player.

The problem with the MVP award is that it has never been
defined. People with baseball opinions have their own notions
of what the award ought to be, and to Mark the MVP was the
guy who made the most difference in the final standings, the
one whom a winning team could least do without. I could

accept that. He said his choice in the National League was Bob Brenly. *Bob What?* He argued that, since the Giants had improved so dramatically at throwing out opposing base stealers, their catcher, the very uncelebrated Brenly, must have been having a terrific year. I charged him with going out of his way to be obscure, and he confessed.

As I well knew by this time, it was just less than a six-hour drive from Cincinnati to Chicago, and carloads of Reds' fans had made the trip for the weekend. Most of them hadn't been at the park on Friday, Cincinnati not being the kind of town where people take off work for baseball games. But they were generously rewarded Saturday when the Reds routed Ed Lynch early and led 7–0 in the fourth.

The Cubs' rookie catcher, Damon Berryhill, pinch hit in the seventh, and no sooner had I noted that his nickname ought to be Blue than the alert Wrigley Field organist was playing the song about the place where Fats Domino found his thrill. Moved by this and the lopsided score, Mark and I entered into a more liberal discussion of nicknames in general, the theme being that the best ones have been left unchosen by the professional sports franchises of America. To wit, we thought that perhaps if Denver got a major-league team, it could call it the Omelette. Or maybe there could be expansion into Alabama—the Mobile Home. Why the redundant Phillies instead of the Philadelphia Cream Cheese? How about the Boston Strangler, or the Baked Beans, or the Cream Pie? The New York New York? Out west, in the Famous Person Division: the Eugene O'Neill and the Helena Rubenstein. Consider the possibilities on the international level: the Peking Duck, the Manila Folders (a team the Cubs could play in September), the Bonn Bons, the Nice Andnephew.

The Cubs knocked out Dennis Rasmussen in the seventh to pull within 7–5, but the Reds scored three more in the ninth against Jay Baller. As the Cubs went down in the bottom of the ninth, dropping to .500 for the season, Mark and I restructured baseball. Though we would never be close on Bob Brenly, we agreed that the ideal number of teams in a division was eight, so that winning it would be an accomplishment worthy of a six-month struggle. We agreed there should be some form of interleague play, so that Atlanta could see Don Mattingly and Baltimore could see Ozzie Smith. We agreed that it would be appropriate to have a team in Mexico City, and possibly in San Juan.

That resolved, what would we do the rest of the month?

Before Sunday's game began, there was a fight on the plaza that drew blood. The incidence of fights seemed to pick up on the last days of series with St. Louis or Cincinnati, particularly if St. Louis or Cincinnati had done well in the previous games, and Sunday afternoon in general was shaping up as a hazardous one. It was hot, the wind was blowing out, and Les Lancaster was pitching for the Cubs against the Reds' Ted Power, the man who had cursed Wrigley Field the last time he had pitched in it against the wind. A woman in a wheelchair was hit in the head by a ball during batting practice.

Meanwhile, in the left-field bleachers, Jerry Pritikin was chatting amiably with his pal on the Reds, Kal Daniels. Earlier in the year, Daniels had thrown a ball to the bleacher fans in left, and Pritikin was so impressed that he wrote Daniels to tell him what a swell guy he was. The Bleacher Preacher gave Daniels his blessing to hit well against all other teams and Lee Smith. Pritikin was in a light mood anyway, because Harry Caray had referred to him on the air as the Cubs' number-one fan.

In right field, Nick Wagener assumed his standing position behind the bleachers and examined the batting averages in the Sunday newspaper. I said hello, and he said, "Did you believe Michael's strategy yesterday, when he had second and third with one out and Larkin up, with the pitcher next? Don't you walk Larkin in that spot?" Larkin had hit a three-run homer. "That's just more fuel to get him fired." His buddy Vic, the forklift operator, showed up in a red hat, and Nick assailed him. "What are you doing with a red hat? Harry will look out here, and all he sees is the color, and he'll say, 'It looks like a lot of Reds fans out there today.'"

Durham, a Cincinnati man who often watches football with Power in the off-season, homered inside the right-field foul pole in the first. In the third, he homered into the first row of bleachers, where a Reds fan caught the ball and threw it back. It was 3–1 after three.

It was still 3–1 after five, the unlikely Lancaster holding off the Reds on a day that seemed suitable for hitting. If the rookie could win, it would be his sixth victory in the major leagues against just one defeat—this, despite the fact that two years before he had graduated from college and was pitching semipro ball back home in Texas. The Cubs had signed him only because they needed arms to fill out a rookie-league roster. Lancaster was, in fact, an explicit example of the kind of athlete who was discriminated against by the sophisticated devices of contemporary scouting. He didn't throw the ball ninety-five miles an hour, but he threw it over home plate.

The lead held through seven innings, and Ronnie Woo-Woo went down the rows slapping hands and signing autographs. Somebody tossed a tennis shoe onto the playing field. After a while, the other shoe dropped. Then came a pair of thongs. The Reds' rightfielder, Paul O'Neill, tossed the shoes back, and then more came down. "O'Neill!" screamed one bleacher fan. "You blatant product of interbreeding!"

"Hey, O'Neill," yelled Nick. "Bend over and say cheese." O'Neill was a young player who might return for many years to Wrigley's right field, and the fans there felt compelled to find out about him. "You get on them, and every now and then they'll overthrow," said Nick. "Especially Jeff Leonard. He hates it, and when a ball comes to him he'll really try to cut loose, and then he'll overthrow. You can see it, too, sometimes, when they go up to hit. There are three ways they can react. They can ignore you, they can laugh with you, or they can give it back. Glenn Wilson likes to give it back. He'll turn around and give somebody the finger, talk back to the fans. One guy called him a bum and he said, 'Yeah, but I'm a million-dollar bum.' O'Neill, I don't know—it looks like he might be a hothead."

The next inning, O'Neill went up and slapped a single. But Lancaster got out of it with a double play, and Smith came in to pitch the ninth. A guy next to Nick said something about another easy save, but he was saying it to the wrong guy. "So this is an easy save, two runs ahead in the ninth?" answered Nick. "What isn't an easy save?"

It was Smith's thirty-fourth, the most in his career, and the Cubs were back over .500 going into the last holiday of the season.

On Labor Day, a small child walked with his family past Yum Yum Donuts on Clark Street, holding a small sign in front of him that said AWESOME DAWSON, and showing it proudly to anyone who went by. Down by the ticket windows, two other kids saw Harry Caray walking toward the entrance to the Cubs' offices, and their mother stood by, buoyantly attentive, as they hurried over for his autograph.

The bleacher ticket window was still open before the game, a sure sign that the summer rush was over and the season had begun to recede. There was little of the normal activity around the ballpark, except on Waveland, where, as always, the neighborhood ballhawks were chasing down batting-practice home runs. As they waited casually by the intersection of Kenmore, a baseball came flying over the left-field wall. The boys and men descended upon it, and the one who grabbed the ball burst out laughing as soon as he looked at it. There was a message written between the seams: Nice Catch, Asshole. It turned out that Jeff Robinson, a Pittsburgh relief pitcher, had tossed the ball to somebody in the bleachers, who in turn had heaved it out of the park. The Bleacher Preacher had witnessed this and promptly identified Robinson as an arch menace.

Pritikin was also not keen on The Chicken, who was at Wrigley Field for the Labor Day game with the Pirates. The Preacher's bone to pick with The Chicken had to do with 1984, when the famous fowl visited Wrigley Field and was quite the fine-feathered friend; but then, when the Cubs played the last three games of the playoffs in San Diego—The Chicken's native city, of course—the big bird was all for the Padres. Pritikin, naturally, had a sign for the occasion: PLUCK THE CHICKEN.

It rained lightly before the game, and under the cover of the scoreboard a young child climbed around on the bleachers while his father stood against the back fence and smoked a joint. Then Jamie Moyer struck out four men in the first two innings. Unfortunately, though, his opponent was the inexplicably difficult Brian Fisher, who had shut out the Cubs twice during a season in which he was considerably less troublesome to the rest of the league. He held the Cubs to two runs for seven innings. Moyer, meanwhile, held the Pirates to two hits over that time, which was the kind of performance that would give Cub fans sufficient reason to be optimistic again in the spring of '88.

But the Pirates got to him for two runs in the eighth, and led 3–2, when The Chicken completed his shenanigans on the field and repaired to the upper section of bleachers to mingle with his constituents and do his part for the Cub cause. In the interest of the latter, he climbed inside the scoreboard, stuck his head through one of the inning holes, then moved the 2 from the Pirate eighth into the Cub eighth. Then he found the 23 left over from the Mets game in August, and slipped that into place in the home team's behalf.

There would be no justification forthcoming from the Cubs, however, as the rascally Robinson took over and became the eleventh man in National League history to strike out the side on nine pitches, buzzing down Durham, Dawson, and Palmeiro. In the ninth, he retired Moreland and Dunston on two pitches, then Mumphrey singled. Chico Walker, back from the minors, was thrown out stealing as a pinch runner. It would be the last out under Gene Michael's term as manager of the Cubs.

That evening, after the rest of the reporters had left, Michael told a radio man named Bruce Levine that he didn't want to be the Cubs' manager in 1988. Amidst all the standard discussion of whether the manager would be rehired for the next year, Levine had been the only one to ask Michael whether he *wanted* the job again. This had happened about ten days previously. The question made Michael pause and brighten. He said he'd never really thought about it that way before; traditionally, a manager's job was one that a man held until fired. Michael told Levine to ask him the same question in ten days or so. Then, after the Labor Day loss that dropped the Cubs back to .500, Michael and Levine sat down in an empty office, and Stick said, "You remember that question you asked me last week?" Levine nodded. "Ask me again."

"Are you sure?" Levine said, explaining that once he made the story public, it would be distributed over the wires in a matter of minutes.

"I've made a decision." Michael told Levine that he'd been to the doctor that day and that his blood pressure was up. Additionally, it was no secret that he and Green had disagreed on several points, not the least of which was the Trout trade. "I'm not coming back next year."

It was a staunch position taken by a man whom many had considered too mild to be an effective manager. In fact, though his willowy frame and soft speech belied it, Michael had been a strong, stubborn manager from the start—at least in his relations with the autocratic Dallas Green. The previous September, after Michael had been hired in mid-season, Green had questioned Stick's commitment to the job. Michael, in turn, volleyed back that there was not adequate talent on the team to make the job workable—a response that demonstrated his resolve and won the point. Even then, though, Michael was never able to plant his feet in the position. In spring training, he had joked openly—it was couched as a joke, anyway—about not being around at the end of the year.

On September eighth, his feeling became self-fulfilling. Green regarded Michael's statements as a resignation, and accepted it immediately. Frank Lucchesi, a baseball warhorse who had been serving as the Cubs' "eye-in-the-sky" coach, watching games from the press box and passing on information to the dugout, was named interim manager. He was sixty years old and, for some time, had been working on a book about his long life in baseball, which included such stories as the time he was ejected from a game in Denver and threw second base into the stands on his way out, and the time he was ejected from a game in Syracuse and climbed a light pole in protest. He had settled down since then, twice managing in the majors, and his appointment seemed to be a wise one for several reasons. Lucchesi was not a candidate for the permanent job, but three of the Cubs' coaches were: Billy Williams, John Vukovich, and Johnny Oates. Green was not ready to name any of them as manager, and allowing one to fill the job temporarily would only have caused tension in the dugout. Also, a man auditioning for the job as manager would have felt compelled to prove himself by winning, and therefore might have been reluctant to award playing opportunities to the Cubs' prospects.

The Cubs' squatty new manager was greeted Tuesday by a rousing national anthem from Wayne and Jane Messmer, the Cubs' silk-throated public address announcer and his operatic wife, and by a bleak crowd of eight thousand—the smallest at Wrigley Field since the Pirates had visited in April. "The day after Labor Day, it's like they all fall into a hole," said Elsie, who, as usual, had come with her eighty-five-year-old friend, Al. Lucchesi's temporary appointment marked the forty-fourth time in Al's life that a new manager of the Cubs had taken over. He wasn't particularly sorry to see Michael leave, but would have preferred a more fundamental change. "Green is the son of a bitch they ought to get rid of," he said. "He's got a cash register for a brain."

A section over, Leonard Becker—who would be at most of the rest of the games now that the crowds were down and the Cubs were out of the race—was typically pleased about what happened. "I was one hundred percent glad to see Michael go," he said. "I was glad when Frey went, I was glad when Elia went, all of them. I wanted Michael gone at the beginning of the year."

While Lucchesi was making his debut as Cubs manager, a rookie right-handed pitcher for Pittsburgh named Vicente Palacios was starting a major-league game for the first time. The Pirates were generally considered to be the dregs of the National League East, but their general manager, Syd Thrift, had loaded their roster with promising young pitchers, of which Palacios was evidently one. He held the Cubs to six hits and one run in eight innings, and beat Sutcliffe 4–1. The Cubs and their new manager both had losing records. It had been a portentous afternoon.

When I got back to my apartment that evening, I thought about the irony of Michael leaving his job just as Jerry Pritikin had started pronouncing his name without an *s*. Just then, an announcer on WGN-TV said that they would be back with more on the resignation of Gene Michaels.

Sherman Redd had been selling peanuts at sporting events around town for four years, but it was his first season at Wrigley Field. It wasn't easy for street vendors to just move in on somebody else's territory; Chicago wasn't like that. Four years before, Sherman had quit his factory job to go into the vending business by himself, and he had done well with it. Bears games were a bonanza, and he said that he could make more from a crowd of ten thousand at Comiskey Park than a crowd of twenty thousand at Wrigley Field. The White Sox fans were more accustomed to seeing him, and also, not being travelers and business people to the same extent that the Cub fans were, probably had better eyes for a bargain. Sherman sold one-dollar and two-dollar bags of peanuts, and he had a little visual display set up to show his customers how many more peanuts they could get for their buck if they bought them before they walked through the gate. He considered everybody who went by to be his customer—he asked them all if they wanted peanuts—and by the end of the season, he had become a fixture, a large, friendly black man in sunglasses and a Cub shirt and cap. He set up on Sheffield, across from Murphy's and near the bleacher gate, and he figured that about thirty percent of the crowd walked past him at some point. The other peanut vendor, a short man named Jerry with a thick mustache, had been working Wrigley Field longer and was better known; he had the busy corner of Sheffield and Addison. But Sherman didn't do badly by the bleacher gate. He said that by June he had already made more money than he would have made in a whole year at the factory. It wasn't easy money, though; he worked at it. He came to Wrigley Field early every game day, and at breakfast it was usually he and eight policemen. It was helpful for the vendors to know the policemen, and also for the policemen to know the vendors. Sherman saw things. One day, he was watching when four guys came out of the park after a game and spotted the tall, skinny scalper who had sold them their tickets—evidently at a price they didn't like so much after a hot day and a few beers. The scalper was just going into one of the portable toilets next to Murphy's when the four men saw him, and when he wouldn't come out, they turned the toilet over and broke the window of a Mercedes parked behind it. The scalper ran off down the street toward the police station on Addison.

I asked Sherman what he thought of Michael leaving, and he did a little kick, like a twenty-two-yard field goal. "I'd like to see them give Green the boot, too," he said.

It was a sunny, breezy, gorgeous day, and the crowd was even smaller than the day before. The bleachers in right-center, though, were lively with regulars who preferred more intimate gatherings. Howard Hankin was still railing about the catch that Eric Davis had made the week before. "I was so disgusted Friday," he said, "I was literally sick to my stomach. Nobody else makes that catch. No other centerfielder. He's the best centerfielder in baseball." From up above, somebody yelled down that Henderson was the best centerfielder in baseball. "I'm talking *defensively*," said Howard, almost shouting by this time. "That guy is the best there is. He specializes in that kind of catch. He's the only guy who could have made that play. I was so disgusted. I lost twice on that game. I lost that one, and then I was so pissed off at the Cubs I bet against them Sunday and they won."

"I see that damn catch in my sleep," said Becker. "It was one of the worst losses I ever experienced."

"What about the Ontiveros game in '79?" yelled Howard. "That was the worst."

"Oh, Ontiveros," said Becker. "That's right. The day that will live in infamy."

Neither of them could remember exactly what it was about the Ontiveros game of 1979 that was so infamous, only that it was. "Ask Craig," said Becker.

Craig was one of the four blind men who had sat with the gamblers—they called them "pleasure players"—in the right-center-field bleachers for almost twenty years. The blind men held radios to their ears to follow the action, but being at the ballpark gave them a sense for the games that they couldn't get listening at home. "I go more as a social thing," said Craig, who also did sportscasts for a local radio station and had attended sixty games during the season. The game with the Pirates was the one thousand eighth that he had been to in his life, dating back to May 15, 1955, when he was five years old and the Cubs split a Sunday doubleheader with the Giants. Craig's friend, Dennis, also blind, had attended Cubs games in seven other National League ballparks. The four of them—Craig, Dennis, Howard, and Bob—knew as much about baseball as practically anybody in the bleachers.

"The Ontiveros game?" said Craig. "August 8, 1979."

Howard Hankin said he thought it was September. "Nope," said Craig. "Bob, wasn't it August eighth?"

"Oh, yeah," said Bob, "August eighth, the day of infamy."

"The Cubs were down by a run in the ninth with one out and runners on first and second," explained Craig. "Ontiveros was on second and Joey Amalfitano, the third-base coach, sent him home on a single, and he was out at the plate. But the thing was, either they had to have a pinch runner in there or stop him at third." It probably wouldn't have seemed so bad if there hadn't been so much at stake in the right-center-field bleachers.

Wade Rowdon, a third baseman called up from Iowa—where he'd been Most Valuable Player in the American Association—tripled in a run in his first at-bat as a Cub. But the Pirates led 2–1 after two innings, going for a sweep of the series. By the third, some of the beer vendors had already given up on the day and changed into their street clothes.

"I thought the old-timers would be here today," said Becker, looking around at the seats where all his bleacher buddies used to be. He shook his head and made a swipe of resignation with his hand. "They're through."

It was 3–2, Pirates, after five, and in the aisle behind section 147, Becker chatted casually with Jerry Pritikin. They were two men with completely different interests and backgrounds in the bleachers; a few years before, they would have had little in common to talk about. Now they did. They both had watched the bleachers change around them. Pritikin missed the kids in left field who saluted Sarge and made up cheers and did crazy, spontaneous things; Becker missed the old-timers in right-center who grumbled about umpires and bad managers and held wads of bills in their fists. They were just like two old men who had walked over from opposite directions to stand with their hands in their pockets and watch the wrecking ball smash in their old neighborhood schoolhouse.

Sanderson pitched well—that was what made him so frustrating: he was good—and the Cubs tied the game in the seventh. But the blond menace, Jeff Robinson, whom Pritikin still had not forgiven for the obscene baseball incident two days before, relieved for Pittsburgh in the eighth, then batted against Lee Smith with two outs in the top of the ninth. He startled everyone in the ballpark—even himself, he said later—with a high game-winning home run against the fence behind the left-field bleachers.

The last-place Pirates had beaten the Cubs twelve out of fifteen times and were only three-and-a-half games behind them. September was lengthening.

"In 1984," said Jeff Odenwald, the Cubs' director of marketing, "somebody asked me, 'Is it going to ruin everything if you win it all?'

"It was a good question. I don't know."

The Cubs were a good example of why, for almost a hundred years, baseball didn't need directors of marketing. This was a team that had actually cashed in on *losing*. Since the sad 1969 season—at which time they were twenty-four years removed from a pennant—the Cubs had been like the little kid who got his lunch money taken every day, and the fans had pulled them to their bosoms like loving mothers: *Aw, it's okay, little Cubbies.* This was a professional sports team that, like no other, sold itself by being adorable. The irony was that the Cubs couldn't win for losing, but they won *by* losing. Would winning a pennant have cost the Cubs their cuteness?

Jeff Odenwald couldn't answer that question, and he probably didn't want to. His concern wasn't winning and losing, anyway, but selling it, whatever *it* was. Baseball was in a marketing age. In the commercial sense, it had moved out of the stadiums and into living rooms and offices, onto backs and ears. Ten years before, only half the teams in the major leagues even had marketing departments; in 1987 the Cubs' marketing department would generate ten to twelve percent of the team's revenues. "It's no longer a game where you can print up the schedule and open the gate," Odenwald said in his Wrigley Field office on September tenth, an off-day for the ballclub. "We've got to realize we're in the entertainment business. The attitude used to be that we're in the sports pages every day; we don't need to advertise. Those days are long gone." In many ways, his job was one that did itself. The Cubs were a precious commodity. All Odenwald had to do was get them to market.

To that end, the Cubs published their own monthly newspaper, *Vine Line*, with a paid circulation of more than twenty thousand; late in 1987, they came out with a cassette tape version. They offered paid memberships in their official Die-Hard Cub Fan Club. They sold Cub merchandise inside and outside Wrigley Field—there were nineteen souvenir stands on the streets adjacent to the ballpark; the Cubs owned the ones within their block. And in 1987, they would send out about one hundred fifty thousand gift catalogs containing more than two hundred items—pins, pens, buttons, watches, clocks, glasses, golf balls, pennants, plates, lamps, chairs, telephones, bedspreads, sweatshirts, shower curtains, coolers, flags, patio furniture, duffel bags, and a Cub-striped Toyota van—all branded by the Cub logo, the blue circle around a big red *C* with *UBS* inside. "The logo is very important," said Odenwald. "We've experimented with a lot of things, but we haven't toyed with the logo. The pinstripes and the bull's-eye logo are as much a tradition as the ivy. I really don't know how much we spend every year just in decals. I do know that we printed up four million WGN-Cubs bumper stickers in four years."

But for all of the catalogs and memberships and newspapers, there was still nothing that could bring the Cubs to the people like television. They were a made-for-TV team. To begin with, WGN had been a pioneer in television technology for baseball. More important than that, though, was the studio. A baseball telecast is a series of moving pictures, and no matter what the teams or the score, the attractiveness of the show depends in part upon the prettiness of the pictures. There was no ballpark as pretty as Wrigley Field. Nor was there one as literally and figuratively colorful. And no other team had Harry Caray.

"Harry is the greatest salesperson we've got," said Odenwald. "He's got a cult following. People like to envision that he runs all night, gets a few hours sleep and is hung over when he gets here—the mayor of Rush Street, all of that. They like to think that Harry is one of them. Ernie Banks in his heyday was what Harry is now."

The next day, the Montreal Expos were back in Chicago, and Al Yellon was in his usual back-row seat in the right-field bleachers. Yellon was a director at a local television station, and an unofficial expert on the Cubs' TV history. "Television helped create baseball in this city," he said. "I believe in it that strongly."

In many ways, the Cubs were not only made *for* television, but *by* television. Cub home games were first televised by station WBKB in 1946—which, fortuitously, was the year following the team's last pennant. The next season, with Whisperin' Joe Wilson and Jack Brickhouse at the mike, WBFB initiated an enduring Cub tradition by broadcasting a full schedule of home games. The new station WGN hired Brickhouse away and began challenging WBFB in 1948, and in 1949 the two of them were joined by yet another station, WENR. But despite the apparent overexposure and a last-place team in 1949, the Cubs still drew more than a million fans, demonstrating that the televising of home games—at least in Chicago—did not borrow from the crowd at the ball-park but instead recruited new customers.

By 1952, the competition had fallen aside and WGN had exclusive rights to Cub telecasts. The same year, Hank Sauer hit a home run and Brickhouse, carried away by the moment, shouted "Hey! Hey!" into the microphone. It was a hokey piece of provincialism that was just right for the ever-hopeful hearts of Cub fans, and he would do it for every subsequent Cub home run until his retirement twenty-nine years later. In 1962, a minute and a half of a game with the Phillies became part of the first intercontinental broadcast over the Telstar satellite, and was seen in Rome, Vienna, and Stockholm. Back in Chicago, though, WGN was televising the home games of both local teams, and the Cubs were losing out in the direct competition with the South Siders. From 1951 through 1967, the White Sox outdrew the Cubs in sixteen of the seventeen seasons.

Chicago was not sworn in its preference for the American League, however, and in 1968 its affections were alienated. The Sox and Cubs both had made runs at their respective pennants in 1967, and afterward each club thought it should have an exclusive television contract. Since the contract between WGN and the White Sox expired after the 1967 season, the station had no recourse but to drop the Sox, who then turned to UHF channel WFLD. The next year, the White Sox finished two games out of last place, and the third-place Cubs drew a million fans for the first time since 1952. Over the twenty seasons that followed, with the Cubs anchored on WGN and the White Sox floating around between various stations, the Cubs had higher attendance fourteen times. It was fortuitous again for the Cubs that when they gained their exclusivity with WGN in 1968, the team that Chicago watched every day was the Banks-Williams-Santo bunch. Coincidence notwithstanding, though, it is apparent that television rights were what swung Chicago to the Cubs. Chicago became a Cub town partly because Ron Santo clicked his heels and partly because the Bleacher Bums wore yellow helmets in left field, but mostly because television was there to take pictures.

"The timing has been right for the Cubs in a lot of different ways as far as TV," said Yellon. "In 1948, WGN just got in under the deadline before the FCC froze licenses for five years. Who knows what might have happened if WGN hadn't been involved? And in '68, when the Cubs and White Sox split off, the White Sox went on a UHF station at a time when not everybody could pick up UHF on their televisions." After the White Sox changed hands in 1981, their announcer, Harry Caray, became available to WGN just as it was beginning to send Cubs games nationwide over the superstation. So successful was the Cub-Caray connection that in 1984 the Cubs were Chicago's top-rated show every day of the season from the middle of June on—regardless of whether they played at Wrigley Field at 1:20, Shea Stadium at 6:35, or Dodger Stadium at 9:35.

Though he didn't get to see the end of many of them—he had to be at work at 3:30—Yellon made it to eighty home games in that memorable season of 1984. He monitored every one of them closely and preserved his scorecards to keep cumulative totals on the Cub games he had attended in his life. He had been doing this since he was a kid, and despite the fact that he had to leave early so often, by late 1987 he had seen more than a thousand home runs at Wrigley Field.

There were four of them Friday, including Durham's twenty-sixth and Moreland's twenty-fifth in the fourth inning, when the Cubs scored three runs against Montreal's Floyd Youmans. Sandberg homered in the fifth, after which the score was 6–1 behind Lancaster, who had suddenly become the most effective pitcher on the staff after Sutcliffe. Actually, Sutcliffe hadn't won in six weeks, primarily due to minor surgery for a growth on the index finger of his pitching hand. For the moment, Lester Lancaster was Chicago's ace.

If he produced a victory Friday, it would be his seventh

against one defeat, and the first for Lucchesi as manager. The latter development would make Jerry Pritikin happy, inasmuch as Lucchesi had phoned the Bleacher Preacher earlier in the day to thank him for the nice note Pritikin had sent the new manager. They had chatted for a while, although not about Lee Smith. Pritikin showed up at the ballpark Friday wearing a black armband in the name of Smith.

It was a cool day and another small crowd. The beer vendors in the bleachers carried only one case at a time. On the other side of Waveland Avenue, somebody had posted a bull's-eye on an apartment building, with a reference to Andre Dawson aiming at fifty home runs. The pennant race was no longer an issue; the objective among the fans now was to see Dawson hit fifty.

In the center-field bleachers, a woman named Lynn Morgan was wonderfully happy not because it was her thirty-sixth birthday, but because she had been at a group breakfast with Andre Dawson. Friday was her day out with the girls, and she arrived at Wrigley Field with her fingernails painted blue and with two American and two Canadian flags to wave while Wayne Messmer sang his booming renditions of both national anthems. "The Cubs are to me what cocaine is to some people," she said. "In 1984, I was having a bad year. Everything was going wrong. For some reason, I started watching WGN, and it happened to be that great season. The Cubs saved me. I've been coming out here whenever I can ever since. I taught my son to read by reading the scoreboard."

The Cubs got two more in the sixth, and a man walked by with a T-shirt that said: I DRANK 200 BEERS AT THE STADIUM. In right-center, Jack Lindenberg pointed to his old bleacher buddy, the gray-bearded Leonard Becker, and said, "This man is forty-seven years old. Look at what the Cubs did to him." Becker's nephew was with them, and commented that he would like to catch a home-run ball. "You can get a hundred to one on that," said Becker.

Drew Hall, the left-handed rookie, relieved Lancaster for the last three outs of an easy 8–4 victory that brought the

Cubs back to within a game of .500, and I left for Milwaukee with Mark Wilmot. We sat in the bleachers as Ted Higuera beat Detroit, and we watched the scoreboard as the Reds held off the Giants 4–3; as the Cardinals scored three in the ninth to tie the Mets and two in the tenth to win; and as Minnesota came from 7–1 down and 10–7 in the ninth to beat Cleveland 13–10 in eleven. The pennant races were unfolding in front of us, inning by inning. That was one baseball thing that didn't happen at Wrigley Field, except on Sundays.

On the other hand, we noticed that nobody in the bleachers at County Stadium had much of a tan.

Bob Henner was a commodities broker, and the exchange closed at one o'clock. September twelfth was his fifty-third game of the year, which said something about the comparative amount of discretionary income available to young people in the 1980s. "When my dad was a kid," he said, "his dad got some tickets to one of the Cubs' World Series games in the thirties. He was looking forward to it for weeks. When they got here, the tickets were selling for so much, and they needed the money so much, that his dad sold them. My dad cried all the way home. That's his biggest memory of coming out here."

Coming out *here*, he said. How many places are there where a young man can talk about his dad coming out *here* as a kid? Wrigley Field was a hand-me-down ballpark. When Bob was a kid, he would go there every Opening Day, and for his parental excuse at school, he would write the score on a piece of paper and his dad would sign it. In 1987, Bob sat in the center-field bleachers with several ballpark friends in their twenties and thirties, and his dad stayed home and watched WGN. "He's one of those guys that got bitter over the years," said Bob. "He'll be watching the game and the Cubs will have the lead, and his attitude is, 'How are they gonna blow it this time?' "

Pascual Perez, the talented and unpredictable former Braves pitcher who in his brief time with Montreal, unlike his Atlanta days, had been neither imprisoned nor lost on a circular freeway, was much more than Jamie Moyer could match on Saturday. With Perez picking on the home team, the Cub fans took solace in the news that the Mets' Ron Darling would miss the rest of the year with an injury. "The thing is," said Mark, "Darling is the Met I can most tolerate. But I still like it." The Mets and Cardinals were playing a day game, and a spontaneous cheer went up when a "5" was posted for St. Louis in the first against Gooden.

In right field, a young woman sat quietly while her boyfriend was off getting concessions. Nearby, Vic, the forklift operator, explained why he didn't keep score like other serious fans. "I feel like life is passing me by," he said. "I work in a warehouse, and I can't see outside. I don't know if it's raining or the sun is shining or what. I get off work, sleep four hours, come out here, go home, sleep a little more, and go back to work. When I sit out here, I don't want to be looking down at a pad."

Mitch Webster homered to left, and the erstwhile quiet young woman cupped her hands around her mouth and shouted, "Throw it back!" They wouldn't. "Boo!" They still wouldn't. She was standing now, shouting independently. "Left field sucks!"

Of the three teams still in the divisional race, most of the Cub fans preferred the Expos to win. On this day, they did, by a score of 7–1.

Sunday was Scarf Day, which said something about the way September is regarded in Chicago. It was also the first day of the NFL season. The Bears weren't playing until Monday night, when the New York Giants would be at Soldier Field—a huge opener between the Super Bowl champions of the previous two years—but the sports fans of Chicago were thinking football; police confiscated more than half a million dollars worth of wagers Sunday. At Wrigley Field, meanwhile, there were twenty-five thousand people to watch Sutcliffe pitch against Bryn Smith—the smallest Sunday crowd since April.

As it often did to the Cubs this time of year, the future had jumped up and down and waved its arms in the eyes of the present, the consequence on September thirteenth being that Mumphrey and Moreland were out of the lineup in favor of Rowdon and Palmeiro. In the first, Rowdon made his third error in his five most recent chances, and a bleacher man yelled, "If we wanted errors, Rowdon, we'd have Moreland in there." Sutcliffe surrendered an unearned run, but no others until the seventh. Meanwhile, the inscrutable Durham, whose expendability had been convincing just weeks before, continued to confuse his detractors with a rally of productive hitting, and Sutcliffe went the distance with a 5–2 lead, making it stick. This was cause enough to account for a great waving of giveaway scarves, a chipper display of fidelity from the twenty-five thousand who preferred not to stay home and watch football.

One of the ushers had said he could get me tickets to the Bears game, and my wife had joined me for the weekend with this in mind. He had been unable to deliver, however, and so we stopped in and caught the White Sox and Twins on our way out of town Monday night. We asked Mark if he and Laurie were interested in joining us, but they had tickets to a speech by Helmut Schmidt.

Actually, Helmut Schmidt ran a good chance of outdrawing the White Sox. We arrived at game time, parked across the street from the ticket window, and bought seats on the first-base line. We could have bought them anywhere, or sat anywhere regardless of the tickets. Two fellows with grandstand tickets asked an usher if it was all right to sit down in the boxes, and the usher just smiled. The attendance was announced at eight thousand, but in the American League— unlike the National, where crowds were determined by the number of people in the ballpark—attendance was figured by the number of tickets sold. In the third inning, I counted the people sitting in half the ballpark, and there were six hundred. One of them held up a sign that said: I'D RATHER BE AT SOLDIER FIELD. Others brought minitelevisions and watched the football game from the baseball park.

There were four people in the bleachers when the game started. By the sixth, the crowd out there had swollen to nine.

My wife read *Wanderlust* by Danielle Steel, and I moved behind the screen to try to figure out why the Twins couldn't hit Dave LaPoint. Bill Veeck's exploding scoreboard showed that the Cubs led the Mets in New York, 4–2. The vendors strolled around the grandstand, pausing to watch the football game whenever they passed one of the little TVs.

A friend of mine, Steve, said he had been to a game like this in Cleveland once. He was sitting there, alone, and the beer vendor walked by and said, "You want a beer?" So Steve bought a beer, but the vendor just kind of hung around. Thinking there must have been a problem, Steve asked the guy if he hadn't given him enough money. "No, everything's all right," the vendor said. "I've got nowhere to go, so I just figured I'd wait till you finished your beer and see if you wanted another one."

Comiskey was a comfortable stadium, the oldest in the major leagues, but there seemed to be little objection to the plan to move the White Sox into a new facility. Without ivy and sunshine and apartment buildings on every side, people just thought of Comiskey as an old ballpark rather than a sacred institution. It was the ballpark for neither the chic nor the corporate, just for people who wanted to catch a game after work. The food and the lines of vision were good. The crowds weren't; but to a baseball fan, that only meant that you could sit closer.

LaPoint was working on a shutout in the ninth, and when he walked his third straight batter, the biggest cheer of the night went up. The Bears had scored. The Sox won 8–2. In New York, the Cubs lost 6–5.

There was no hollering on the ramp—there was no hollering and no ramp—and in less than a minute we were at our car. A kid was already there waiting to wash the windows for a buck. In another minute, we were on the Dan Ryan South, listening to the Bears pound the Giants. My wife closed her eyes, and I switched over to hear Schmidt beat the Cardinals with a hit in the eleventh.

I had to wear socks and a sweatshirt to Wrigley Field on Monday, September 21. Baseball's cycle had nearly com-

pleted itself; it felt like it had in April. In that way, baseball
has a symmetry unlike any other sport. It picks people up on
one end of summer and drops them off at the other. Football
is not nearly so considerate, luring its fans into the fair air of
early autumn and then dumping them into the snow of the
new year. Professional basketball has no seasonal integrity
whatsoever. The college game does, warming its followers
through the coldest months, but, being a game played in
shorts, after all, it doesn't take people *through* the winter, but
out of it.

Sad to say, baseball, too, had been climate-controlled in
many cities, but Chicago was thankful not to be one of them.
On September twenty-first, Elsie and Al moved back to the
section of right-center-field bleachers protected from the
wind, and the New York Mets played the last-place team in
the National League East.

It had happened the day before, when the Cubs lost in St.
Louis while the Pirates beat the Mets in fourteen innings. The
team that had been in first place in May, and had played the
Cardinals for first place in June, was last. Dawson was still an
MVP candidate, and Sutcliffe still had a shot at the Cy
Young, and Martinez was looking better every day, and Palmeiro was beginning to hit, and Lancaster was quite a sur-
prise, and Durham and Moreland were hitting the long ball,
and Sandberg was still one of the best, and Smith had all
those saves. But the Cubs, who hadn't finished last since
1981, were last.

Funny—all year long people had been saying, Where would
the Cubs be without Dawson? And here they were, with Dawson and in last. Dawson had hit his forty-fifth home run in
Sunday's loss in St. Louis. Somebody asked Whitey Herzog
where the Cubs would be without Dawson; he said, "Triple
A."

The Monday crowd was eight thousand, and they were
good fans. When Veeck had owned the White Sox, he used to
walk around the ballpark this time of year taking names—
keeping a list of fans he'd seen all season, so that they were on
the priority list for tickets. Marcy, the woman I'd met at

spring training, had prearranged to take a week of vacation for the last homestand—Mets, Phillies, and Cardinals—knowing that even if the Cubs were out of the race, the weather would probably be pleasant and the bleachers agreeably unpopulated. "Don't you think, with the Cubs being last, it might help Dawson in the MVP voting?" she said, thinking—hoping—that perhaps a last-place finish might call attention to Dawson's island of accomplishment. Leave it to a Cub fan to find a four-leaf clover in the wasteland of last place. Marcy, however, was more than a Cub fan: she had just gotten cable TV installed at her apartment in Rogers Park and was already looking forward to the Cardinal-Met series the last weekend of the season. Although we didn't discuss her eating and drinking habits, it was a fact that she slept baseball. "I dreamt that the Cubs got Von Hayes," she said on September twenty-first. "But I can't remember who they traded for him."

Norb Kudele was in Europe and Mark Wilmot had taken a part-time job with a messenger company because of the teachers' strike, but most of the hard-core were there. Steve Herzberg, the tie-dyed friend of leftfielders, like Marcy had reserved his vacation for the final week of the home season, and it was the first time all year he'd been to Wrigley Field without his wife. Dancing Annie was there with her friend's son, teaching him how to keep score and heckle Strawberry. To the weekday September crowd, last place was no reason to give up on baseball. "I hope they finish last," said Leonard Becker. "It would be a distinction."

And high up in center field, I saw my friend the nacho man. He was wearing his painter's cap and the old plaid jacket he had been wearing in April, when I saw him last. Where had he been all summer? Was he working? He seemed too old to work. Did he dislike the hot weather? The crowds? Was he all right? What did he think of Dawson? Lancaster? Did he think the Cardinals would hold on? Did he want lights? I knew he wouldn't tell me any of these things. I remembered that back in April I had been determined to get to know him a little bit, to make him talk, but April was a long time ago. I looked at him sitting up there by the scoreboard, all by himself, chewing his nachos, and I conceded.

In right field, meanwhile, somebody yelled that left field sucked, but there was little interest. Jerry Pritikin walked behind the bleachers and shouted, "We're number six!" Somebody had a sign that said: BACK UP THE TRUCK—GOOD-BYE, DALLAS. People talked about 1988, which looked more promising every time Lancaster pitched, as he was doing Monday against Gooden.

It was 1–1 through the middle innings, and the rookie retired fourteen batters in a row. In the fifth, Mike Brumley led off with a single for the Cubs, stole second, and stayed there. Marcy was frustrated by the Cubs' inability to move their runners along. In the sixth, they had two on and two out with Durham batting. From right-center, you could see Gooden's big curve catching the outside corner, and as the count went full, Marcy and I tried to guess what pitch was coming up. All through the crowded days of summer, I had never discussed what pitch was coming up. I decided that September was the best time of year at Wrigley Field, and Durham struck out on a fastball.

In the eighth, Strawberry broke Lancaster's string of outs with a single up the middle, and Kevin McReynolds batted. Somebody shouted, "Get this asshole out," but Lancaster walked him intentionally. "Oh, no," said Pritikin. "Now they'll take him out if there's another hit." Lucchesi had been suspended for two days for a run-in with an umpire in St. Louis and, sure enough, Johnny Oates, the acting manager, replaced Lancaster with Ed Lynch after Gary Carter got an infield single to load the bases. In right-center, opinions were undivided that it was the wrong move. Lancaster had retired fourteen in a row, given up one decent single and another scratch one, and the two guys in the bullpen—Lynch and Drew Hall—had earned run averages of 5.06 and 7.27. Lancaster said later that he had a little blister on his finger, but he also said he would have liked the opportunity to pitch to Howard Johnson with the bases loaded.

Johnson, a switch-hitter batting left-handed against Lynch,

hit several foul balls hard down the left-field line, and the count went to 3 and 2. It was a good battle, but through it all, there prevailed a sense that the upper hand was Johnson's. Lynch walked behind the mound to rub the ball and think through what he was going to do; Johnson stood and waited. The impression was that Lynch was trying too hard, making his own job too difficult. There was no way to know this, of course; it was just a feeling picked up from watching a lot of ballgames. Johnson hit a grand slam that landed close to where we sat.

When it did, a blonde woman nearby rushed toward the guy who had caught the ball and demanded that he throw it back. She was quite serious about this. He kept the ball, and she moved closer to him, adamant. I thought of the gung-ho female in the play *Bleacher Bums* whose character had been the only one I couldn't match up with anybody I had seen in the bleachers. Now I could. Dramatized by an acceptable degree of literary latitude, this could have been the woman. She was smartly dressed in clean white jeans and matching jacket and had come to Wrigley Field with three other women—none of which had any mitigating effect upon her passion for the Cubs and bleacher protocol. Finally, the man succumbed and threw the ball back, and when the woman in white returned to her seat, her jaw was set in stubborn satisfaction. The final was 7–1, and when it was over, she said, "Thursday's a Jewish holiday. My boss will let me off and I'm coming back here, because I'm not going to end the season on a loss."

Outside Gate N afterwards, I saw a guy I recognized from the center-field bleachers. His name was Jim Cote, a broker at the Chicago Mercantile Exchange, and he almost always sat with baseball buddies in the bleachers despite the fact that he had weekend season tickets in the box seats. He had bought the season tickets primarily so he could qualify for playoff and World Series tickets, in the event.

Jim was not one to partake of what was trendy—he had moved to center field from left to get away from the goings-on—and his favorite neighborhood bar, consequently, was an unassuming Japanese-American place on Sheffield, where he invited me for a delicious and prodigious bowl of *yet ce mein* soup. As we sat down, Jim said hello to a guy named Al, who was a regular at the bar because his buddy owned it and his wife worked at the diner next door. The first thing Al said was, "They should have never taken Lancaster out in that situation."

Jerry Pritikin arrived early Tuesday and brought his Frisbee to throw with Roger McDowell, the Mets' relief pitcher. There was almost nobody in the bleachers other than Pritikin and a security guard when the Bleacher Preacher stood by the right-field wall and reached into his duffel bag. "Don't do it," said the security man. Pritikin suggested he turn the other way, and then flung the Frisbee in the direction of McDowell. For that, he was removed from the ballpark.

It would be the first game Pritikin would miss all year, and he couldn't stand the idea of it. He called Dallas Green, who sighed and told him to come into the Cub offices and meet with one of his assistants. But when Pritikin stepped through the office door, he was greeted by his security friend, who once more turned him off the premises and this time threatened incarceration.

Inside, where Pritikin longed to be, Sutcliffe went for his eighteenth victory, and Marv Blum—another one taking a week of vacation—noted that the Cubs were in danger of finishing with a worse record than the rallying White Sox. A banner hung from the scoreboard: STICK A FORK IN 'EM, THE CUBS ARE DONE. Craig, the blind man in right-center, said, "This reminds me of the Cubs in '78. Remember that, Bob?"

"Oh, yeah, they really died that year."

In an unlikely fashion development, there were two men in the bleachers—independent of each other—wearing hats of the St. Louis Browns, who had moved to Baltimore in 1954. One of the men was from Toronto and said he had a collection of forty hats from teams that no longer existed.

Sutcliffe took a 3–2 lead into the late innings, and in right field Al Yellon reflected on some of the people who had sat near him over the years. "Somebody asked me once about the seat next to me, and I said it was saved," he recalled. "Without a word, the guy in front of me turned around and slugged me in the mouth. Then he declared he was Jesus Christ." There was also a rather unsanitary fellow who used to sit in front of Papa Carl and would move his body about in curious ways, after which it seemed there would often be a stolen base or a hit-and-run or something else strategic.

A section over, Debra Cagan caught up with old friends. She had been a bleacher regular before she left Chicago to take a job in Washington with the State Department, and she was a little concerned about what might become of her beloved Wrigley Field. "Tell me," she said to one of her friends. "They're not going to double-deck this place and turn it into a geek park, are they?"

The Mets put a runner on second with one out in the eighth, and Oates came to the mound to talk to Sutcliffe. "No! No!" screamed the fans. "Leave him in!" Sutcliffe worked out of the inning, then drove in two runs with a single in the bottom of the eighth. Durham turned a dazzling double play in the ninth, touching first base with his glove and then diving after Howard Johnson and tagging him in a rundown. He had an astounding nine unassisted putouts in the game, and Sutcliffe's eighteenth victory was by the score of 6–2.

Afterward, Jerry Pritikin was still standing outside the team offices trying to state his case to somebody sympathetic. Steve Stone walked by, and Pritikin said, "Steve, guess what—I got kicked out of the ballpark."

"Good," said Stone, hardly slowing down.

"Good?" screamed Pritikin.

I took him over to the Japanese bar for a bowl of *yet ce mein* soup.

That night, about five hundred residents of Lake View gathered at LeMoyne School for a rally against lights at Wrigley Field. Most of the local television stations were on hand with cameras, and the event was a good show. The anti-lights people, careful not to come off as anti-baseball—they had, after all, chosen an organizational name with the acronym C.U.B.S.—played baseball music over the loudspeaker, including the late Steve Goodman's "Dying Cub Fan's Last Request":

Do they still play the blues in Chicago
When baseball season rolls around?
. . . When the snow melts away
Do the Cubbies still play
In their ivy-covered burial ground?

It was an ironic message, inasmuch as the Cub threat to leave Wrigley Field was predicated upon the prohibition of lights. Although they knew it was an inadvisable political move to try to push the Cubs out of Wrigley Field, many of the anti-lights activists were willing to accept that consequence. "People like having the Cubs here," said state representative Ellis Levin, "but if it comes down to a choice between the community and the Cubs, the community is more important."

On the other hand, the C.U.B.S. people were also unwilling to acknowledge publicly that the baseball club was vital to the maintenance of the neighborhood. "The ballpark makes the neighborhood run," said Bill Westman, the Clark Street realtor. "The residents would probably admit that under the influence of drugs."

Without drugs, though, they talked about trash on the street and how hard it was to even go to the grocery store when there was a ballgame in progress because there was no place to park upon returning home. "I think it really adds something to live near a ballpark," said Mike Quigley, the alderman's aide who lived on Magnolia Avenue, a few blocks from Wrigley Field, and was a vice-president of C.U.B.S. "But when people say this neighborhood is nothing without Wrigley Field, I say, 'Hey, look around.' "

The neighborhood, actually, was several neighborhoods within one, the several being represented at the rally Tuesday night by people holding signs for the Halsted Street Merchants, the Hawthorne Neighbors, the Triangle Neighbors, the North Lake View Neighbors . . . any pocket of merchants or neighbors that could be a name on a sign. The plan was to walk around the ballpark carrying lights. Mark Atkinson, the president of C.U.B.S., led the march in blue jeans, a baggy sweater, and an old tweed hat. As they prepared to set out, Atkinson said, "If you want to pick up trash from today's game along the way, we have trash bags available." One woman was selling eyeglasses with small flashlights affixed to them for twenty dollars, batteries included. Another man wore a hat that said CUBS SUCK.

They walked down Addison past the liquor store, the taco stand, and the el stop, shouting, "No lights, no way!," then turned right on Sheffield and marched past the bleacher gate and Murphy's. I thought about one of Murphy's friends, a big man named Tom Hickman, who had sat at Murphy's bar one day and said, "All that noise pollution business is bullshit. Shit, there were games going on here long before these people moved in. If you don't like baseball games going on, why do you move into a neighborhood with a ballpark? I can't see the Cubs moving out of here because of a few assholes."

They turned left at Waveland, and a little boy and girl looked out through an apartment window and said, "We want lights." At another house, people stood on a porch and applauded. The five hundred walked past the firehouse on Waveland and turned left on Clark, the procession stretching on for nearly three blocks: old men and women who had lived in the neighborhood when P. K. Wrigley promised there would never be lights, mothers with strollers, young professionals still in their business clothes, kids in sweatshirts. At Clark and Addison, they walked past the big red sign that said WRIGLEY FIELD HOME OF CHICAGO CUBS, and the electronic message board that touted the upcoming Fan Appreciation Weekend.

They held signs of yellow cardboard with red lettering that said NO LIGHTS!—just like the signs in the windows of so many houses in Wrigleyville. One of the marchers held a sign

that said NO LIGHTS OR NO BOOZE—alluding to the threat
that they could vote the precinct dry if the Cubs were permitted to have night games. Another sign said WE ELECTED YOU,
HAROLD, THE TRIBUNE DID NOT. Back at LeMoyne School,
Mark Atkinson stood up to the microphone and declared,
"We're fighting for our lives as a community tonight. We're
going to make the decisions about what happens in this community, not Harold Washington." Then Mike Quigley stood
up to the microphone and said, "The bottom line is, the Cubs
want to take the equity out of your house for their bottom
line."

It was so complicated. What would really happen to the
neighborhood with night games? What would really happen
to the Cubs without them? Whose rights were basic here? Did
the fans matter? Did the rest of Chicago? The interesting
thing was that, if the very people who rallied around Wrigley
Field on September twenty-second had lived in other parts of
town, it is likely that they would have been indifferent about
lights, or possibly even favored them. It wasn't a principle
they were fighting for; it was an investment. It wasn't a question of what was best for everybody, but what was best for
them. It was the same with the Cubs. There would be no right
resolution or wrong resolution to the issue of lights at Wrigley
Field; there would only be a winner and a loser.

Jamie Moyer pitched against Bruce Ruffin on Wednesday,
and the Cubs couldn't score. In center field, Jim Cote talked
about getting a higher draft choice for finishing last. In right-
center, Marv Blum said there was a pig farmer who bought
rotten potatoes from the produce warehouse where he
worked, and the pig farmer had bet Marv at the first of the
year that the Cubs would finish third place or higher. Marv
hadn't heard from the guy.

John Radzikowski, an unpretentious bleacher veteran who
wore a Cub hat, said, "I don't blame the pitching. I don't
blame the hitting. I blame the whole goddamn team. I'm so
goddamn pissed. I keep coming out here all these years. I've
been coming out here thirty-eight years. Why? I'm crazy."

On the end of the bench, Elsie's eighty-five-year-old friend, Al Barrett, was looking disinterested as the Phillies fashioned a 5–0 lead in the fifth. "Al, you tired?" Elsie asked.

"No, disgusted."

I asked Al if there was any hope for the Cubs in the foreseeable future. He shook his head. "What are they gonna do next year?" he said. "What have they got to trade? The main thing is to get rid of that son of a bitch Dallas Green."

Damon Berryhill, the rookie catcher, struck out for the second time, and John Radzikowski yelled, "Great, kid, go back to Iowa." Wade Rowdon made a sharp play at third. "Hey, Moreland," shouted Radzikowski. "We got a third baseman."

In the eighth, Berryhill hit into a double play. "Geez, look at him run," said Elsie. "He's slower than Davis."

It was about that time that Howard finished selling Frosty Malts and reported to right-center field. Howard was loud and could be irritating—in 1976, a lady broke a batting helmet over his head because he wouldn't shut up—but he also had a way of loosening up a dull September day. Becker was in the mood, anyway. He was starting to get a little frisky, trying to bring back the spirit of the old days. "All right, a little walk here, we got 'em now," Becker said, upon which Howard and the blind guys behind them all joined in. "All right, a little walk, a little walk."

"What time is it almost?" yelled Howard—not because it was almost time for anything, but because that was what they used to yell. The small crowd and the standings reminded them of the way it used to be. "It's almost *Sutter* time. Remember that? What would Three Hundred Sam say now? Waaaaaaalk him! Waaaaaaalk him!"

Three Hundred Sam was called that because he bet three hundred dollars all the time. Almost all of the old gamblers were known by sobriquets. There was another guy named Charlie who was seventy-seven years old, so Becker called him Charlie Seventy-Seven. The next year, he was Charlie Seventy-Eight, and by the time he stopped coming to the ballpark he was Charlie Eighty-Nine. They said that Charlie

Eighty-Nine sold seat cushions at the old ballpark in 1906. There was a cab driver they called Pip who always thought he was being cheated. Mama Doll wore funny socks. There was a liquor salesman who wore a leather jacket, arrived late every day, and bet everything in his pocket. He would stand over by the rail and say, "All right, who wants to lay a price?" The blind guys would smile when they heard him, and in a voice like the liquor salesman's would say, "All right, who wants to lay a price?" A guy they called San Diego Jerry once made fifteen or twenty different bets against the Cubs, and when the Cubs took the lead in the seventh inning, he disappeared. None of the bleacher guys ever saw him again. They presumed he went to San Diego.

There were usually two or three bookmakers among the bettors. One of them was rumored to have lost an apartment building betting in the bleachers. The vice squad would come down on them occasionally, but the bleacher boys would pass the hat, put a dollar in, and give it to their cop friend outside to keep them out of trouble.

Ruffin took his shutout into the ninth, and Becker tugged on his trousers. "You know what a pants lifter is?" he said. "A pants lifter is a guy who always bets the favorite. Then he pulls up his pants, 'cause he's all confident and cocky for betting the favorite."

"You shoulda been here fifteen years ago," Howard told me. "There's nothing here anymore."

I said that there was more to the bleachers now than gambling. "What do you mean, more to it?" he said. "That's what it is."

In the next section, Norb compared old hat collections with the guy from Toronto, who was envious that Norb had the Seattle Pilots. Chris James made a diving catch on a ball hit by Dernier in the ninth, and Norb said, "As the Phillies clinch fourth place in the National League East. . . ."

The last-place Cubs had been shut out by an undistinguished Philadelphia pitcher on a Wednesday in front of seven thousand people, and afterward fans were lined up three-deep by the fence enclosing the players' parking lot on

Waveland. They were quiet, vigilant, and when a Cub walked out of the stadium door, there would begin a great whispering, "Who is it? Who is it?" Then the name would go skipping down the line. "Baller. It's Baller. Jay Baller." Boyish Greg Maddux came out. "Who's that, the batboy?" "Aw, we got his already." Lee Smith appeared, and there was no booing. "Lee! Lee! Lee!" His 4 × 4 red Blazer was near the door, and he ducked into it without looking at the crowd. Dunston's matching truck was right next to Smith's, and they drove off together. Another player came out of a different door and got into a car parked a couple hundred feet from the lot, and two guys stole silently in his direction, careful not to alert the competition. There were kids among the crowd, of course, and young couples, and middle-aged couples, and three women in their fifties or sixties who had little cubby bears pinned to their jackets. One of the women wore several buttons with pictures of her and Jody Davis.

As long as a few cars remained in the lot, people stayed. There was nothing they would prefer to do with their time than wait for a chance to get an autograph from a Cub. Chunks of minutes passed uneventfully. A vendor rolled away his ice cream cart, and it was perfectly still in the parking area. The fans put their fingers through the chain link and waited.

September twenty-fourth was the anniversary of when the Cubs clinched the division title in 1984. It happened in Pittsburgh, but there were Cub fans there, of course, and the thing most people remembered was Harry Caray saying, "I'd like to drink half of what they're throwing." Another thing people remembered was that a woman took off her shirt.

Three years later, the Cubs were headed for last place. It was interesting to note that three years after they won their most recent National League pennant, at the end of World War II, the Cubs had also hit the bottom of the standings. They and the White Sox hadn't both finished last in the same season since that lamentable one of 1948.

In right-center, a Northwestern student with three days of

facial growth and a T-shirt with the words SOBER UP bought a beer before he sat down. "This is the first beer I've bought legally," he announced. Then he sat down and said, "What the fuck is wrong with the Cubs, man? Every single year."

Through four innings, Greg Maddux allowed no hits and struck out eight Phillies. It was the kind of performance that September is about—a kid pitcher looking like he could pitch—and in the seventh, Mike Schmidt came up as a pinch hitter with two outs, the bases loaded, and the score tied 2–2. Lucchesi had made up his mind before the game to go as far as he could with Maddux, and he let him pitch to the great slugger. One of the guys on the rail in center field said, "This is where we see what Greg has hanging in his jock." Schmidt fanned.

For the song in the middle of the inning, the center-field guys had their own words. They substituted White Sox for Cubbies and sang, "If they don't win, it's the same. . . ." The thing was, though, the White Sox had begun to win, and were only four and a half games in arrears of the Cubs with ten days left in the season.

It was a close group that sat in the first row over the concession stand, young men who had met in the bleachers and were the best of buddies there, although they seldom saw each other outside the ballpark. The seats they had chosen were good ones, providing a sweeping view of the field and also a nice overhead shot of everybody who walked past in the wide back aisle below. They said the best-looking women were at Friday 3:05 games, and they kept an unofficial top-ten list for the season. They were also genuinely interested in the ballgames. One of the guys in center, a restaurant manager named Dick, had his own intricate system of scorekeeping, dividing each space in half in order to leave room for extra innings and using a number code that only he could understand. He had to leave in the eighth to get to the restaurant Thursday, and he said to his friends, "I might see you this weekend." After Dick was gone, Bob, the commodities broker, said, "We'll see him in April. April to September, that's it. Opening Day, we'll all be here."

The game went extra innings, and more people left. Howard wasn't around and Becker got bored. Mark said he thought about leaving, but he had confidence that Baller would blow the game quickly. As he spoke, Darren Daulton hit a home run leading off the eleventh and the Phillies won 3–2. The Cubs had not scored in nineteen of the twenty innings they had played in two days with Philadelphia. They had fallen below .500 at home.

That night, I listened on the radio as the Cardinals rallied against Pittsburgh in the bottom of the ninth. They were down 2–1 with no outs and two men on when the phone rang. It was Jerry Pritikin. In a solemn voice he said, "At the end of the year, I'm becoming a generic fan. I'm going to be a free agent.

"I've decided that just because they're the Cubs is not reason enough to give them your loyalty. They've got to earn it. It's just a little awakening on my part. The Frisbee incident really brought it to light. . . . This has nothing to do with it, but you know, I think a Frisbee in the air is one of the most beautiful sights there is. That and a diving catch. By the way, I'm going to donate the Frisbee to Harry Caray's new restaurant.

"But there comes a time when fans should not be automatic. This has been a rotten season. It's like the little lady said that I always see on the el. She said they should get that truck up to the building the last day of the season and just fill it up. She's right. It's gotten to the way it used to be, where you come out to the ballpark expecting them to lose. I didn't expect much this year, but they showed me they had something. They should have done something with it. There are some players on that team who don't deserve my loyalty.

"I really mean this. I'll take my voodoo doll this weekend, but after the season, I'm wide open. I'm going to start merchandising myself. I'm going to be a free agent. Maybe I'll be a White Sox fan, who knows?"

As he spoke, the Cardinals scored two to win.

The sweet, silent, soft part of September was over. The Cardinals were in for a weekend series that would end the Cubs' home season.

For the first time in two weeks, the bleachers were teeming with revelers and vendors. The regular Old Style man, a hustling salesman with yellow-gray hair and a piercing voice, walked by another Old Style guy and said, "Hey, they need you in the upper deck." I heard the deep voice of young Howard, the photographer/vendor: "Any beers?" He said he had made two hundred seventy dollars one day over the summer, which had been a good one for the regular crew of bleacher beer men: Harry, who carried only one case on hot days because his beers stayed colder that way; Mark, the young guy with braces who competed with Howard to see who could sell the most; the two dark-haired brothers who always chewed gum; the law student; the guy who said, "Beeeeer," in a low, semicircular manner, out of the side of his mouth; the guy with big arms who said, "Bud Bud Lite! Bud Bud Lite!"

Jerry Pritikin was in a better mood than he had been on the telephone the night before. His Frisbee story had received national publicity, and he had been on a New York talk show that morning. But the changing state of the bleachers did nothing for his spirits. He strolled down to left field, looked around, and said, "There's not one person here from last year." Mary Ellen, the weekend regular who usually stood by the steps to center field, described left field as a nice place to visit but no place to stay.

In right field, Dick Jones, a seventy-year-old grocer from Morris, Illinois, was wearing a flannel shirt and suspenders and sitting in the bleachers for the first time. He had been coming to Wrigley Field since 1929, though, and had fond memories of the great Cuyler-Stephenson-Wilson outfield and the deep chocolate voice of field announcer Pat Pieper. "I would have never imagined they wouldn't be in another Series after '45," he said. Jones had been on his way home from Europe after World War II, and he ducked into Winchester Cathedral to plug in his little plastic radio and listen to Claude Passeau throw a one-hitter at the Tigers in game three. All his life he had been a Cub fan, but he had never been in the bleachers. "It shows what I've been missing all these years," he said. "These are the really true fans."

I sat in aisle 153 in left, between an actor and a machinist. In front of me was a kid who checked out his braces in his reflecting sunglasses. Dawson hit a two-run homer over our heads in the first, and with that a pennant race suddenly seemed like such a whimsical thing. The Cardinals were three and a half games ahead of the Mets, but Jack Clark was still out of the lineup with his bad ankle, and the momentum could swing to New York if the Cubs could sweep the Cardinals at Wrigley Field—which they easily could if Dawson got hot again. Players get hot and then they're not; it's a cyclical, capricious thing, and if Dawson—or even Durham or Davis or Moreland or Sandberg—happened to find a groove over the weekend, the Cardinals could have their season dashed. With Clark out, they had nobody like the sluggers on the Cubs—nobody who could drive in ten runs in a three-game series.

The guy in the groove Friday, though, was Sanderson, and he kept the Cardinals off the scoreboard until the sixth, when they scored one and were deprived of another one or two when Moreland made a skillful play on a sharp grounder by Willie McGee. "Not bad, Moreland," yelled the Bleacher Preacher. "One out of a hundred." He was bitter.

It was still 2–1 in the late innings, and in the bleachers there was heavy sentiment that the game would go to St. Louis. It was a Cardinal kind of game, after all—tight and low-scoring—and they had won one just like it the night before. "The Cubs are gonna blow it," said Marv. "It's as sure as death and taxes."

Frank DiPino relieved Sanderson in the eighth, and was still pitching in the ninth when, with two outs, Whitey Herzog sent up Clark to pinch hit. To the Cub fans, it was interesting that Lucchesi broke precedent and allowed the left-handed DiPino to stay on instead of bringing in Smith for the save; to the Cardinal fans, Clark at the plate was what they had been waiting to see. The feeling was that the Cardinals, with speed, pluck, and Herzog, might hang on to win the division without Clark; but, lacking power as completely as they did in his absence, they would be overmatched by the Giants in the playoffs and, if somehow they wriggled into the World Series, certainly by Toronto or Detroit or whoever represented the muscular American League.

Clark hadn't batted in more than two weeks, and he wasn't sure how his ankle would handle it. But he wanted to try, and he stepped into the box, turned the back of his left shoulder to DiPino in his exaggerated closed stance, twisted his spikes into the turf, and took a ball. Then DiPino threw a slider that Clark thought he could put onto Waveland Avenue, and he swung with the force of a man who had thirty-five home runs. He missed, and he dropped to the ground, his ankle unable to stand up to the might of his whiff. Then he got up and walked into the dugout.

Tony Pena replaced him and grounded out to end the game, after which Clark said that he had just slipped and that his ankle was no worse than it had been. He would not bat again in 1987.

On September twenty-sixth, the crowd was cheering before the game even started. Pittsburgh had scored four against Gooden in the second. Cardinal and Cub fans colored Wrigley Field like stripes on a barber's pole, but they bled together in their rancor for the Mets, whom the Cardinal fans feared on a competitive level and the Cub people loathed on general principle.

The bleachers were chaotic on the final Saturday. The first game and the last weekend were the only times when seats were reserved in the bleachers, and on the last weekend in particular the concept was not a viable one. It was done so that prizes could be awarded by seat number, but the bleacher fans were not appreciative. The regular ones considered their seats reserved by custom and early arrival, and Elsie, for instance, was not about to give up her spot to some suburban weekender because of a few letters and numbers on a ticket that he probably bought in a mall.

As their first Saturday home game had been, the Cubs' last was also on national television. The networks didn't need good reasons to broadcast from Wrigley Field—the chromatic environment was enough—but New York had won the night before, and the Cardinals' lead was only two and a half games. Jerry Pritikin tried to get his big blank check for Dawson in front of the NBC cameras, and in left field, friends of a little street hustler who was serving time on a drug-related charge held up a sign that said FREE LUKE. Luke had said he didn't mind the sentence so much, but he was awfully sorry that he had to miss the Cardinal series.

John Tudor, the reliable left-hander who had missed three months of the season in the dugout accident, pitched for St. Louis against Sutcliffe, who would probably have three more chances to win the two games he needed for twenty—a number that, in a bad year for starting pitchers in the National League, would make him a favorite for the Cy Young Award.

Sutcliffe was 2–0 since he had been wearing his new T-shirt under his uniform. A few weeks before, he had seen the best of the Cub T-shirts—WORLD CHAMPIONS, 1908—and ordered four of them. "It really had an effect on me," he said. "I got them to wear when I pitch and when I'm working out. When I'm in Kansas City in the winter and I've got to go out twice a day and do my running, it's not easy. I got them to motivate me. When I saw that shirt, my first reaction was sadness. These fans haven't had a world champion in all that time. I think it's a shame."

Of all the players on the team, Sutcliffe was probably the one who most appreciated what was special about the Chicago Cubs. If he had grown up in Chicago, he would have been a bleacher guy; in fact, when his friends came to Wrigley from Kansas City, they wouldn't take the box-seat tickets Sutcliffe could get for them but would go right for the bleachers instead. When he told Dallas Green he would give one hundred thousand dollars of his own money if it would help the Cubs sign Dawson back in March, he wasn't grandstanding; he was being a Cub fan. "I was offered more money to play other places in 1985," Sutcliffe had said in the Cub dugout a few days earlier. "And it's not that they weren't places I'd like to go, either, because I had the same offer from Kansas City. But there is something about the Cubs, and it goes beyond what I can describe. This is without a doubt a unique situation in baseball. Los Angeles and New York might draw more fans, but no other place has the feeling that this does. When I first got here in '84, I hadn't even pitched yet, and I'd gotten more letters than I did monthly in Los Angeles or Cleveland. You really feel like part of their family here. I can remember when I came here with the Dodgers, I just thought of this as an old ballpark. Really, this place is kind of ugly until you get the fans in it. You come out here and you wonder what people see in it. But there's something about this place that attracts people. The ballpark has more to do with it than the players. There's no question that I'd be a Cub fan if I lived around here, but if they were ever to leave this park, I'd have to think again."

Sutcliffe walked Vince Coleman to begin the game, but Jody Davis threw out the great base stealer at second. "Hit the road," yelled Marv, removing his cigar. "Fifty-five south, hit the road." Three batters later, Dan Driessen, a worn veteran who had been added to the St. Louis roster to fill in for Clark, lifted an innocuous-looking fly ball to left field that hitched onto a channel of wind and landed in the seats. I thought of how the NBC camera would show the ball carrying over the ivy wall, and the packed-in bleacher people rising together as it fell into them; it was the image that had intrigued me about the Wrigley Field bleachers: Who were all those people? What brought them out on all those hot and disappointing days? What was it like among them? I had spent the summer finding out, and I had six notebooks and a file drawer full of answers. Still, I knew none of the people whom Dan Driessen's two-run homer had fallen amongst.

There was no more scoring until the sixth, and Sutcliffe was removed in the seventh. He would have to make good on his last two starts to win twenty; the Cardinals led 5–2 going into the ninth. By that time, the menacing Todd Worrell was pitching for St. Louis. The Cubs loaded the bases with one out, and Worrell faced Dawson. A grand slam would win the game; it was perfect. Bob Henner, the commodities broker, shouted, "Is there magic in the park today? There's magic in the air today at Wrigley Field." People chanted, "MVP! MVP!" Jerry Pritikin was so excited that he tripped over something in the aisle. Dawson hit a ground ball on which Ozzie Smith, not surprisingly, made a difficult play and threw the batter out by a step at first.

It was 5–3 with two outs, and Herzog brought in left-hander Ken Dayley to pitch to Durham. Durham had gone through a difficult series the week before in St. Louis. He'd met one of the Cardinal rookies, a kid named Lance Johnson from Durham's hometown of Cincinnati, and Johnson had told Durham that he knew the Bull's little brother. Only Johnson hadn't known that Durham's younger brother had been killed in an auto accident the summer before. Durham had just about worked his way through the tragedy when it hit him all over again. But he had been swinging the bat well through most of the past month or two, and in the ninth inning of the final Saturday game of the season at Wrigley Field, he had a chance to make the fans forget his earlier failures. In right-center, Mark and two friends, Judy and Colleen, watched tensely as Durham dug in against Dayley.

"Come on, Leon," said Mark. "One time, one time."

"Please, Leon," said Judy.

Durham struck out looking.

"What a useless piece of shit," said Colleen.

In the *Tribune* Sunday morning was a column by Jerome Holtman in which Dallas Green said:

> I want to apologize to the fans of the Chicago Cubs. The reason I have to apologize is because we quit, with a capital Q: Q-U-I-T. There is no other explanation for it. . . . I have done everything I could possibly do for the players and their families. I didn't expect them to quit on me, to give up with 30-some games to play. I was slapped in the face, and so were the Cub fans . . . Chicago is one of the easiest cities to play the game of baseball. . . . If you just give effort, these people will

love you. But our players have shown no feelings for the fans of Chicago. . . . For the last month, all the players have been talking about is their hunting and fishing trips and the damn cruises. They forgot we had another month to play. No, they didn't forget. They didn't care.

In many cities, such words by a general manager would have been eagerly consumed by a baseball public quick to find fault with those who had failed them. Cub fans had been thinking along the same lines; it had occurred to them, too, that the team had lost its initiative. But if there was one thing that they abhorred more than bad or even lazy teams, it was excuses. Having remained steadfast through the longest championship dearth in the history of professional sports, Cub fans would not tolerate excuses. That was why they turned on Ron Santo in 1969. Santo was a good, spirited, and popular player, but when he blamed Don Young for missing that fly ball, the fans of Chicago took it out on *him*, not Young. If there were any excuses to be made concerning the Cubs, their fans reserved for themselves the right to make them.

"He can't conceive of the fact that there could be a difference in talent between the Cubs and the other teams," said Mark Wilmot, who couldn't stand Green anyway. "I think I might write him a letter. I don't normally do that, and I wouldn't expect a response, but I might write him a letter."

A week remained in the season, but Sunday's was the Cubs' last home game. They went into it a game and a half behind the fifth-place Pirates, and one game under .500 at Wrigley Field. Despite this, they had two million fans in the fold— Saturday's crowd had put them over that mark for the third time in their history and the third time in four years. Attendance was at a peak all over the major leagues. On Sunday, as the Cubs drew thirty-four thousand, baseball reached fifty million for the first time ever. Of course, that included Jerry Pritikin seventy-nine times. On the occasion of the last game, he showed up in a new T-shirt. On the front, it said FREE AGENT. On the back, it said THIS SPACE FOR RENT, with a phone number.

In the right-field bleachers, Mary Ellen had brought a tin of cookies for her friends. She took account of all the Cardinal fans in the ballpark and said, "If they announced that John Deere was double-parked, it would clear the place out." Elsie moaned about the Northwestern football game the day before. "Boy, I get all the losers, don't I?" Ronnie Woo-Woo went by slapping hands. "Get out of here, you jerk," Elsie said. And in the back row of section 144, Mike Bojanowski was attending his thirty-fourth game of the season and six hundred forty-fifth of his life at Wrigley Field. He said that thirty-five or thirty-six games was the most a person could get to in a year—counting weekends and a little vacation time—if he worked a nine-to-five job.

Bojanowski was a thin, blonde commercial artist, and for all of the educated baseball fans I'd met in the bleachers, there were none more informed. To begin with, he kept an impeccable scorecard that befitted a man who was both an artist and a student of baseball. When he got home he filed each card, and at the end of each season he compiled them into nine typed pages of personal records. He knew not only how many games he had been to in his life, going back to 1964, but how many of those the Cubs had won and lost (323–303, the discrepancy in the total resulting from his games as a small kid when he didn't know how to keep score); how many home runs he had seen by the Cubs and opponents (526–536); the most home runs he had ever seen in a game (9); the number of times he had seen a team score fifteen or more runs (11); the most runs he had ever seen in the ninth inning (7); the most consecutive triples he had ever seen (3); the number of six-RBI games he had seen (8); the number of Hall of Famers he had seen (15—he expected the list to triple within ten years); the number of different Cubs and opposing players he had seen hit home runs (92, 243); the Cub and opposing players whom he had seen hit the most home runs (Durham, 43, and Schmidt, 21); the shortest game he had ever seen (1:30); the number of times he had seen a game with no changes in the lineups (4); and so on, ad infinitum in an exhaustive listing of custom-made minutiae.

Serious baseball fans are sort of like arm wrestlers: when they come across another one, they can't resist sitting down at the table to find out what the other guy's got. Mike and I tossed around some trivia and, feeling smug because I'd been doing research on the Reds, I asked him if he happened to know what player had the most hits of all those who were eligible for the Hall of Fame but not in it. He said Vada Pinson, 2,757. I was astonished. He wondered if I knew what pitcher had the most wins of any eligible for the Hall and not in it, and I didn't. The answer was Tony Mullane—an old Red whom I'd been reading about. Was there a treasury of baseball knowledge under the rowdy surface of the bleachers? I wondered how many other fans there were like Mike whom I'd seen all year but never met—it was the last day; I might have easily missed him. How many hours were devoted by how many people to the passion called baseball? "It's how you pass the long, boring winter," Mike said.

Lancaster, the undrafted rookie who had started the season at Iowa, pitched the home finale for Chicago against Danny Cox, the big veteran who had started the season by blowing down the Cubs at Wrigley Field. On this day, though, Lancaster looked to be the better man, shutting out the Cardinals through five innings as the Cubs built a 5–0 lead. On the steps to the center-field bleachers, a Cub fan named Grubby was slowly, dramatically, pulling little shocks of red from a Cardinal doll for which he had paid twelve dollars, and letting them float weightlessly to the ground below. Steve Schanker stood up on a bleacher seat, grabbed his neck, and yelled, "Choke! Choke!"

St. Louis scored a run in the sixth, and an inning later it was registered on the third-base scoreboard. By that time, though, the Cardinals had scored two more. The Cubs added one on Moreland's twenty-sixth home run, and it was 6–3 when Lee Smith started the eighth inning. Marv moaned. When somebody suggested that he should have faith, Marv answered, "If I had faith in something like that, I'd get married again." But Smith pitched out of the eighth uneventfully, and with two outs in the bottom of the inning, Dawson batted in front of the fans at Wrigley Field for the last time in 1987.

Perhaps in other ballparks there would not have been the same awareness, a week removed from the end of the season, that the hero of the home team was making his final appearance at the plate; but at Wrigley Field, the people stood and made the place ring with anticipation. "MVP!" they chanted thunderously. "MVP!" Old men and yuppies and regulars and a girl in front of me in a swimsuit all chanted "MVP!" (At one point, the girl in the swimsuit turned to the guy next to her and said, "What's that?") Bill Dawley was pitching for St. Louis, and when the count went to 3 and 1, Mark Wilmot said he was afraid Dawson was going to walk. The last-place home team was ahead by three runs with two outs and nobody on base in the bottom of the eighth, and not a soul in sight was sitting down. "MVP! MVP!" And on the 3 and 1 Dawson sent an awesome drive onto the eastbound lane of Waveland Avenue.

When he got to the dugout, people all over the ballpark raised their arms up and bowed to the meritorious rightfielder, and Dawson, a man of estimable dignity and suppressed emotion, came out of the dugout, raised his arms up, and bowed back. It was purely a baseball moment. Only baseball pauses for times like those. In football, a clock is always running, and the players, in their pads and helmets and in their obstructed and distanced separation from the seating areas, are not humanly connected to the crowd. Time must go on in basketball, as well. But baseball doesn't hasten away its passionate moments with ticks and tocks. Baseball leaves open the garden gate so that its roses may be smelled.

All over again, the fans shouted "MVP! MVP!" I looked over at Marv. His cigar was gone from his mouth, but he wasn't shouting like the others. He had removed his glasses to accommodate the slow flow of tears from his eyes. He smiled happily and shook his head.

When the game resumed, people said they *knew* Dawson was going to hit a home run, that they could just feel it, as if they and Dawson were terminals charged by the electric occasion. At a bar downtown, Dawson received a standing ovation.

Smith got the Cardinals out in the ninth for his thirty-fifth save, and the Cubs had won forty and lost forty at Wrigley Field. For all the beers that had been drunk in the bleachers, all the lines drawn on all the scorecards, all the fights, all the friends made, all the nachos put away, all the home runs caught and thrown back, all the songs sung, all the shouting, all the kissing, all the cursing, all the cheering, all the booing, all the bowing, all the skin browned and hair bleached, all the wind, all the bright days and rainy, all the emotion, all the devotion, all the time and money spent, all the blue worn, all the heartbreak, all the hope, all the silliness, all the second-guessing, all the rich and rampant Cubness to which the people of the Wrigley Field bleachers had been party in 1987, the Cubs were right back where they started.

Norb looked at his schedule for 1988 and said, "April fifteenth against the Pirates."

Postlude

IN THE END, they were three-and-a-half games behind the Pirates. It was the eleventh time in their 112-year National League history that the Cubs had finished last.

Across town, meanwhile, the White Sox pushed ahead of Texas and California in the American League West and won seventy-seven games, one more than the Cubs (although both lost eighty-five), while drawing about sixty percent as many people. By leaving last place to the Angels, though, the White Sox did manage to finesse the Cubs in one small way pertaining to attendance. The Cubs and Angels—who tied with Texas—were the first teams ever to draw two million fans while finishing last, and the record, by all poetic standards, should have been set at Wrigley Field. California got it instead. Of course, the Angels were coming off a division championship and Chicago was coming out of fifth place.

The Cubs secured sixth place for 1987 when they lost two out of three at Pittsburgh in the last week. Sutcliffe, beaten there, packed it in with eighteen wins, Dawson got as far as forty-nine in home runs, and the Cardinals clinched the division before the Mets even visited them for the final weekend.

In the postseason championships, the Ex-Cub Factor held true. The theory is that the team with the most ex-Cubs loses. The San Francisco Giants went into the playoffs with three of them (Rick Reuschel, Mike Krukow, and Chris Speier), which was simply too many, considering that the Cardinals countered with only reserve catcher Steve Lake. The Detroit Tigers were caught with former Cubs Willie Hernandez and Bill Madlock on their side for the American League playoffs, while the Minnesota Twins had but Joe Niekro. In the World Series between the Cardinals and Twins, the games were even until Minnesota won the seventh, which Lake started and Niekro didn't pitch in (the Twins lost the fourth game, which Niekro *did* pitch in).

What really doomed the Cardinals, though, was their failure to win even once in four games at the Metrodome in Minneapolis, a place that clamored for power. To that end, St. Louis, in effect, lost the World Series on September twenty-fifth at Wrigley Field, when Jack Clark buckled under the slider from Frank DiPino.

While the Twins were winning the first World Championship in their history—which put them one ahead of the Cubs over the past eight decades—there was a drama developing inside the white walls of Wrigley Field. Dallas Green, uncertain of how to fill the vacant manager's job, had decided to return to the field and do it himself. This, of course, would extend his imperious influence over the baseball matters of the Cubs—he would be a one-man triumvirate of president, general manager, and field manager—and what ensued was a classic boardroom power struggle between a willful executive and a corporate administration threatened by autocracy from a hired hand. Sensing that a daily withdrawal to the dugout would leave his presidential flank unprotected, Green backed off the move and decided instead that coach and protégé John Vukovich would be his manager. But the Tribune was still not willing to leave the front office unchecked by one of its own, and it was mutually agreed that Green should excuse himself.

There was no mourning in Chicago over his resignation, but neither was there any suggestion that the Cubs were not better off for his unshrinking leadership. Under Green, the Cubs had won a division title, rebuilt their farm system, and made money. Despite their dramatic three-year decline, they were not at a hopeless distance from either competitive parity or their peak of popularity. The big guy left the club in good shape for Jim Frey, whom he had hired as manager in 1984 and fired in 1986, and who, less than two weeks after Green's departure, was transferred from one Tribune subsidiary, WGN, to another, taking over as director of baseball operations.

Frey was a baseball man who entertained no pretenses of being anything else, and there were no significant objections to his appointment. Nor were there any when Frey named as manager his old buddy from the West Side of Cincinnati, the round-cheeked Don Zimmer. In a lifelong baseball career, Zimmer had been beaned in the head and face—the first occasion being so serious that the major leagues made batting helmets mandatory soon thereafter—called a gerbil by one of his players, and, as a three-time manager, lost his best shot at a pennant one black day in 1978 when Bucky Dent homered and Carl Yastrzemski popped up. At one point, Zimmer had been the most abused man in New England; but he had color and courage, and he said he would make the Cubs run the bases. Together, the changes were sufficient to make Mark Wilmot a Cub fan again.

Baseball lines itself up that way in the off-season, fixing attitudes and affiliations. In the autumn of 1987, Frank Lucchesi was let go, Billy Williams turned down the manager's job at Iowa, Bob Dernier joined the Phillies, Brian Dayett signed a four-year contract with the Nippon Ham Fighters that made him wealthy, and Jerry Pritikin pondered his future as a fan. Meanwhile, Norb and Steve and Marv and Dancing Annie wondered whether Palmeiro would be the full-time leftfielder—he finished with fourteen home runs in less than half a season—and whether Frey would trade Durham or Davis or both or anybody.

In the same way that a baseball season never really begins, it never really ends either. For the twenty-six teams of the two

major leagues, 1988 would take its shape directly and precisely from two things: the first being the way each of them
reacted and learned from 1987; and the second being the
volition of the game's eternal commissioner, whimsy, which
presides in such a hands-on manner. In concert, they kept the
good fan humming along through the winter. There would be
trades, squabbles, reports from the Latin American leagues.
Always, there were variables and possibilities.

In the case of the Cub fans in the postseason of 1987, there
was also an announcement they were eager to hear. I remembered Marcy Schauwecker, her eyes red with good-bye to
another unfaithful sweetheart of a season, leaving the bleachers on the day of the last home game and saying, "If Andre
gets the MVP, I'll be happy." He got it, 269 votes to 193 for
the spectacular Cardinal, Ozzie Smith. Dawson was the first
man ever to win the award while playing for a last-place
team—it had to be a Cub, of course—and outside Chicago
some said it wasn't right. How valuable could a man be if his
team was beaten by all the others?

It was a legitimate argument, but if the vote had been
carried out to include every player in the National League,
the fairness of it would have been demonstrated. For instance,
Clark of the Cardinals finished third, and he and Smith together far outpointed Dawson. In a full man-by-man ac-
counting, all of the Cardinals combined, and all of the Mets
and Expos and Giants and Reds, would have totaled many
more points than all of the Cubs. It made sense in the full
perspective. The Cubs may have been last in the East, but
Dawson was first in deed, indeed.

Another way to reach the same conclusion would have been
to watch him from the bleachers all year. From there, it was
vividly apparent that nobody was more valuable to the well-
being of baseball in 1987 than the rightfielder of Wrigley. The
real irony would have been if Sutcliffe had won the Cy Young
Award to go along with Dawson's MVP. As it happened,
Philadelphia's reliever, Steve Bedrosian, won in the closest
vote ever, fifty-seven to fifty-five for Sutcliffe and fifty-four
for the ex-Cub Rick Reuschel.

A last-place team had never been so generously decorated, but it didn't change the standings or the outlook. The Cubs could not remain the same, and Jim Frey was well aware of it. Late one Tuesday afternoon in December, my phone rang in Cincinnati, and when I picked it up, Jerry Pritikin said, "Did you hear about the trade?" No. "They traded Lee Smith to Boston." Who'd they get? "I don't even know who they got. I was so happy to hear that he had been traded that I didn't pay attention to the rest. Yes, Virginia, there is a Santa Claus."

It had been two months since the season had ended, and the disillusionment that the Bleacher Preacher had felt so acutely in September had begun to meander down the same well-traveled way out taken so many postseasons by the Cub-fan blues of so many Chicagoans. "I've been doing a lot of thinking," he said. "You know, this is the last day for players to declare whether they're free agents. I've decided that with everything that's happened—with Dallas leaving and Frey, I like Frey, and now with Lee Smith being traded—I've decided I should be where I belong. In the bleachers."

The trade was for a pair of pitchers, Calvin Schiraldi and Al Nipper, neither of whom had credentials anything like Smith's. In Boston, the deal sounded so good that people thought the radio stations were playing a practical joke. In Chicago, Jerry Pritikin's attitude was the exception. Fans who all season had complained that Smith was overrated in performance complained anew that he had been undervalued in barter. It was like: Hey, he might be a bum, but he's *our* bum. There was something else, though, more subtle, that made such a big trade difficult for the fans. Deep down, they knew that something radical had to be done with the team, but the hard thing was admitting it. Could the Cubs—their Cubs—really be that bad? What about all those good players, all those good moments?

With the Cubs, more than with other teams, it was particularly hard to accept the testimony of the final standings. It had been heady there for a while, and the team had hit well; it just didn't seem right. The Cubs had set a team record with

209 home runs while the Cardinals hit 94, and they had even batted a point higher than St. Louis, and they had scored fewer runs by 78. Did somebody add up all the numbers wrong? After contending in June, they had finished nine games under .500. How did it happen? How could all of it have amounted to a *bad season*?

As to the last question, I didn't believe that it could. There was a big difference between a bad team and a bad season. All through September, as the Cubs blundered and back-tracked, people said to me what a shame it was that the summer I picked to sit in the bleachers had turned out, in the end, to be such an ordinary one. But I thought it had been a perfectly fine summer. I thought it was a quintessential Cub summer—and, in that sense, a quintessential baseball summer.

It was a baseball summer the likes of which might never be experienced again, because the best bleachers in baseball were in transition. Leonard Becker missed his old buddies. Mark Wilmot had to conduct an investigation to find out what a batter did in the fifth. Jerry Pritikin wasn't having any fun. Howard Hankin couldn't get a bet. The bleachers were still what baseball was all about, they were still baseball's sketch in America's mural, and there was still no other place like them; but they weren't the place they used to be either, except for here and there, now and then—in May, in September, in the rain, against the Padres on Tuesdays, on the big weekends with the Cardinals and Mets. Those were the times when the bleachers were a charming American anachronism. Those were the times when 1987 was a great, important season.

It would never be the same if lights come to Wrigley Field. Baseball would never be the same. Lights going up around Wrigley would be like the last dinosaur getting the electric chair. Maybe there would only be eighteen night games, but that wouldn't matter; Wrigley Field's place in the natural order would be lost the moment a substitute checked in for the sun. The moment Wrigley Field had lights, it would no longer not have lights.

Shortly after the 1987 season ended, the results came in on the survey that Mayor Washington had commissioned. Some—specifically, those in Lake View who opposed lights—thought that the numbers were ambiguous, but they provided Washington with the data he needed to come out in favor of lifting the ordinance that precluded night games at Wrigley Field. Citywide, the great preponderance of those polled favored lights at Wrigley, and an overwhelming majority said they favored lights if the Cubs met four conditions: that there would be no more than eighteen night games; that no games would start after 7:05 P.M.; that no beer would be sold after the seventh inning of night games; and that the number of 3:05 games would be reduced. Even residents of Lake View favored night games under those conditions. Don Grenesko, the Cubs' vice-president who was in charge of their lights brigade, said that the results of the survey were a mandate for Washington.

On November thirteenth, the mayor endorsed a plan by which the Cubs would be permitted eighteen regular-season night games in each of the next fifteen years. To minimize the impact on local clubs, restaurants, and theaters, it was agreed that none of the night games would be on Fridays and only two on Saturdays—the Cubs had no attendance problems on weekend dates, anyway; to them, night games were an alternative to the neglected weekday games of May and September—and as a compromise on the parking situation, the Cubs consented to reducing their 3:05 starts to seven.

The mayor's political influence had been widening since his reelection on Opening Day, and the general belief was that, despite the expected lobbying efforts of Wrigleyville residents and aldermen, opposition to his proposal would only be token on the City Council. If the city lifted its ordinance, the Illinois law would still have to be dealt with, but it was unlikely that the state would stand in the way; the state restrictions applied only after 10:00 P.M. anyway. Finally, if the city and state capitulated, there was the last-ditch threat that the neighborhood would vote the precinct dry, prohibiting beer sales at Wrigley Field and perhaps forcing the Cubs out, but the *Sun-*

Times and Gallup conducted a survey of the precinct that indicated only thirty-three percent of the neighbors favored such a drastic measure. It seemed quite possible that Wrigley Field would have lights by the beginning of the 1988 season. The Cubs were ready to go ahead with plans to add five thousand seats to the ballpark.

And then, on the day before Thanksgiving, Harold Washington keeled over in his City Hall office and died. Chicago politics being what they are, the scramble for power was on, and as far as lights at Wrigley Field were concerned, all bets were off. Lights had lost their champion downtown. The prospect of night baseball was proving to be as tantalizing and elusive to the Cubs as the National League pennant.

But there will be lights at Wrigley Field eventually—before there will be a pennant, in all likelihood—and after that, things will be irreversibly different. Eighteen times a year, Wrigley Field will fill up on the dark side of dinner. Eighteen times, nobody will have to skip school or cut out of work to take in a ballgame. There will be no more shadows at five o'clock or homers in the gloamin'. Nobody will get drunk in the sunshine.

Maybe at night the bleachers will be nothing but cheap seats, and maybe they won't sell out. Then people will be able to lie down on them before the ballgames and take little naps, like they did back when Cal Koonce pitched for the Cubs and Doug Clemens played in the outfield. Some of Becker's buddies will probably trickle back. A few guys might strike up some camaraderie in left field and throw their beers in the air or something when somebody hits a home run. Maybe there won't *be* as many home runs, because they say the wind doesn't blow so hard at night. Maybe then the Cubs will get some players who can run and play ball, and maybe then they'll win a pennant.

It's bound to happen. There will be lights at Wrigley Field, and the Cubs will win a pennant, and on that day a new era will begin at Clark and Addison, even as the old one shuffles away from the happy bleacher crowd, head down, hands in pockets, and disappears into the past. From that day on, people will try to remember what it was like in 1987.